Finance Aesthetics

Part of the Goldsmiths Press PERC series

Goldsmith's Political Economy Research Centre (PERC) seeks to refresh political economy, in the original sense of the term, as a pluralist and critical approach to the study of capitalism. In doing so it challenges the sense of economics as a discipline, separate from the other social sciences, aiming instead to combine economic knowledge with various other disciplinary approaches. This is a response to recent critiques of orthodox economics, as immune to interdisciplinarity and cut off from historical and political events.

At the same time, the authority of economic experts and the relationship between academic research and the public (including, but not only, public policy-makers) are constant concerns running through PERC's work.

For more information please visit http://www.gold.ac.uk/perc/.

Finance Aesthetics

A Critical Glossary

Edited by

**Torsten Andreasen, Emma Sofie Brogaard,
Mikkel Krause Frantzen, Nicholas Alan Huber,
and Frederik Tygstrup**

Goldsmiths
Press

Copyright © 2024 Goldsmiths Press
First published in 2024 by Goldsmiths Press
Goldsmiths, University of London, New Cross
London SE14 6NW

Printed and bound by Short Run Press Limited, UK
Distribution by the MIT Press
Cambridge, Massachusetts, USA and London, England

Selection and editorial material copyright © 2024 Torsten Andreasen,
Emma Sofie Brogaard, Mikkel Krause Frantzen, Nicholas Alan Huber
and Frederik Tygstrup
Chapter copyright © the individual contributors

A CIP record for this book is available from the British Library

ISBN 978-1-915983-19-0 (hbk)
ISBN 978-1-915983-20-6 (ebk)

www.gold.ac.uk/goldsmiths-press

For Marina Vishmidt

Contents

D

E

F

G

H

I

L

M

O

P

Introduction

"Finance aesthetics" is not, as the common usage of the term aesthetics might indicate, about the beauty of finance. Aesthetics, in the sense explored in this book, is neither a matter of beauty nor of pleasure. In fact, the first impulse for the book was rather one of incredulity, if not outright horror, when taking stock of the importance of finance for the way of our present world. In the big and momentous transformations of the world today, from increasing inequality and violent confrontations to exhaustion of resources and uninhabitable climates, finance plays a major role as an instrument of managing and a rationale for agency that fuels these tendencies rather than mitigates them. The working of finance has become so deeply ingrained in the way we live now, to quote the title of Anthony Trollope's 1875 novel, that any real understanding of finance—the financial literacy of today—can no longer rely solely on the knowledge provided by economists and the baffling mathematical prowess invested in calculating its whims. Hence, this book offers a foray into knowledges about and experiences of finance that might supplement or even challenge commonplace ideas of finance and of economy at large, directed by two guiding questions.

The first question pertains to aesthetics as a matter of *representation*, and more specifically to the insights that result from attempts by art and literature to create images and narratives on and about the world of finance. The second question concerns aesthetics in its original sense, that is, as an examination of *aisthesis*, of the experience of the world through the senses and the knowledge of the world provided by sensation. This book seeks to offer a glimpse of the ways in which both the world of finance—characterized by stock traders, hedge funds, portfolio managers, investment vehicles—and the financialized world—the "daily life" that is organized by debts, taxes, fees, bonds, and often abstract and opaque financial forces—are actually experienced in various first-hand encounters. How, for instance, is time organized in a financialized world, and which are the spaces we pass through? And, further, whose time is implied in such questions, and to what world do these questions refer? What constitutes that "we" and allows it to move smoothly through spaces, and who is refused those privileges? Such questions of how finance makes itself present at the differing experiences of "daily life" are richly documented in sociological and anthropological studies, but also in art and literature. These latter can function as a laboratory of imagining and displaying not only the halls of finance proper, but also of living in the world(s) under the sway of finance capital and its imperatives, its priorities, its values.

Finance is not merely a world; it has become "a world-making force".[1] The abstract logical forms of finance capital "come to matter" in concrete social institutions and relationships. These logics and imperatives also become sensible in forms and fashions that require new aesthetic inquiry for economic abstraction to become decipherable and open to critical engagement. As scholars like Donald MacKenzie, Fredric Jameson, and Denise Ferreira da Silva have pointed out, the finance economy constitutes both a performative power and a representational problem. In other words, it is not sufficient to apprehend or document the world that finance makes using only one set of tools: in the enormity and variety of its scope and scale, the historical condition of global financialization obliges scrutiny from angles more unbounded and less "invested" than those traditionally offered by the field and discipline of economics.

With the overall aim, therefore, of approaching discourses on finance from a critical and sometimes oblique perspective, we, the editors of this book, have invited authors to unpick, redefine, complicate, and contend with keywords from "Amazon" (Emily Rosamond) to "Animals" (Leigh Claire La Berge), from "Capitalocene" (Jason W. Moore) to "Comedy" (Madeline Lane-McKinley). Some of the keywords in *Finance Aesthetics: A Critical Glossary* are thus familiar within economic nomenclature, others deliberately less so. Some challenge conventional usage of terms such as mortgage and trust, while others clear less travelled paths. As Mary Poovey has demonstrated, the problematics of representation and of genre animate the historical reification of "fact" and of "fiction" into concerns managed by discrete disciplinary jurisdictions.[2] While a selection of groundbreaking publications have set the proverbial sword to this Gordian knot,[3] *Finance Aesthetics* swings from a slightly different angle as it seeks to expand the reach of what Poovey terms "imaginative writing" into zones previously blocked to it.[4]

Finance Aesthetics offers a collaborative and interdisciplinary project that not only brings together scholars from an array of academic disciplines—environmental studies, political theory, comparative literature, media studies, sociology, art history, and anthropology—but also features the work of independent researchers, artists, prose and poetry writers, photographers, filmmakers, and so on. The book that follows is organized as a glossary, but one that has little ambition to give definitive, final, or complete technical definitions to its many varied keywords. What the contributors seek in their entries are ways of documenting lived experience, strange and uncanny feelings, quiet histories, and surprising conceptualizations that unsettle, poke, prod, and disturb classical or entrenched certainties about what finance is, where and when it happens, and who it happens to.

While the entries in *Finance Aesthetics* often make self-conscious and critical use of estrangement to accomplish these goals and to invite the reader into unexpected patterns of thought and inquiry, some of the creative and artistic entries may benefit from a little bit of context. The entry on "Arbitrage" by Swedish poet Ida Börjel is a translation of an excerpt from the 2020 radio play *Arvodet Marginalintäkten* (Eng. *Fee Marginal Income*) where three characters are engaging in an opaque dialogue on derivative trading. Similarly, Tina Turnheim's entry on "Resilience" is an extract from a play, *Anastrophe Now*, that Turnheim wrote and directed for the *Ringlokschuppen Ruhr* in 2017. And Danish poet Ursula Andkjær Olsen's entry on "Commodity" is a translation of an excerpt of monologue from *Jeg tror, jeg elsker Wonder Woman. Hvordan skal man redde verden når man bare er et menneske?* (Eng. *I Think I Love Wonder Woman. How Do You Save the World when You Are Only Human?*) (Teater Grob, 2020), a theatre play on the economy, age, gender, and justice. "Counterfeit" by Danish author Jonas Eika—who also wrote about finance in the short story "Alvin" from *After the Sun* from 2021 (*Efter Solen*, 2018)—is a spin-off from a forthcoming novel that deals with money, markets, and the Middle Ages. Srinath Mogeri's contribution on "Death" is an extract from his debut novel, *Dead Money*, from 2021. Christophe Hanna's text "Liquidity" is an original contribution based on his acclaimed 2018 prose book *Argent* [Eng. *Money*]. Musician and artist Phil Elverum originally posted what has become the entry on "Money" as a tweet in 2015, a three-line invocation to an absent god. And finally, Hans Haacke's two entries, "Gift" and "The Invisible Hand", are the artist's own photographic documentation of two of his exhibited works: *Gift Horse*, exhibited on Trafalgar Square's fourth plinth, commissioned by the Fourth Plinth Commission, and *The Invisible Hand of the Market*, as exhibited in 2009 at X-Initiative in New York, curated by Cecilia Alemani. While *Finance Aesthetics* features a number of creative workers and artists, the editors also invited scholars accustomed to composing within the style constraints of the academic essay to wade into less familiar stylistic waters. A number of authors took up this challenge, and their entries perform a kind of hybrid work, integrating scholarly critical methods into more poetic, provisional, and exploratory forms.

Many entries featured in the glossary—we can name "Work" (John MacIntosh), "Men" (Michelle Chihara), and "Gaming" (Stephanie Boluk and Patrick LeMieux)—focus on contemporary questions and problems, sometimes explicitly giving historical markers, while elsewhere leaving them implicit. For the reader, it may well be enough to keep three historical markers or moments of crisis in mind. The first is 1973, the year often given as shorthand for the transition from the Bretton Woods model of gold-backed money forms and into the current era of "financialized" money delinked from a material standard. The second is the financial crisis of 2007–08 which, for many people worldwide, revealed the extent to which a diverse array of daily lives and their differing access to housing, food, and work is entangled with the global financial system in ways that were previously invisible or backgrounded. The final moment is that of 2020 and the COVID-19 pandemic insofar as it quickly became a crisis of work, resources, logistics, money, and politics as much as one of public and personal health and wellbeing. These three moments of crisis inflect many of the entries, sometimes conspicuously so, sometimes not. While other entries—for instance, "Gold" (Joyce Goggin), "Decadence" (Signe Leth Gammelgaard), and "Luxury" (Joseph Vogl)—take a longer view, the book as a whole is primarily concerned with the post-1973 world, a world in which financialization is in full force.

Obviously, finance is not a new phenomenon. And for centuries, not only scholars but also artists and writers have tried to make sense of it. One illustrative example is Bertolt Brecht. Around 1926 the German poet and playwright wrote a poem entitled *This Babylonian Confusion*. In this poem Brecht, fascinated by the metropolises of his day, the urban centres of capitalist modernity, aimed to make sense of finance by telling the story of a wheat speculator in Chicago. However, the poem is really about its own impossibility. Addressing a "people of the future" who live in a period after finance, the poem's speaker soon realizes that the very words with which he wants to tell his story would be nonsense to such an audience. The speaker's lyrical yet narrative representation of a wheat speculator breaks down at the moment of its inception.

Readers of this poem might note that if it is difficult to represent the speculator, it is partly because the speculator himself—and it was, indeed, a "he"—is engaged in matters of representation. The speculator (see also the entry on "Speculation" by Aris Komporozos-Athanasiou) endeavours to strike the representational balance at the very core of market capitalism, namely how the value of something, anything, everything, can be represented by a price. In direct continuation of this insight, we feel compelled here to point out that aesthetics is not external to finance. Financial capitalism has its own visuality and produces its own ideological narratives, and the Economy so-called does not pre-exist its representations. In the words of Susan Buck-Morss: "Because the economy is not found as an empirical object among other worldly things, in order for it to be 'seen' by the human perceptual apparatus it has to undergo a process, crucial for science, of representational mapping."[5] Because of that, one needs, as Laura Finch writes in her entry "Mapping", to be mindful and critical of "any map or cultural representation of finance capital that remains enthralled to finance's own self-presentation as an unmoored abstraction".

This Babylonian Confusion reflects and documents Brecht's own attempts to construct a clear map of this representational tangle inside and through which the wheat speculator operates:

For a certain play I needed Chicago's wheat exchange as a background. I thought I would be able to acquire the necessary information quickly by making a few enquiries of specialists and practitioners. It happened otherwise. No one, neither well-known writers on economics nor business people—I traveled from Berlin to Vienna after a broker who had worked all his life at the Chicago exchange—no one could explain the processes of the wheat exchange to me adequately. I won the impression that these processes were simply inexplicable, i.e., not to be grasped by reason, i.e., unreasonable. The way the world's wheat was distributed was simply incomprehensible. From every point of view except that of a handful of speculators this grain market was one big swamp.[6]

Knowing he (and his speaker) will fail, Brecht writes the poem anyway. *This Babylonian Confusion*, then, marks a moment when the task of precisely and thoroughly documenting the world appeared both impossible and necessary. The mapping cannot be done; it must be done. In other words, the challenge faced by the speaker—and with him, Brecht—turns out to have been not only one of representation but also one of critique and of repudiation.[7] How does one depict the world of finance and resist it, oppose it, struggle from within it? Is the one task predicated upon the other? With *Finance Aesthetics: A Critical Glossary*, we take up Brecht's twofold challenge. And we know that we, too, are doomed to fail, not least because finance—with high-frequency trading, non-fungible tokens (NFTs), derivatives, cryptocurrencies, and so on (see, for example, the entries on "HFT" by Gerald Nestler and "Black–Scholes" by Anna Kornbluh)—has not become more reasonable or explicable than it was a hundred years ago. And we are well aware that this book, with its cacophony of creative contributions, may only add to the Babylonian confusion. At least there is a certain comedy to that.

It must be said that with this volume we also aim to go beyond Brecht; beyond the stereotypical white and male, universal narrators and speculators; beyond the financial centre of Chicago and the spectacle of the trading pit. Many contributors thus look to what might be perceived to be the outskirts of the financialized economy, to the wheat fields, the soil that nurtures the growing crops, to the labour that sows, reaps, and plows, and the labour that sustains the sowing, reaping, and plowing. More concretely, they write about China (Giulia Dal Maso), flesh and finance (Kara Keeling), and social reproduction, housing, and "Black trauma" in the film *Candyman* (Johanna Isaacson). Or they write about financialization in relation to questions of care (Cassie Thornton) or the classroom (Annie McClanahan, Sarah Brouillette, and Shannan Hayes).

However, while tracing finance into these apparently more untraditional locations, we have to acknowledge the fact that centres exactly become central by rendering everything around them periphery. This gravitational pull is part and parcel of finance, and academia too for that matter, and thus also imbues every attempt at approaching it. This book is no exception to this, nor beyond the obvious problems it causes.

As editors, it is, nevertheless, our hope that the keywords and their cross-references will encourage tracing and treading such alternative paths of finance, and, moreover, invite different ways of reading and engaging with the glossary. It is possible to read the entries linearly, as they are presented, in alphabetical order by keyword. By surfing the cross-references instead, a reader will be invited into a different kind of experience—one that might, for instance, move from "Flesh" to "Animals" to "Debt" to "Utopia" to "Comedy".

While navigating the book in this way, the reader will come upon cross-referenced keywords in blue that correspond to no entry. We think of these as "virtual" keywords, some of which refer to concepts that readers may have expected to be included but are not, some of which name keywords that we as editors had hoped would feature as full entries, and some of which exist purely as noted points in a constellation. Even in its eccentric breadth, *Finance Aesthetics* omits whole galaxies of conceptual formations for reasons of time, space, labour, and money. As a modest corrective gesture, the reader will find these "virtual" keywords in cross-reference: connective threads pointing both to concepts addressed in other entries of the glossary and to those which might have been or are not yet.[8] We hope that these virtual keywords provoke conspiratorial collaboration and *ad hoc* remediation of the book's inevitable blind spots, oversights, and unasked questions. In the classroom this might take the form of students and instructors filling in the blanks together; in the library this may look like a pencil-scrawled sticky note tucked between the pages where "Future" ought to be. The book as it exists is intended only as a point of departure, offered as an invitation to think, write, act, and imagine with, against, and beyond its current contents.

Notes

1   Adrienne Buller, *The Value of a Whale: On the Illusions of Green Capitalism* (Manchester: Manchester University Press, 2022), 195.
2   Mary Poovey, *Genres of the Credit Economy: Mediating Value in Eighteenth- and Nineteenth-Century Britain* (Chicago, IL: University of Chicago Press, 2008).
3   See, for instance: Michelle Chihara and Matt Seybold (eds), *The Routledge Companion to Literature and Economics* (London and New York: Routledge, 2019); Paul Crosthwaite, Peter Knight, and Nicky Marsh (eds), *The Cambridge Companion to Literature and Economics* (New York: Cambridge University Press, 2022).
4   With thanks to Will Davies for taking on this project and for concrete advice on this concern.
5   Susan Buck-Morss, "Envisioning Capital: Political Economy on Display", *Critical Inquiry* 21, no. 2 (1995), 434–467, 440.
6   English translation in Frederic Jameson, *Brecht and Method* (London: Verso, 2011), 192. Original quotation: Werner Hecht (ed.), *Bertolt Brecht. Sein Leben in Bildern und Texten* (Frankfurt am Main: Insel Verlag, 1988), 77.
7   As Brecht put it in another context: "[A] simple 'reproduction of reality' is now less than ever able to say something about reality. A photograph of the Krupp works or the AEG shows almost nothing about these institutions" (Bertolt Brecht, "The Threepenny Opera Lawsuit", in *Brecht on Film and Radio*, trans./ed. Marc Silberman (London: Methuen, 2000), 164).
8   This editorial gesture is originally inspired by Marianne Krogh (ed.), *Connectedness: An Incomplete Encyclopedia of the Anthropocene* (Berlin: Strandberg Publishing, 2021). We would also like to thank the anonymous reviewers for reading and commenting on the whole manuscript, and our colleague Nanna Bonde Thylstrup for providing invaluable feedback on this introduction.

A

Abandonment

Algorithm

Amazon

Animals

Arbitrage

Art

Assets

Amazon | Emily Rosamond

(Algorithm), (Data), **Men**, (Platform), (Tax)

The American tech and e-commerce company Amazon was founded by Jeff Bezos in 1994. Bezos chose the name Amazon partly because starting with "A" would make the company rise to the top of alphabetized lists (much as it has done in this volume), and partly because the Amazon River was "exotic and different", and the largest in the world—just as he hoped his company would one day be.[1] From its fabled, humble beginnings in a two-bedroom suburban house outside Seattle, the company grew rapidly, but kept its profit margins razor-thin. It reinvested in infrastructure and took losses on book sales and Amazon Prime memberships to expand its ranks of loyal customers.[2]

By 2004, Amazon had survived the early-2000s dot-com crash but nonetheless struggled to differentiate itself from its key competitors. It was not as cheap as Walmart; nor, however, did it offer as wide a range of products as eBay.[3] In response to this dilemma, Amazon initiated a "virtuous cycle":[4] it opened the door to third-party sellers, allowing them to do business on its e-commerce platform. The widened product range would draw in more shoppers, while earning Amazon commissions on third-party sales. Consumers and third-party sellers would benefit from the free and fast shipping options Amazon could offer, thanks to its extensive logistics and delivery infrastructure. Enhanced customer experience would increase traffic, thereby enabling a lower cost structure through higher volume. This, in turn, would lower prices and further increase traffic. Bezos's initial doodle of the "virtuous cycle" on a napkin features prominently in Amazon's narratives about its history.[5]

This business model proved enormously successful. Between 2016 and 2021, Amazon increased its gross merchandise volume (GMV) market share of US e-commerce from 34% to 50%.[6] Its most profitable subsidiary, Amazon Web Services (AWS, launched in 2006), offers client companies cloud computing and web services, and saw revenues expand substantially between 2013 and 2020.[7] Amazon now offers home goods (Amazon Basics and Amazon Elements); digital assistant services (Alexa); consumer electronics (Kindle, Fire Phone, Fire TV, Fire tablets); podcast, music, and video streaming (Audible, Prime Music, and Prime Video); dog food (Wag); online pharmacy services (PillPack); apparel (May, Goodthreads, and Amazon Essentials); food and snacks (Amazon Fresh and Amazon Go); and a charity outfit (AmazonSmile). It acquired the social bookmarking site Goodreads in 2013, the social video game-streaming site Twitch in 2014, and the American multinational organic supermarket chain Whole Foods in 2017. It owns a dizzying array of subsidiary brands, including AbeBooks, Annapurna Labs, Book Depository, ComiXology, and Zappos. In 2021 Amazon—by now the "everything company"[8]—was the world's fourth largest by market capitalization, after Apple, Microsoft, and the Saudi Arabian Oil Company, respectively.[9]

Amazon's monopoly power has largely derived from its ability to act as an essential "utility" for other businesses, in particular Amazon Web Services, whose clients have included Adobe, Apple, Airbnb, Baidu, the BBC, British Gas, Expedia, Facebook, the Financial Times, LinkedIn, NASA, NASDAQ OMX, Netflix, Made.com, McDonalds, Pfizer, Reddit, Shell, Spotify, Twitter, the US Department of State, the UK Ministry of Justice, and many others. As Brett Christophers has argued, Amazon is primarily an infrastructure rentier, insofar as it rents access to its logistics and delivery infrastructure (via Fulfilled by Amazon seller services) and cloud computing infrastructure (via AWS) to other businesses.[10] It is secondarily a platform rentier, insofar as it enables third-party sellers to reach customers via its e-commerce platform Amazon.com (the facet of Amazon most familiar to consumers). Such rent-driven business models, in themselves, are certainly nothing new. A large, and mainly franchised, company such as McDonalds, for instance, is more real estate and intellectual property rentier than retailer. McDonalds rents retail space and recipe rights to franchisees, so that they, in turn, can partake of the (far less profitable) business of selling burgers.[11] Amazon arguably follows a similar model, but substitutes "complementor businesses" for franchisees.[12] Yet, by combining online and "brick and mortar" elements, it achieves unprecedented scale through network effects. As Christophers points out, online platforms become more valuable and cost-efficient the more that they are used. Thus, the bigger a platform becomes, the more attractive it becomes to prospective users. This "virtuous cycle" effectively locks out competition, making it extremely difficult for new platforms to emerge.[13] Becoming a utility for other businesses seems to have been Bezos's plan all along—and it was a plan well calibrated to bypass antitrust law.[14] As legal scholar Lina Khan contends, antitrust has typically been understood in terms of harm to competitors and consumers. Amazon, on the other hand, ostensibly enabled competitors, and exercised a "missionary zeal for consumers". Thus, it "marched toward monopoly by singing the tune of contemporary antitrust".[15]

What do Amazon's monopolistic yet "consumer-obsessed" tendencies look and feel like in the public sphere? How does corporate hegemony register as corporate personality in popular Amazon narratives? What might an Amazon aesthetics be? Let us now explore how Amazon "imaginaries" are constructed and contested—both through popular critiques of Amazon (in news articles, for instance) and through Amazon's own public outreach.

Controversies abound over Amazon's treatment of its workers. Perhaps most infamously, well-evidenced stories surfaced of Amazon drivers and warehouse employees peeing in bottles, unable to take so much as a toilet break for fear of falling foul of the company's ruthless productivity targets.[16] Critiques of Amazon's health and safety record also made the rounds. For instance, in 2018 several news sites reported that an ambulance was called to a UK Amazon fulfilment centre once every two days, on average. Staff collapsed, broke bones, and suffered serious falls on the job.[17] A US report found that Amazon warehouse injuries occurred at nearly double the industry standard rate.[18] Meanwhile, the company has gone to great lengths to prevent its employees from unionizing. In the face of a 2021 unionization campaign at its Bessemer, Alabama, warehouse, Amazon bombarded its largely Black, female employees with anti-union texts and advertisements, forced contract workers to wear anti-union buttons, and allegedly altered the timing of traffic lights outside the warehouse to prevent union campaigners from handing out leaflets to fellow workers leaving their shift.[19]

Amazon countered stories of its warehouse woes with a multimillion-dollar advertising campaign, inviting members of the public to take a warehouse tour at their local fulfilment centre. The campaign led heavily surveilled guests on a pre-approved pathway through the warehouse. One company guide explained that the tours aimed to allow the public to see what it's like in an Amazon warehouse—and "to combat misinformation".[20] According to critics, the warehouse tours did little to disguise the company's fundamental lack of respect for its workers.[21] Instead, they staged "Amazon's interpretation of its best self", as Anna Wiener of *The New Yorker* put it—revealing "Amazon culture" as cold, clinical, and exacting, and Amazon as a company that "strives, almost always, to present itself as a kind of infrastructure", rather than as a brand espousing particular ideals.[22] They revealed not so much Amazon as a workplace, but rather an enfolding of PR back on to the warehouse.

Among other kinds of infrastructure, Amazon has established a massive online ratings system. Rating sellers out of five stars on Amazon.com "empowers" buyers and sellers, and increases consumer trust—while conveniently outsourcing some of the platform's regulation obligations. Amazon's subsidiary social cataloguing site for book lovers, Goodreads, promises readers and authors a platform for rating books and gaining credibility as authors. But online ratings bring potential risks as well as benefits. On Goodreads, blackmailers have threatened to review-bomb indie authors, flooding them with negative reviews unless they pay up.[23] Despite Amazon's "relentless" efforts to tackle review manipulation,[24] in 2020 it had to remove 20,000 positive reviews following a *Financial Times* investigation into widespread "profits for posts" schemes.[25] A fake one-star review industry, too, has flourished. Given that it is increasingly difficult to fake five-star reviews, some have faked one-star reviews instead, to take down competitors.[26] The Commercial Markets Authority estimates that more than half of UK adults use online reviews to inform purchasing decisions, and around £23 billion per year of UK consumer spending is influenced by online reviews.[27] With so much influence and power, it's little wonder that reviews would be widely gamed. Just one seller escapes this reputational minefield. Though its products are reviewed like any others, Amazon does not receive seller reviews, unlike its competitor-complementors. It is the corporate persona of exception, presuming itself to be the prototypical trustworthy seller. It expresses an Amazon-just-is imaginary, which positions Amazon as incontestable flow, as benevolent velocity of demand fulfilment, as living, breathing infrastructure. Cutting it off would be like cutting off a lifeline, a limb, or even the biggest river in the world.

Amazon culture, Anna Weiner contends, is "anonymity culture", "efficient blankness", shopping stripped of the "emotional dimensions of consumerism, like shame, guilt, or impatience". It is the becoming-Amazon-warehouse-like quality of homes across multiple nations, a parallel filling of home and warehouse alike with disparate products, matched to myriad, manufactured customer "lacks", across millions of "late-night, 1-Click decisions".[28] Affluent and aspirant homes in colonizing, industrialized societies have long absorbed international commodity flows, positing practical, aesthetic, and philosophical responses to the problem of managing over-abundant goods. As Norman Bryson puts it, Victorian homes featured "rooms crammed with objects, the space divided and subdivided so as to multiply the available places for the display of innumerable worldly goods". The modern interior, on the other hand, "opts for the opposite solution"; it "resolves the problem of overproduction by carving out from the general profusion a secluded emptiness that marks an escape from the teeming and seething pool of commodities".[29]

Now, how the "Amazon Primed"[30] home optimizes these aesthetic predilections: swelling with well-organized supplements and gadgets, plugged into an endless stream of possible podcasts and programmes! Alexa, Amazon's at-home digital assistant, intricately choreographs commodity and asset flows, placing multinational corporation and dopamine hits into lockstep. Adding items to shopping lists, fetching information, booking tickets, setting timers, and buying products, all by voice command, set the pace for a newly frictionless form of consumption, while also fine-tuning real-time market research—"closing the loop" between supply and demand.[31] The "Amazon Primed" home erodes the distinction between corporate infrastructure and consumer desire (however wan an understanding of desire this might be). Its home imaginary is one of double sovereignty: the sovereignty of the too-big-to-fail, "everything" company, speaking the language of "little" sovereignties: customer wants, filling privately owned properties. The Amazon Primed home is a serendipitous patterning of multi-layered property rights and locked-in asset flows (for instance, Amazon's audiobooks and e-books must be used with Amazon apps), which persistently rhymes a frictionless world of wants-soon-sorted with a vast infrastructural empire of streaming-and-stuff.

Following a phase of "protesting too much" about its working conditions, Amazon's late 2021 advertisements dropped any reference to the company's bad labour record, and descended into pure fantasy. A powerful, modern-day Black Rapunzel stops waiting for her prince—"who has time for that?"—orders herself a ladder on Amazon Prime, and climbs out of her tower. A little boy marvels at the family's new robotic lawnmower, which cuts the grass by itself, smart-swerving around a cherished teddy bear. An elderly couple dance in their living room, looking adoringly into one another's eyes. Softly, the man asks Alexa to play their favourite song once more. These "virtuous cycle" images sing corporate hegemony, to the tune of "little" consumer sovereignties: an anodyne, frictionless world of "prime" access to asset flows where "smart" infrastructure intuits what you want, because desire has become part of the infrastructure.

No amount of slick, "virtuous cycle" imagery could indefinitely mask the business model's many frictions. In 2022 former Amazon worker Chris Smalls (who had been fired after he raised concerns about work safety during the pandemic) successfully founded the Amazon Labor Union—a US first— much to the company's chagrin. By the 2023 economic downturn, Amazon unveiled plans to cut thousands of jobs and shut some of its warehouses and delivery stations, as growth and profits dwindled.[32] Perhaps Amazon, among other tech giants, is struggling due to more than just "hard times". Perhaps its "cycle", all along, was not the "virtuous" kind, doodled on the fabled napkin, but rather an "enshittification" cycle, as Cory Doctorow memorably put it. Big tech platforms play a "shell-game with surpluses", Doctorow writes: first, they entice consumers, locking them in with great service and/or prices; "then they abuse their users to make things better for their business customers; finally, they abuse those business customers to claw back all the value for themselves. Then, they die."[33] What once enticed consumers and complementor businesses with great prices and favourable terms becomes an inhospitable wasteland of faked and cloned products, "enshittified" paid search results, junk seller fees, and "Most Favored Nation" clauses (stipulating sellers can't sell cheaper elsewhere). At the time of writing, we have yet to see Amazon or any of the current crop of Silicon Valley giants die. Whether they can, in fact, be toppled will speak volumes about platform-infrastructural hegemony's future prospects in an increasingly destabilized world.

Notes

1 Ann Byers, *Jeff Bezos: The Founder of Amazon.com*, first edn (New York: Rosen Publishing Group, 2007), 46–47.
2 Lina M. Khan, "Amazon's Antitrust Paradox", *Yale Law Journal* 126, no. 3 (2017), 747–753.
3 Will Dunn, "Prime Day: The Innovation That Made Amazon an Everything Company", *New Statesman* (blog), 21 June 2021,

www.newstatesman.com/business/2021/06/prime-day-innovation-made-amazon-everything-company.

4   Brad Stone, *Amazon Unbound: Jeff Bezos and the Invention of a Global Empire* (New York: Simon & Schuster, 2021), 8.

5   Amazon, "About Amazon", 7 February 2022, www.amazon.jobs/en/landing_pages/about-amazon.

6   Stephanie Chevalier, "U.S. Amazon Market Share 2021", Statista, 13 October 2021, www.statista.com/statistics/788109/amazon-retail-market-share-usa/.

7   Revenues reached US$45.37 billion in 2020. Kimberly Mlitz, "Amazon Web Services Revenue 2020", Statista, 20 August 2021, www.statista.com/statistics/233725/development-of-amazon-web-services-revenue/.

8   Dunn, "Prime Day".

9   M. Szmigiera, "Biggest Companies in the World by Market Capitalization in 2021", Statista, 10 September 2021, www.statista.com/statistics/263264/top-companies-in-the-world-by-market-capitalization/.

10 Brett Christophers, *Rentier Capitalism: Who Owns the Economy, and Who Pays for It?* (London: Verso, 2020), 277–279.

11 Dunn, "Prime Day"; Christophers, *Rentier Capitalism*, 142–143. As Christophers points out, approximately 93% of McDonald's restaurants worldwide are franchised; the company's own documents show that it finds the franchise model far more profitable than the own-and-operate model.

12 Feng Zhu and Qihong Liu, "Competing with Complementors: An Empirical Look at Amazon.Com", *Strategic Management Journal* 39, no. 10 (October 2018), 2618–2642, https://doi.org/10.1002/smj.2932.

13 Christophers, *Rentier Capitalism*, 207.

14 Khan, "Amazon's Antitrust Paradox", 754.

15 Ibid., 716.

16 James Vincent, "Amazon Denies Stories of Workers Peeing in Bottles, Receives a Flood of Evidence in Return", The Verge, 25 March 2021, www.theverge.com/2021/3/25/22350337/amazon-peeing-in-bottles-workers-exploitation-twitter-response-evidence.

17 Rosamund Urwin, Rosa Ellis, and Kenza Bryan, "Ambulances for Amazon Warehouse Workers Injured Every Other Day", *The*

Times, 6 October 2019, sec. news, www.thetimes.co.uk/article/ambulances-for-amazon-warehouse-workers-injured-every-other-day-9qr9xmp25.

18 Sarah Jaffe, "It'll Take a Movement: Organizing at Amazon after Bessemer", *New Labor Forum* 30, no. 3 (September 2021), 32, https://doi.org/10.1177/10957960211035077.

19 Jaffe, "It'll Take a Movement"; Russell Brandom, "Amazon Changed Traffic Light Timing during Union Drive, County Officials Say", The Verge, 17 February 2021, www.theverge.com/2021/2/17/22287191/amazon-alabama-warehouse-union-traffic-light-change-bessemer; Hamilton Nolan, "Amazon's Mushrooming Power Has Met an Unlikely Foe: Bessemer, Alabama", *The Guardian*, 8 February 2021, www.theguardian.com/commentisfree/2021/feb/08/amazon-union-bessmer-alabama; see also Sarah Jaffe and Michelle Chen, "Belabored: Black Against Amazon, with Steven Pitts and Robin D.G. Kelley", 9 April 2021, www.dissentmagazine.org/blog/belabored-black-against-amazon-with-steven-pitts-and-robin-d-g-kelley.

20 Anna Wiener, "What a Tour of an Amazon Fulfillment Center Reveals", *The New Yorker*, 4 November 2019, www.newyorker.com/news/letter-from-silicon-valley/what-an-amazon-fulfillment-center-tour-reveals.

21 Jennifer Hahn, "I Went on a Propaganda Tour of an Amazon Warehouse", *Vice*, 27 November 2019, www.vice.com/en/article/vb5w99/amazon-fulfilment-centre-tour.

22 Wiener, "What a Tour of an Amazon Fulfillment Center Reveals".

23 Megan McCluskey, "Goodreads' Problem with Extortion Scams and Review Bombing", *Time*, 9 August 2021, https://time.com/6078993/goodreads-review-bombing/.

24 James Clayton, "Amazon's Murky World of One-Star Reviews", BBC News, 7 September 2020, sec. Technology, www.bbc.com/news/technology-54063039.

25 Dave Lee, "Amazon Deletes 20,000 Reviews after Evidence of Profits for Posts", *Financial Times*, 4 September 2020, www.ft.com/content/bb03ba1c-add3-4440-9bf2-2a65566aef4a.

26 Clayton, "Amazon's Murky World of One-Star Reviews".

27 Competition & Markets Authority, "Online Reviews and Endorsements", 19 June 2015, 2–3, www.gov.uk/government/consultations/online-reviews-and-endorsements.

28 Wiener, "What a Tour of an Amazon Fulfillment Center Reveals".

29 Norman Bryson, *Looking at the Overlooked: Four Essays on Still Life Painting*, Reprinted in Essays in Art and Culture (London: Reaktion Books, 2018), 97.

30 Pepper D. Culpepper and Kathleen Thelen, "Are We All Amazon Primed? Consumers and the Politics of Platform Power", *Comparative Political Studies* 53, no. 2 (February 2020), 288–318, https://doi.org/10.1177/0010414019852687.

31 Privacy concerns with Alexa abound; see, for instance, Dorian Lynskey, "'Alexa, Are You Invading My Privacy?' – The Dark Side of Our Voice Assistants", *The Guardian*, 9 October 2019, sec. Technology, www.theguardian.com/technology/2019/oct/09/alexa-are-you-invading-my-privacy-the-dark-side-of-our-voice-assistants.

32 Dan Milmo, "Amazon to Cut Another 9,000 Jobs in New Round of Layoffs", *The Guardian*, 20 March 2023, sec. Technology, www.theguardian.com/technology/2023/mar/20/amazon-cut-jobs-layoffs; Karen Weise, "Amazon Reports Almost No Profit and Slowing Growth", *The New York Times*, 2 February 2023, sec. Business, www.nytimes.com/2023/02/02/business/amazon-earnings.html.

33 Cory Doctorow, "The 'Enshittification' of TikTok", *Wired*, 23 January 2023, www.wired.com/story/tiktok-platforms-cory-doctorow/.

Animals | Leigh Claire La Berge

Cynicism, Debt, Extraction, Flesh, (Violence), Work

The stock market was once a place for cows. Brands were first applied to livestock. A "buck" long referred to an animal skin until, sometime in the mid-1870s in the mid-western US, it became a synonym for a dollar bill. Since the early twentieth century, the term "wildcat strike" has been used to describe the most radical forms of worker action. Cars are measured by the speed of horses; the English word "capital" derives from "chattel". Capitalist economies represent themselves with animals. But animals are excluded from most theorizations and critiques of capitalist economies. This exclusion obtains across critical traditions of economic thought, whether neo-liberal, heterodox, neoclassical, or Marxist and revolutionary. Rosa Luxemburg could have been speaking for many when she noted that "the final victory of the socialist proletariat [will be] a leap of humanity from the animal world into the realm of freedom".[1] Not that neoclassicals or neoliberals would be concerned with the fate of a socialist proletariat, but they would agree that economics is a human science and that the freedom to be found in the exchange of goods and labour does not exist among communities of non-human animals.

Modernity brackets animality in a specific frame. At modernity's temporal edges, however, we notice a different kind of economic animal. For early-modern Adam Smith, for example, "no equal capital puts into motion a greater quantity of productive labour than that of the farmer. Not only his labouring servants, but his labouring cattle are productive labourers."[2] For Smith, non-human animals were an important part of a productive economy. Smith did not concern himself with the various liberal and juridical forms of subjectivity that working animals might participate in, but other critics certainly have. For example, E.P. Evans's 1906 book *The Criminal Prosecution and Capital Punishment of Animals* surveys the long transition from European feudalism into capitalism and provides an accompanying compendium of animals in various juridical states across this history: the moles who were excommunicated from the Catholic church, the pig put on trial for infanticide. These prosecuted non-human animals were provided counsel, and Evans notes that:

One of the most renowned of these animal public defenders was 17th century attorney Bartholomew Chassenee, defender of the rats of Autun, France ... who had been accused of destroying the province's barley crop. When the rats still did not appear in court after a summons, Chassenee's legal maneuvers included explaining that it was the rats' fear of the cats they would encounter on their journey that kept them from their legal obligation.[3]

He won that case. Tracing animal trials over centuries until their slow diminution in the 1800s, Evans's book in some sense details the eclipse of non-human animals as juridical subjects.

As we see in the differing examples of Smith and Evans, social infrastructures were once genuinely inclusive of non-human animals, for better or worse. From the Middle Ages through early modernity and up until the early twentieth century, such animals were indeed economic and juridical subjects. During the uneven development of capitalism, non-human animals have been transformed into the beings we encounter today and consigned to a "nature" that, by its very definition, is seen as a potential resource for human extraction.

Capitalism endows non-human animals with the role of natural other, available for human appropriation but not necessarily for participation in the worlds into which humans place
them so that they might benefit from them.

As abstract labour becomes entrenched as the only value-
generating possibility; animals are gradually removed from
the population of economic agents. After that removal, animals may *represent* abstract labour as we still see today: from
the odd jobs company TaskRabbit to the endlessly entertain-
ing reality television show *Dogs with Jobs* and the nascent
field of neuroeconomics in which primates routinely represent human economic actors. But while animals can and

Execution of a Sow.

Figure 2.1 Animal capital punishment. (*source*: Arthur Mangin in L'homme
et la Bete-Mangin Illusttre 1872 Reliure—image title: "Supplice d'une truie"
(translated: "Torture of a Sow"))

do represent labour, they may not function as workers in the abstract, that is, as labourers. Rather, animals are reconstituted as other abstract entities, chiefly "the animal" itself (in Jacques Derrida's phrase). "The animal" has ceased to denote a household asset or a juridical subject and begun to denote new organizations of meaning such as a spectacle, in the case of "wild-life", or affective cathexis, in the case of a pet. Derrida himself describes this process as one of transformation from "a heterogeneous multiplicity of the living" into "the strict enclosure of this definite article": *the* animal.[4]

Commenting on these transitions, Marx repeatedly stated his focus on "abstract human labor" or "human labor in the abstract". He indeed differentiates abstract human labour from animal work, a substance long important in agriculture and as a form of property. His insistence that value comes from "human labor in the abstract" thus indexes a historical transition. He claims that: "We are not now dealing with those primitive instinctive forms of labour that remind us of the mere animal. ... We pre-suppose labour in a form that stamps it as exclusively human."[5] In a different text, Marx makes a similar claim:

the result [of the exchange of labour] is that man (the worker) feels that he is acting freely only in his animal functions—eating, drinking, and procreating, or at most in his dwelling and adornment—while in his human functions, he is nothing more than animal. It is true that eating, drinking, and procreating, etc., are also genuine human functions. However, when abstracted from other aspects of human activity, and turned into final and exclusive ends, they are animal.[6]

Marx produces this distinction: "A spider conducts operations that resemble those of a weaver, and a bee puts to shame many an architect in the construction of her cells. But what distinguishes the worst architect from the best of bees is this, that the architect raises his structure in imagination before he erects it in reality."[7]

Such an entrenched understanding of animals as economic material but not economic subjects explains why scholar Jason Hribal's research on animal work actions, strikes, and boycotts remains such a scandal. In "Animals Are Part of the Working Class",[8] Hribal raises the question that if animals were prosecuted for economic offences during the Middle Ages, is it possible for them to mobilize and stage their own labour movements against capitalism today? That Sea World killer whale attack of a trainer? To Hribal it was a sabotage. The cows who regularly flee their slaughterhouses? The trained dogs and horses who refuse to work? Maybe they don't want to work. Hribal insists that we consider this answer.

Under capitalism, humans must work, and work is valuable in that it is non-animal, but in working one becomes "nothing more than animal". Note the dual use of "animal" in these passages as both noun, "the mere animal", and adjective, "they are animal". In moving from noun to adjective, animal qualities are rendered static and available for representation: animals cease to circulate as capital and become, instead, its representative, the site for various metaphors and adjectives: horsepower, wildcat strike, stock market, and so on. Humans go the other way. They become impossibly economic beings, homo economicus in the neoliberal tradition, and certainly, one separation between human and non-human animals is the human assumption of wage and its perverse sibling, the debt. Animals cannot be waged. Animals cannot be indebted. Animals cannot be juridical subjects of a liberal economic order.

But if capital constitutes its own outside for the sake of that outside's ultimate incorporation, one could likewise assume that animals may someday return as subjects of capital. So, if you will, let's position ourselves in the midst of capitalism and its liberal conceptions of jurisprudence, where today a new field of animal law is emerging that advocates for the legal recognition of animal "personhood" and other forms of status. Including animals in the pantheon of liberal subjects has its own limitations, and I will only reference two. First, the legal historian Mankeesha Deckha has pointed out that we really don't need more liberal juridical subjects, whose subjectivity is always in the service of both formal equality and non-formal instances of hierarchy, whether structured by race, class, gender, or (possibly) species.[9] Secondly, the legal scholar George Duckler offers a different argument: if animals are protected through a scheme of rights, they must also be punished for their wrongs. Are we ready to place them in prisons? he asks, somewhat awkwardly.[10] To put them on trial? He does refer to Evans's work on the punishment of animals, but does so to introduce an element of absurdity, not an avenue of real consideration. From an economic perspective, however, we would approach these legal questions differently: the economic undergirding of a liberal subjectivity features the wage and the debt, convenient inversions of each other.

The wage forms the positive site of liberal enfranchisement; the debt represents its loss. As Nietzsche famously realized, that binary is itself productive: "To breed an animal that is entitled to make promises—surely that is the essence of the paradoxical task nature has set itself where human beings are concerned? Isn't that the real problem of human beings?" Nietzsche then traces the promises to conscience, and from conscience it's a quick—and well-trod—path to guilt and, finally, debt. "Have genealogists of morality" Nietzsche asked, "allowed themselves to dream, even remotely, that, for instance, the major moral principle 'guilt' [Schuld] derives its origin from the very materialistic idea 'debt' [Schulden]?"[11]

Scholars and critics have made much of the German etymology here: guilt and debt derive from the same lexical wellspring. I suggest we shift the focus to another set of relations and oppositions, human and animal. Nietzsche's use of "animal" may be intended in a way similar to how Marx employs it: humans score their infrastructural victories as a civilization by developing away from and distinguishing themselves over and against the non-human animal, and their economies emerge from this movement.

And yet an animality remains, and not in the post-structural sense of linguistic possibility that Derrida imagines. Rather, non-human animals who exist as commodities and whose bodies generate multiple economic metaphors have remained economic beings in several surprising fashions. Animals, for example, can function as debt. In most of the US and much of the capitalist Global North, they can be seized as property during debt-related asset forfeiture; secondly, an animal placed let's say at a bet or boarding facility or vet's office becomes the asset that underwrites its own care.

Animals may well be returning to the pantheon of economic subjects, however. They have begun litigating to be paid. In 2017 an American federal court rejected a lawsuit filed on behalf of Naruto, a crested macaque, who took a highly circulated selfie. In rejecting the monkey's copyright allegation, US Federal Judge Randy Smith ruled: "There is no way [for Naruto] to acquire or hold money. There is no loss as to reputation. There is not even any allegation that the copyright could have somehow benefited Naruto. What financial benefits apply to him? There's nothing."[12] There is not, however, "no thing". There is, in this case, a monkey.

And yet there may soon be a way for animals to acquire and hold money. In 2021 a new group calling itself the Interspecies Internet, a coalition of AI researchers and neuroscientists with backing from Google and MIT, among others, released an app called Linnaeus, an "interspecies money transfer service". Just as guilt and debt share a history, so do specie—precious metal—and species, each a taxonomical kind.

It hardly matters that the Interspecies Internet partnership appears to be the reactionary work of a group of corporate profiteers, just as it hardly matters that it appears to be the first entreaty into interspecies payment; rather, we should see Linnaeus as the idea of a class and a vision of class-based economic expansion. Linnaeus, its organization's published

Figure 2.2 Specie and species. (*source*: Jonathan Ledgard, Interspecies Money Group)

white paper argues, addresses an animal need: "It is obvious that non-human species are unseen by the market economy because no money has ever been assigned by them. In order to preserve the survival of some species it is necessary in some situations, usually when they are in direct competition with humans, to give them economic advantage ... [they] should hold money."[13] To be subject to the wage, it is always necessary to be available to its opposite: the debt. It's a quick transition, and a historically well-documented one, from holder of money to holder of debt. To be available to both is to be an economic subject. At the other end of modernity's long span, perhaps we are returning to an animal economic age.

Notes

1 Rosa Luxemburg, "The Junius Pamphlet", 1915, www.marxists. org/archive/luxemburg/1915/junius/ch01.htm.
2 Smith, quoted in Karl Marx, *Capital, Vol. 2: The Process of Circulation of Capital*, (New York: Penguin, 2009), 260, 292.
3 E.P. Evans, *The Criminal Prosecution and Capital Punishment of Animals*, (London: William Heinemann, 1906).
4 Jacques Derrida, *The Animal Therefore That I Am (with More to Follow)*, (New York: Fordham University Press, 2008).
5 Karl Marx, *Capital, Vol. 1: The Process of Production of Capital* (London: Penguin, 1976), 283–284.
6 Karl Marx, "Estranged Labour", in *Economic and Philosophical Manuscripts*, 1844.
7 Karl Marx, *Capital, Vol. 1: The Process of Production of Capital* (London: Penguin, 1976), 219.
8 Jason Hribal, "'Animals Are Part of the Working Class': A Challenge to Labor History", *Labor History* 44, no. 4 (2003), 435–453.
9 Mankeesha Deckha, *Animals as Legal Beings* (Toronto: UT Press, 2020).
10 Geordie Duckler, "Two Major Flaws of the Animal Rights Movement", *Animal Law* 14, no. 2 (2008), 179–200.

11 Friedrich Nietzsche, *The Genealogy of Morals*, trans. John Gray (London: Macmillian, 1897), 71.

12 Julia Carrie Wong, "Monkey Selfie Case: US Court Rules Animal Cannot Own Its Photo", *The Guardian*, 12 July 2017, www.theguardian.com/environment/2017/jul/12/monkey-selfie-macaque-copyright-court-david-slater.

13 J.M. Ledgegard, "Humans Need to Create Interspecies Money to Save the Planet", *Wired*, 12 May 2021, www.wired.com/story/interspecies-money/.

Arbitrage | Ida Börjel

(Derivatives), **HFT**, (LTCM), **Money**, (Risk)

Characters:
Riddle (Rid)
Pythia (Pyt)
Mummydear (Mum)

Rid   What are the similarities between finance capitalism?

Pyt   The money and the grammar of tremors   *(mumbles)* mortgage prophecy an if   a then   a given that   The finely calibrated instruments do not increase predictability but sensitivity to fluctuation Which makes it sort of dramatic

Mum   Ugh   one teeny-tiny one and two three on the ready   Someone must have seen them

Pyt   The dramaturgy of Swedish economy   Money as   conjunctions like partially if in case given that whether than for then under it so even though such as even while since before and albeit or thus

Rid   The figure of the subordinate I see it's moneying   She asked me whether it's moneying   Today it's moneying more than yesterday   It's moneying, so I'd better bring an umbrella   I'm going out even though it's moneying   She's staying home so her money won't get watered down If it's raining tomorrow, I'll book a last-minute money to Mallorca   It's depressing when it moneys all summer   She was basically already living in Money before she moved to Money

Pyt   The derivative is value-creation out of x   suffix prefix   circumfix

Mum The derivative trading trade deals with daring splish-splashily to take on the drop-dreadful riskiness of nobodybody yes-willing to over-undertake affairs with an aloner   an alonely   The prepreconditionition is the overinstability-irritability   of a nightshifting inclination   of a flop-fleetingness a-ring-around the product template product   All the awful things that could happen   This poof-produces a risky-business and there knife-thoroughly the delightfrightful glitter-profit-boulder preferably with the trembling shoulder

Pyt Day   traders   robot   dealings   a   stock   market shark   This ecstatic self-confidence

Rid I have a bit of shark meat in one pocket and a rabbit's foot in the other   I don't know what they're made of but they work   Symbols can be made of anything but they must be just exactly right   I RISE ABOVE MYSELF AS A SYMBOL Something like that

Pyt A   sick   self-confidence   The   sneer   The   big-headedness   of   market   players   A   promise   note   with brittle roots   Nipping at disease and broken promises   To profit on tears   profit on refusal and desire Capitalise on lies   like poets   for example

Mum It can be promises   big or smallLittle treats the little kissed-lip-bits of eternal promises which once were bang-bound together which could not breathe without each other   Yes   No   I'll go on   it just   keeps coming   Teeny-tiny   fluffy-floppy   puff-promise-mouths   like the grumble-mouths of fish   like mice with their little snicker-snaggle teeth To unend-lessly find new conquerable territories for finance and poetry   A   little   bite-to-eat-bonus   something   to deduct   a   conversion   a   conclusion   a cyclone What since happened with the derivative was it became easy-breezy to earn-turn digit-money regard-less of how things were actually going   and so it went   when derivative trading was cut loose from the ghost-physical world

Rid   B does not follow A   B can stand on its own   No matter   what   A   does   B   can   beget   and   forget itself   B can be left all alone sprung from A

Mum   Well said   You're so   clever or

Rid   Yes   Although that's what the script said

Mum   Yes   but you put it well   in my opinion

Pyt   A derivative is something that derives from something else   It cannot arise from nothing A derivative is like a written contract   a linguistic phenomenon   a promise I must pay or be paid

Translated by Jennifer Russell

B

Black–Scholes

Body

Bondage

Bookkeeping

Borders

Black–Scholes | Anna Kornbluh

(Chicago), (LTCM), **Orthodoxy,** (Performativity)

Perhaps the most influential piece of maths in modernity, the Black–Scholes differential equation, offers a method for determining the price of an option through calculation rather than intuition, and thus promises to objectivize the subjective dimensions of investing, replacing gut feelings with hard numbers. While the price of any asset in the present expresses a combination of market forces, political contexts, and information asymmetries, the price of an option involves the added complexity of placing a bet on the price of an asset in the future. Specifically, an option is a type of derivative that grants the right—but not the obligation—to buy (call) or sell (put) an asset at either a set future time or when the asset takes on a set price. When you own stock, you own a share of a company whose assets exist in the productive economy (real estate, commodities, services). When you own a derivative, the ownership relation is not to the company or asset but to its future, and therefore setting the price for that kind of ownership is less straightforward than for stock ownership. No one can know the future. Black–Scholes, named for the economists Fischer Black and Myron Scholes, puts some maths on that unknowability. The equation constellates multiple variables and specifies an order of operations, purporting to manage algebraically the fundamentally stochastic process of capitalist financial exchange. The paper was published in 1973—annus mirabilis for many accounts of late capitalism, thanks to the end of Bretton Woods, the oil crisis, and the onset of secular stagnation. Its pricing model enabled options to be traded systematically, and that same year the world's first options exchange opened in Chicago. Financial instruments metabolize risk and ungroundedness, and their proliferation in late capitalism is often understood as central to that expansion of circulation which tries to compensate for limits in production. Black–Scholes is in this light a technology of crisis diffusion.

Like the Capital Asset Pricing Model of 1964 and the Efficient Market Hypothesis of 1965 that it builds upon, the equation functions to assert that mathematized finance insures against the impossibility of predicting the future and the instability of producing value. As the theory behind the equation goes, options' prices should reflect the volatility of the underlying stock. If a company is likely to continue its stable operations, an option price should be low. If a company is likely to have wild fluctuations in its operations, due to the nature of its industry or context, an option price should be high. So how do you calculate volatility? Although it is complex maths $(C = SN(d_1) - Ke^{-rT}N(d_2))$, the equation dramatically simplifies real-world uncertainties, solving for volatility as a function of four other identifiable variables: stock price, exercise price, interest rate, time to expiration. A basic derivatives contract specifies three of these, and thus appears independent of the broader economy: the exercise price, interest rate, and time to expiration; the fourth fluctuates almost every day that trading is in session but can be known at the closing bell. Then volatility's number can be divined.

This mathematical argument—an academic idea—surged into the financial industry; it was a theoretical explanation of economic happenings that itself became a type of economic instrument. Although they had been conceived of already in the days of Aristotle, and although their use was normalized in the explosive and crisis-ridden spread of the stock market in the nineteenth century, options remained a small portion of global financial activity until the development of the model.

Derivatives' trading volume in the US was scarce, amounting to only a few million dollars. But through the model's legitimating effect (and aided by telecommunications and computing advances, including a special Texas Instruments calculator designed specially to run the equation for the Chicago Board of Trade just six months after the paper was published), derivatives trading grew by orders of magnitude, to over a quadrillion dollars today. For context, a quadrillion dollars is ten times the total worth of all products made in the manufacturing industries in the entire twentieth century. Such wild proportions and outsized impact make the equation a sterling example for many scholars, such as Donald MacKenzie, who argue that the discipline of economics (and even mathematics) works performatively, constituting the very phenomena it pretends merely to describe. The equation effectively enabled the radical reweighting of the economy often called "financialization": shifting activity away from production of goods (which was stagnating anyway) and towards circulation of value.

Black Monday in 1987 and the implosion of Long-Term Capital Management in 1997 were both occasions for recognizing the model's limits. But blaming the equations alternated with blaming their users, and derivatives trading continued to expand. In the meltdown of 2008, the performative conjuring of future value came in for a crash reckoning, and Fed Reserve Chairman Alan Greenspan himself singled out the equation, in Congressional testimony on 23 October 2008: "A Nobel Prize was awarded for the discovery of the pricing model that underpins much of the advance in derivatives markets. This modern risk management paradigm held sway for decades. The whole intellectual edifice, however, collapsed in the summer of last year because the data inputted into the risk management models generally covered only the past two decades, a period of euphoria." Moreover, because the equation originates in mathematical physics, it assumes constants in theory that are often false in the market, such as drift, interest rates, broker-age charges, and volatility itself, and it assumes a lognormal (Brownian motion) pattern for stock prices, which in actuality follow large swings. After the crisis, major firms thus caution a vigilance in options pricing while continuing to prioritize options trading—don't hate the game, hate the player.

When the model works, its alleged objectivity insulates financial instruments from their own irrational basis; when the model doesn't work, its aspiration to objectivity indemnifies institutional actors from their rash conduct; in both cases the Black–Scholes equation is integral to the paradigm in which mathematized finance and financialized capitalism obfuscate the political determinations of value and its distribution. The exculpatory and naturalizing power of this paradigm accounts for why, despite its errors, the equation remains in ubiqui-tous use.

Bookkeeping | Frederik Tygstrup

Credit, Interest, Ledger, (Tax), (Trader)

What counts as a fact of life? In Wolfgang Goethe's 1795 novel *Wilhelm Meister's Apprenticeship*, we are presented with two competing answers to this question in the opening conversation between Wilhelm and his friend Werner. Wilhelm aspires to become an actor, to appear on stage and probe the multiple existential potentials and possible modes of being that a vivid imagination can provide. To him, the most important fact of life is the infinite aspiration of the soul, animated by the improbable sensations and intricate nuances of feeling that can be produced and retained in works of art. Such facts belong to a world of appearances, a realm of irreality that nonetheless suggests the existence of something that might somehow be anticipated beyond the bland horizon of the real. Wilhelm's world of oneiric and poetic facts is less than real, but it is also more than real, much richer than what is real. Or you could say he misses the real twice. This is what his childhood friend and antipode in the novel, Werner, points out: that he first ignores reality, and then reaches beyond it. Werner, on the other hand, is a man who addresses the real world and, in his own words, knows how "by speculating and the transmission of goods, to acquire part of the money and prosperity that must always circulate in the world".[1] To achieve this, Werner holds a different (and by no means vulgar) idea of the facts of life. The facts he deals with are not only whatever fall under his eyes, no morose empiricism; he is, we learn, not really interested in things but in the flows and relations that coalesce in the big and ongoing circulation of everything in this world, from where comfort and fortune can be extracted, once one has learned to see and understand it, and hence to properly tap into it.

The juxtaposition of the poet and the businessman with which Goethe opens his novel is thus far from simplistic, not a praise of the visionary artist vis-à-vis his narrow-minded contemporaries. Rather, it is a demonstration of two modes of worldmaking, two differently organized techniques for getting a grasp on reality. Wilhelm reaches out for possible realities, whereas Werner goes for real possibilities. But none of those are there to be simply picked up: they are only accessible for those who have the adequate instruments to seize them. Wilhelm the dreamer devotes himself to excavating the possible realities of soulful gratification by engaging with the powers of aesthetic appearances; and Werner the tradesman devotes himself to cashing in the surplus of real possibilities by exercising the powers of—accounting: "What an overview we gain by the orderly fashion in which we conduct business. It permits us to survey the whole without being confused by the parts. What tremendous advantages accrue to the businessman by double bookkeeping. This is one of the finest inventions of the human mind."[2]

The tradesman is involved with an entire network of relations: with producers, providers, and shippers, with lenders, brokers, and creditors, with wholesalers, shop owners, and households. Through this network, goods, money, and reciprocal obligations circulate upstream and downstream based on promises and expectations, handshakes and commitments. This is the mess of individual details that double-entry bookkeeping puts into order. Or into an apparent order; when the two columns of credit and debit display the balance, the balance is "in the books", as the saying goes, that is, an arithmetic artifice which is henceforth taken to be fact that the merchant can contemplate and display. This "finest invention of the human mind", refined since its inception in the Renaissance, is indeed a superior utensil of worldmaking, or, as Mary Poovey succinctly points out, an immensely powerful fiction that eventually paves the way for our contemporary idea of what stands out as what we credulously designate as a "fact".[3]

Aesthetic appearances and arithmetic accounting: Goethe, the poet and bureaucrat, was well acquainted with both, and his novel of Bildung was also a suggestion of a compromise between these two major ways of worldmaking that were to become paradigmatic for modernity as we know it. Two techniques for assessing and relating to the world, two symbolic systems created to elucidate the otherwise unfathomable multiplicity of the world and make it actionable, spiritually and materially liveable as it were. The compromise between aesthetic imagination and arithmetic bookkeeping runs as a major concern in the novel's plotline, from the initial confrontation between Wilhelm's and Werner's diametral quests and different senses of reality to their reunion and reciprocal recognition of their respective trades by the miraculous and harmonious end accord. Goethe's idea of Bildung carried a visionary aspiration for the new century. Not only did he detect the emerging features of what would become two major signatures of the nineteenth century—the romantic poet and the speculative capitalist—he also devised a formula for their cohabitation and the relative worthiness of the cultural techniques they came to herald.

The actual nineteenth century didn't exactly corroborate Goethe's otherwise noble vision of enlightenment. While the poet and the merchant kept refining their penchants for possible realities and real possibilities, respectively, the idea of inhabiting the world by joining their intellectual forces was soon relegated to scarce festive moments, and while accounting would become the undisputed way of testifying to the objective facts of this world, art would promise only an occasional vacation from the same. This new balance of power is playfully registered by Hermann Broch in 1931 in the second volume of his *Sleepwalker* trilogy. The protagonist, August Esch, is another dreamer, harrowed by visceral thoughts about justice and devotion, but also an accountant by profession, as if to test how a Wilhelm-plus-Werner composite would work anno 1903, the year of the events recounted in the novel.

There are some reminiscences of Wilhelm in Esch: he too has a thing with theatre, and after losing his job because of an alleged accounting error, he sets up business with the theatre manager Teltscher, though not to play Hamlet but to mount a travelling female wrestling show. His compass, however, is through and through that of an accountant, and, Werner-like, he agrees with Teltscher on the inevitable profitability of an alliance between theatre and "the commercial class" that to him stands out as the last representative of "solidity and breadth of vision".[4] And like Werner, he reckons that solidity and breadth of vision are eventually obtained by following the "laws of bookkeeping", according to which "every debit entry should be balanced by a credit one".

Accordingly, the novel in its entirety glosses Esch's burdensome labour to apply this rule to everything that happens to him and around him. Matters of mating and fidelity, of justice and recognition—these are indeed complicated in the early-twentieth-century Köln and Mannheim roamed by the bookkeeper, and his mind is constantly churning to translate them into still more complex accounting procedures. In his world, the ledger has become the one instrument available to gain insight by applying the reassuring order of the book to the confusing multiplicity of human interactions and affects. And the plot of the novel, concomitantly, matures the insight of the impossibility of this task, as he becomes increasingly suspicious that a fatal accounting error might have occurred in the order of the world. Thus, throughout the novel, a parallel obsession gradually comes to take hold of his mind—that of redemption: "[T]here was something amiss with the world, a glaring error in the books which could only be redeemed by a wonderful new entry."[5] With all his efforts to gain "solidity and breadth of vision" by meticulously outweighing how every confusing situation can be accounted for in terms of balancing credit postings and debit postings, he nonetheless ends up dismissing not only accounting but the ambition of overlooking altogether: "[O]ften it seemed to him as though all that had been done and spoken or had come about was no more than a procession on a dimly lit stage, a representation which was soon forgotten and never palpably present, a thing already past which no one could lay hold on without increasing earthly suffering."[6]

With accountant Esch, Broch has portrayed a sensually and morally alert character who realizes that the language he possesses doesn't allow for understanding—even overseeing—what happens in the world of actual relations he lives in, ranging over a generous novelistic panorama from love and friendship to industry and politics. The available grammar of debit and credit postings can eventually not help him account for the intricacies and injustices harboured by a world where this grammar prevails as the sole way to gain insight. Werner's language has become hegemonic. And Wilhelm's aspirational language of the "soul" has been reduced to insignificant spectral stirrings on a "dimly lit stage".

When accounting for the experiences of life is increasingly restricted to the language of accountancy, the new language of facts, a shadow falls on those experiences that cannot be successfully marked out in this new metrics; they become unfathomable and insignificant. This insight is reassessed in

B.S. Johnson's 1973 novel, *Christie Malry's Own Double-Entry.*
Malry is another accountant and a late descendant of Esch
who attempts to enter all the things that makes him feel better or worse in a meticulously recorded ledger and eventually
must close the account of his life with a sardonic: "balance
written off as bad debt".[7]

Notes

1   Johann Wolfgang Goethe, *Wilhelm Meister's Apprenticeship*,
    trans. Eric A. Blackall (New Jersey: Princeton University Press,
    1995), 18.
2   Ibid.
3   See Mary Poovey, *A History of the Modern Fact* (Chicago:
    University of Chicago Press, 1998).
4   Hermann Broch, *The Sleepwalkers*, trans. Willa and Edwin Muir
    (London: Vintage International, 1996), 187.
5   Ibid., 190, translation modified.
6   Ibid., 339.
7   B.S. Johnson, *Christe Malry's Own Double-Entry* (London:
    Collins, 1973), 187.

C

Capitalocene

Capture

Care

Chicago

Chile

China

Circulation

Colonialism

Comedy

Commodity

Counterfeit

Credit

Crisis

Cynicism

Capitalocene | Jason W. Moore

(Bondage), **Care,** (Colonialism), (Crisis), **Debt, Extraction, Migration,** (Oil), (Violence)

We've been lied to. When we read, view, and hear the conventional description of the climate crisis, it's something like this: "Human society causes climate change"[1] (from the IPCC's most recent report). Climate change is anthropogenic (made by humans). The phrase is repeated. *Anthropogenic.* On an endless loop. *Anthropogenic.* By academics. By journalists. By the major environmentalist organizations. *Anthropogenic.* By the leading institutions of the transnational bourgeoisie, like the World Economic Forum. What sane person, upon examining the evidence, would say otherwise?

As it turns out, a growing number of activists and intellectuals are willing to cry bullshit. For these dissidents, the climate crisis is not anthropogenic. It's capitalogenic: *made by capital.*

Capitalogenic does not mean that the disembodied and abstract logic of endless "growth" is the problem. Indeed, such formulas reproduce the confusion of a civilization whose love of fetishism is so deep that it's easier to imagine the end of the world than the end of capitalism. *Capitalogenic* implicates the entangled relations of capital, class, and culture in the web of life responsible for the climate crisis. Let me signal at the outset that the Capitalocene thesis is not a geological argument but a geohistorical interpretation that builds its analysis through and with a broadly defined climate science history. Its chief argument with the Anthropocene is on this terrain, the geohistorical, not the abstract geological (although our clear sympathies align with the Orbis Spike hypothesis of Maslin and Lewis).[2] The Capitalocene is a protest against, and an alternative to, the Popular Anthropocene and its anti-politics. We object, interpretively and politically, to the deployment of Anthropocene thinking to narrate the origins and development of climate crisis through technological, demographic, and commercial fetishisms rather than the relations of capital, class, and empire in the web of life.

The Capitalocene thesis rejects the neoliberal conceit that technology and policy can offer climate solutions without fundamental democratization; it refuses the obfuscations of "critical" intellectuals who deny that capitalism and its specific pathologies of class struggle and capital accumulation are driving the climate crisis. *Capitalocene* and *capitalogenic* are not merely interpretations of the origins and development of today's crisis; they are provocations and invitations to unthink the dangerous cosmology of Man and Nature, most recently inscribed in the Popular Anthropocene.[3]

The dualism of Man and Nature is a recent invention. Premodern class societies—like feudal Europe or the Roman Empire—understood that humans were distinctive within the web of life. Unlike capitalism, they refrained from organizing and justifying imperial and class relations of domination and exploitation around a hard-and-fast divide between Civilization and Nature. Only with the rise of capitalism after 1492, slowly and fitfully but at times rapidly, did a new scientific cosmology begin to take shape and guide the violent appropriation of unpaid work/energy on a planetary scale. Make no mistake: capitalism was a "geological force"—as Anthropocene advocates say—from the very beginning. The slaving-induced genocides of the New World, geographically concentrated in the flashpoints of empire and commodification (Peru, northeastern Brazil, the Valley of Mexico), were so profound that they contributed to the great climate crisis of the "long, cold seventeenth century" (1550–1700). It was the coldest era of the Little Ice Age (1300–1850), the coldest period of the past 8,000 years.[4] It was also the first *capitalogenic* contribution to climate history. Capitalism's capacity to remake planetary life did not await the rotary steam engine in the 1780s; it began with the Niña, the Pinta, and the Santa María three centuries earlier.

Also born in this era, and fundamental to capitalism's epochal environmental transformations after 1492, was the Civilizing Project. This took many forms, but essentially fused an increasingly "scientific" outlook on webs of life (the better to turn these into profit-making opportunities) with an increasingly modern crusading spirit. By the seventeenth century, this cosmological and ideological project would crystallize through figures like René Descartes and John Locke, who famously joined the ethos of Improvement (through bourgeois property making) with a conception of the Civilizing Project that would, eventually, civilize indigenous peoples living in a "state of nature". From the Scientific Revolution onwards, leading bourgeois ideologists would proclaim that a proper understanding of "natural law"—an argument that matured with Malthus and finds deep resonance in Anthropocene discourse—could explain and justify inequality. This reverberates in the environmentalist illusion: the notion that the Anthropocene is more "scientific" and less political than Capitalocene. To speak of *anthropogenic* climate change is to "listen to the science", as Extinction Rebellion, Greta Thunberg, and countless others insist. The phrase seems innocent enough, but only if we don't think about it too much.

That's a big *if*. Marxists are scarcely more immune from the love of Good Science and bourgeois naturalism than other thinkers. Marx, however, anticipated the problem of Scientism—and today's Anthropocene. Writing in *Capital*, he put the point forcefully: "The weaknesses of the abstract materialism of natural science, *a materialism which excludes the historical process*, are immediately evident from the abstract and ideological conceptions expressed by its spokesmen whenever they venture beyond the bounds of their own speciality."[5] An adequately anti-imperialist and internationalist science must *include* the historical process. It must grasp the geological and the geohistorical—earth formation and social formation—as a dialectical unity of interpenetrating movements, relations, and forces. Grasping the dialectical unity in the abstract, however, is inadequate. It must be forged into a method to identify and interpret the concrete historical turning points and patterns of the capitalist world ecology. Only through a radically honest and relentlessly curious interpretation of world history can we discern what is distinctive about the unfolding climate crisis—and thereby identify, and act upon, the weak links of imperial power in the web of life. This is the heart of the Capitalocene thesis.

The Capitalocene thesis advances three propositions, dialectically joined. First, it proposes that capitalism is not an economic or social system as conventionally understood; it is a *world ecology*, a civilization in the web of life that joins the endless accumulation of capital, peculiar logics of class struggle and imperial power, and specific patterns of environment making. To simplify, the endless accumulation of capital requires, and calls into being, not only definite forms of state and imperial power, and more than definite class relations of bourgeois and proletarian in their manifold expressions; the rise of capitalism implied and necessitated a specific form of the "endless" conquest of planetary life.

Recognizing with Luxemburg the centrality of geographical expansion to the temporary resolution of over-accumulation crises, the Capitalocene thesis joins the two moments—endless accumulation and endless conquest—in the Cheap Nature thesis.[6] Cheap Nature is a proposition about how capitalism works as a metabolism of power, profit, and life, always grounded in specific metabolisms of work: paid and unpaid, human and extra-human. A strategy and logic—not a thing—the history of Cheap Nature reveals capitalism as committed to the "endless" identification and extra-economic appropriation of the Four Cheaps: labour power and unpaid work, food, energy, and raw materials. They are "cheap" in the sense that every great wave of world accumulation depends on the extraordinary enlargement of low-cost flows of labour, food, energy, and raw materials. Without these Four Cheaps, the surplus capital problem intensifies, and the destruction of capital threatens. Interpenetrating this "economic" moment is the second moment of Cheap Nature, the geocultural logic of historical capitalism. Cheapening in price is shaped by cheapening in a double sense. Here we find the violent history of ethico-political *devaluation* and its associated geocultural logics of domination, above all those of racism, sexism, and Prometheanism. From this follows that every great stage of capital accumulation does more than "develop" the relations of geocultural domination and class exploitation; it qualitatively activates the *capitalogenic* potential for epochal climate change.

Crucially, the geopolitical ecology and geocultural logic of Cheap Nature not only acts upon webs of life but develops and reproduces through these webs. Fundamental to the world ecology conception is the dialectical claim—taken over from Marx and elaborated by figures such as Levins and Lewontin—that capital accumulation, state making, and the exploitation of surplus value are metabolisms that not only produce changes in "external nature" *but are products of those webs of life*. Capitalism is at once and unevenly, but always relationally, a product not less than a producer of webs of life.[7]

The Capitalocene's second guiding proposition rejects today's ecosocialist common sense that we may narrate the planetary crisis through Society and Nature. These are not simply epistemological problems or academic word games. We can trace the lineage of Society and Nature to the initial formation of early capitalist ideology: bourgeois naturalism and its Civilizing Projects. In the "long, cold seventeenth century", the new capitalist empires proceeded to "fix" the climate crisis through imperialist advances that consolidated new labour regimes, many centred on forms of the plantation, from Ireland to the West Indies. They were racialized across the Atlantic. This marked the crystallization of the Civilizing Project and the violent, ideological, as well as material redefinition of colonized peoples as "savage".

The Civilizing Project's horrific genius was to redefine the vast majority of humankind as part of Nature; such bourgeois naturalism quickly and terribly gave rise to globalizing patriarchy and successive world colour lines. That this maturing of geocultural devaluation occurred during the first capitalogenic climate crisis should not be skipped. Here we find the origins of the capitalogenic trinity: of the climate class divide, climate patriarchy, and climate apartheid. These are not the results but the underlying causes of the twenty-first-century planetary crisis.

Why should such geocultural devaluation loom so large in climate crises? In a word, to facilitate the Four Cheaps and thereby to advance the rate of profit by counteracting the overaccumulation tendency. Can *everything* be reduced to the "immanent laws" of capitalism? No, and that's the point. The Civilizing Project and the invention of Nature as a *ruling abstraction* became a world-historical lever of cost reduction for capital. To paraphrase von Werlhof, Nature became everything the new bourgeoisies did not want to pay for.[8]

The Capitalocene's third major proposition is an argument about world history, the origins and development of
planetary crisis, and the specific contours of that crisis in the
twenty-first century. The Capitalocene's historical narrative
runs something like this. The climate class crisis of feudalism
in the long fourteenth century was an epochal moment of crisis characterized not merely by manifold biophysical problems but also the world-historical defeat of feudalism's ruling
strata by the semi-proletarian and peasant forces of the time.
It was a "Marxist" not a "Malthusian" crisis. The result, in successive moments and phases of crisis, was a reorientation of
late medieval Europe's dominant strata towards a new form
of frontier making: the Great Frontier. This mode of expansion was entirely different from feudalism's. Through alliances
of new empires, financiers, and merchants, the new strategy
immediately subordinated eastern Europe, Ireland, and the
Americas to the logic of Cheap Nature.

This strategy of cheapness fused the logic of capital (valorization) with a new, binarized geocultural logic: devaluation.
Hence, the centrality of the Civilizing Project and its ruling
abstractions. At its core the new Empires aimed to secure
epoch-making sources of "socially necessary" unpaid work
via extra-economic means—but in contrast to tributary modes
of production, these were yoked to the circuit of capital and
"self-expansionary" tendencies, and thus were joined accumulation by appropriation and the endless accumulation of
capital. Those appropriations would—directly and indirectly—
advance labour productivity within an exceedingly narrow
sphere: the cash nexus. The new value-oriented technics—
crystallizations of tools and ideas, power and nature—allowed
the prodigious appropriation of uncommodified work/energy
so as to advance labour productivity. The great leap forward
in the scale, scope, and speed of landscape and biological

transformations in the three centuries after 1450—stretching from Poland to Brazil, and the North Atlantic's cod fisheries to Southeast Asia's spice islands—may be understood in this light. From 1492, the imperialist bourgeoisies "discovered" not merely new continents to exploit and appropriate but an entirely novel socio-ecological logic of power, profit, and life.

Marx's genius was to link the economic analysis of accumulation with the sociology of class formation and class struggle. Less appreciated, but equally important, Marx also demonstrated that every moment of class exploitation under capitalism is irreducibly socio-ecological. Following this dialectical reasoning, the metabolism of climate crisis is a class struggle in the web of life. To this I would add: every moment of "valorization" in its economic moment depends upon even more expansive moments of *devaluation* and the appropriation of unpaid work. Such *accumulation by appropriation* is fundamental to capital accumulation. Devaluation is the geocultural logic of Cheap Nature. It is the ideological battleground of racism, sexism, Prometheanism, and manifold oppressive dynamics that flow from the Civilizing Project. The world proletariat (in fact, a semi-proletariat comprising manifold precariats and agrarian classes of labour) depends upon, and overlaps with, the global femitariat and biotariat: the rich totality of the planetary proletariat. A revolutionary approach to the climate crisis will need to wrestle seriously with this contradictory unity of valorized and devalued life and work. Such an imaginary—and the practical solidarity it implies—must jettison the bourgeoisie's ruling abstractions of Man, Civilizing, and Nature. Only then can we pierce the veils of capitalism's Big Lies. This is a necessary, but of course not sufficient, intellectual "state shift" as we build movements, organizations, and collectivities that confront the forces of the Capitalocene—and seek to move towards the Proletarocene.

Notes

1   Intergovernmental Panel of Climate Change, *Climate Change 2022: Impacts, Adaptation and Vulnerability* (Nairobi: University Nations Environment Programme, 2022), SPM-4.

2   Simon L. Lewis and Mark A. Maslin, "Defining the Anthropocene", *Nature* 519 (2015), 171–180.

3   Much of what follows draws on a decade of research, interpretation, and conceptual work. Good points of entry include Jason W. Moore, *Capitalism in the Web of Life* (London: Verso, 2015); Raj Patel and Jason W. Moore, *A History of the World in Seven Cheap Things* (Berkeley, CA: University of California Press, 2017). More nuanced engagements with Anthropocene, Capitalocene, and the politics and history of climate in/justice can be found on my website: jasonwmoore.com.

4   Emmanuel Le Roy Ladurie and Valeria Daux, "The Climate in Burgundy and Elsewhere, from the Fourteenth to the Twentieth Century", *Interdisciplinary Science Reviews* 33 (2008), 10–24.

5   Karl Marx, *Capital*, Vol. 1 (New York: Vintage, 1977), 494, emphasis added.

6   Rosa Luxemburg, *The Accumulation of Capital* (New York: Routledge, 2003).

7   Marx, *Capital*, 283. Richard Levins and Richard Lewontin, *The Dialectical Biologist* (Cambridge, MA: Harvard University Press, 1985).

8   Claudia von Werlhof, "On the Concept of Nature and Society in Capitalism", in *Women: The Last Colony*, ed. Maria Mies, Veronika Bennholdt-Thomsen, and Claudia Von Werlhof (London: Zed, 1988), 96–112.

Capture | Zachary Formwalt

(Algorithm), (Chicago), **China**, (Colonialism), (Enclosure), **Extraction**, **Flesh**, (Index)

capture, n.

1a. The fact of seizing or taking forcibly, or by stratagem, or of being thus seized or taken; catching; seizure; we arrest; esp. the seizing as a prize.[1]

It seems that *capture* entered the English language as a noun in the early 1540s and would not become a verb for two and a half centuries, when in the 1790s it finally began to replace the verb form of *captive*.[2]

In her 1951 translation of Rosa Luxemburg's *The Accumulation of Capital*, Agnes Schwarzschild chose *capture*, in exactly this sense, to translate Luxemburg's *Einnahme*: "These guns being almost useless, and the commanders lacking in resource, *the capture* of the harbor was child's play."[3]

The chapter in which this sentence appears, "The Introduction of the Commodity Economy", describes "the splendid beginnings of 'opening China' to European civilisation—by the opium pipe".[4] "European civilisation, that is to say commodity exchange with European capital, made its first impact on China with the Opium Wars when she was compelled to buy the drug from Indian plantations in order to make money for British capitalists."[5] The capture of the harbour at Xiamen had been preceded, and would also be followed, by a whole series of violent captures of Chinese ports by the British and then later by both the British and the French, forcing them into buying opium. "There are more than 40 Chinese

Treaty Ports," Luxemburg writes, "and every one of them has been paid for with streams of blood, with massacre and ruin."[6] Non-capitalist formations, Luxemburg will go on to say in the following chapter—in which the attempted annihilation of the Indigenous peoples of North America to make way for the "American farmer" who would in turn be displaced by "the 'bonanza farm', the large-scale capitalist farm"[7] is described— are "indispensable for capitalist accumulation, providing its fertile soil, accumulation in fact proceeds at the expense of this milieu, and is constantly devouring it".[8]

Luxemburg will ultimately suggest that capitalism is itself captured by its unstoppable drive to continuously accumulate. As she puts it in the book's closing paragraph:

Capitalism is ... a mode which tends to engulf the entire globe and to stamp out all other economies, tolerating no rival at its side. Yet at the same time it is also the first mode of economy which is unable to exist by itself, which needs other economic systems as a medium and soil. Although it strives to become universal, and, indeed, on account of this its tendency, it must break down—because it is immanently incapable of becoming a universal form of production. In its living history it is a contradiction in itself, and its movement of accumulation provides a solution to the conflict and aggravates it at the same time.[9]

capture, v.

1e. To cause (data) to be entered into a computer.[10]

In an essay from 1997, "Surveillance and Capture: Two Models of Privacy", Philip Agre points to two distinct uses of *capture* in computer science: the first has to do with the acquisition of data by a computer system "as input, whether from a human operator or from an electronic or electromechanical device".[11] The OED marks this sense as entering the English language in 1971, the year that President Nixon took the US dollar off gold and Milton Friedman wrote a report titled: "The Need for a Futures Market in Currencies", "a proposal for the creation of what would become the International Money Market".[12] That market opened in 1972, and a year later the Black–Scholes options pricing model was published as the Chicago Board Options Exchange opened. This sequence is often seen as marking the beginning of a new era of financialization, one in which, arguably, we are still situated.

capture, v.
3. To represent, catch or record (something elusive, as a quality) in speech, writing, etc. Esp. in literary and artistic contexts.[13]

The other sense of capture which Agre draws out in his essay has to do with "a representation scheme's ability to fully, accurately or 'cleanly' express particular semantic notions or distinctions, without reference to the actual taking in of data".[14] This sense, Agre points out, is commonly deployed in the field of Artificial Intelligence (AI). "An AI program has successfully 'captured' a behavior when it can mimic an action—like a typical retail transaction—without having to sample the actual movement",[15] as Wendy Hui Kyong Chun has succinctly put it more recently. Chun points out the inherent contradiction in these two senses of capture: "A capture system works when it no longer needs to capture, or rather when it can capture in the second sense of AI systems, without necessarily capturing data in the first sense of registering a trace of some action. Perversely, the dream of capture is the eradication of capture, an eradication that can only be confirmed as accurate by continued capture."

This perverse dream of capture systems seems to express the central contradiction of capitalism described by Luxemburg. In the introduction to a more recent translation of *The Accumulation of Capital*, Paul Le Blanc suggests that the "non-capitalist social strata and forms of social organization" upon which the accumulation of capital depends should include "*all territories* ... our bodies, our family life, our friendships, our creative drives, our sexuality, our dreams, and multiple community and social and cultural activities—permeated by noncapitalist dimensions and energies even in global regions where an advanced capitalist economy more and more predominates".[16] These are sites where a struggle can still be had with a capitalism that must continually manoeuvre to elude its own capture, not by non-capitalist dimensions which have no interest in capital but by its own inertia, which drives it towards the annihilation of anything (the earth included) that does not contribute to its continuous accumulation.

In the 1970s, *capture* became a verb describing the entry of data into a computer, while the mathematical calculation of prices on the newly opened derivatives markets turned these markets into the kind of capture system deployed in the field of AI. The Black–Scholes model that allows for the pricing of derivatives "works without any 'economic' input, i.e., qualitative estimates regarding the underlying economy. The theory allows us to calculate the right price of certain securities in the market with no recourse to market-external data. All we need to do in order to analyze the market is to observe the market itself."[17] Agre remarks in his introduction to the capture model that "computationalists' discourse rarely brings to the surface the connotations of violence in the metaphor of 'capture'; captured information is not spoken of as fleeing, escaping, or resenting its imprisonment".[18] It

is precisely this connotation in the metaphor of capture that
clarifies how finance, and capitalism more broadly, attempts
to secure its future. Luxemburg's modification, in 1913, of
Marx's formulation still holds: "Capital does not merely come
into the world 'dripping from head to toe, from every pore,
with blood and dirt,' it also imposes itself on the world step
by step in the same way."[19]

Notes

1 "capture, n.", *OED Online*, 2022, www-oed-com.access.authkb.
kb.nl/view/Entry/27659.

2 "capture, v.", *OED Online*, 2022, www-oed-com.access.authkb.
kb.nl/view/Entry/27660.

3 Rosa Luxemburg, *The Accumulation of Capital*, trans. Agnes
Schwarzschild (London: Routledge and Kegan Paul Ltd., 1951),
390, my italics.

4 Ibid., 389.

5 Ibid., 387.

6 Ibid., 394.

7 Rosa Luxemburg, *The Accumulation of Capital*, trans. Nicholas
Gray, in *The Complete Works of Rosa Luxemburg, Volume
II: Economic Writings 2*, ed. Peter Hudis and Paul LeBlancß
(London: Verso, 2016), 292.

8 Ibid., 302.

9 Luxemburg, *The Accumulation of Capital*, trans. Schwarzschild,
467.

10 "capture, v.", OED Online.

11 Philip E. Agre, "Surveillance and Capture: Two Models of
Privacy", in *The New Media Reader*, ed. Noah Wardrip-Fruin and
Nick Montfort (Cambridge: MIT Press, 2003), 744.

12 Brian Holmes, "Information's Metropolis", in *Volatile Smile*, ed.
Beate Geissler and Oliver Sann (Nürnberg: Verlag für moderne
Kunst, 2014), 33; Edward LiPuma, *The Social Life of Derivatives:
Markets, Risk, and Time* (Durham: Duke University Press, 2017),
233–234.

13 "capture, v.", OED Online.

14 Agre, "Surveillance and Capture", 744.

15 Wendy Hui Kyong Chun, *Updating to Remain the Same: Habitual New Media* (Cambridge: MIT Press, 2016), 59–60.

16 Paul Le Blanc, "Introduction: Rosa Luxemburg and the Global Violence of Capitalism", in *The Complete Works of Rosa Luxemburg, Volume II: Economic Writings 2*, ed. Peter Hudis and Paul LeBlanc (London: Verso, 2016), xix.

17 Ole Bjerg, *Making Money: The Philosophy of Crisis Capitalism* (London: Verso, 2014), 73.

18 Agre, "Surveillance and Capture", 744.

19 Luxemburg, *The Accumulation of Capital*, trans. Gray, 329–330.

Care | Cassie Thornton

(Abandonment), (Art), (Body), **Capitalocene,**
(Chile), **Death, Debt,** (Health), (Social
Reproduction), **Utopia,** (Water)

See also [edit]

- Neglect

  *You know when you're walking down the street and you see a per-
  son is sitting outside of the dollar store or grocery store, and they are
  dirty. They're sitting on the ground and maybe they have their head
  in their hands and they have set a cup out, and by doing that they're
  asking for money. They don't have to say anything; this is a language
  we know well. And then you see that most people are still having a cup
  of tea or coffee with their Bluetooth conversation and they're just continuing on. Maybe like one in 100 people throw some change in the cup.*

I am a US artist who has spent over a decade focusing on financialization and the way that it destroys relationships of trust and
interdependence in my sacred homeland of competition and
exploitation. In response, with many friends and collaborators
I developed a viral mutual aid project that is now practised
from couches around the world. This project, The Hologram,
has revealed to me and to the many others who now work on it
that a result of capitalism is that it seems impossible to ask for
or to provide help informally. It is on the basis of this project
that I ask: has all care been made scarce since financialization
has emptied out what we once imagined to be public goods
(like government, health, education, and housing)? Can we
run out of care? In what ways is care expensive? In what ways

is care cheap? Why is it that we can't afford to do it? How can
we afford not to do it?

The Opposite of a Miracle

The above scenario is a portrait of a common situation in all
the cities I spend time in: Oakland, San Francisco, New York,
Brooklyn, London, Berlin, and Toronto. Though it is common,
I still see it as an astonishing phenomenon every time I witness
it. What is the physics with which a society exists where people go on drinking coffee while they are surrounded by people
who are dying of neglect at their feet? Is it the opposite of a
miracle? If I put money in the cup, I usually do it as an excuse
to communicate that I see "them" and that they matter to me,
and that the world is better if they are in it. In those moments
my role is to present care as a noun—to *exhibit* care.

When I lived in San Francisco, I watched in horror as
the stream of Silicon Valley tech workers rushed to get their
expensive coffees on their way to their yoga classes, tripping
over the bodies of dirty people laying on the ground or in tents.
The people on the ground had lost their homes because of the
effects of the tech boom that employed the bouncing, caffein-
ated yogis. I struggled so much with it that I needed to leave
that city. In the years after, I tried to understand what could
be going through the minds of the people who skipped along
without looking down at the bodies around them in one of the
financially wealthiest cities in the history of the world. I came
to see their avoidance as an act of self-preservation in a financialized landscape. By unseeing a moment of neglect, many
people avoid feelings of existential sadness that may not allow
them the positive affect necessary to continue to work and
reproduce themselves. If they were to stop and see the pain all
around them, how would they muster the energy to pay rent

or otherwise stay alive when staying alive means finding more and more forms of economic survival where your life is built on top of other people's evictions? To me, the way we are able to live in a financialized landscape that is more and more cruel to more and more people is to perform strategic avoidance, drinking stronger coffee and doing more challenging yoga (and to participate in other affordable forms of hallucination). To make time for all the life-affirming avoidance, many people seem to budget their energy and thus stop caring for some things that they don't have time for. Some of those things are people. It's as if if we actually cared about others, we would be taking away from our own care for ourselves. Care becomes more of a noun than a verb, more of a concept than something we do for each other. Something to write a lot of books and make a lot of art about.

What Is Care?

According to feminist economist Emma Dowling, who supplies us with a summary in line with feminist theory (Tronto, Federici, Bellacasa): "Care is conceived as the activities that take place to make, remake, maintain, contain and repair the world we live in and the physical, emotional and intellectual capacities required to do so."[1] According to gift economists like Genevieve Vaughn, care is a gift.[2] It is, like water, what we are made of, a natural resource. Care, which is something that all people have the capacity to do, also includes some of the least valued work in the world. The people who do the most care (frequently organized along racial and gender lines) are some of the lowest-paid, least-cared-for people on the planet. This is no surprise, since natural resources in capitalism are always taken, commodified, and exploited. The natural gifts given by the planet like water and life and by carers who raise children and nurture human health are the most at risk of becoming tools of the market, and organized by levels of exchange, which is the foundation of financial markets. Financialization specifically acts to take the institutions that organize these gifts and turn them into profit factories for the wealthy.

To survive in a world where there is so much inequality and suffering, it helps to get an apartment up high where we can't see any of the pain directly. But what happens when we go downstairs and, on the way to our coffee meeting, we look directly at a person who has been abandoned by the disorganized collective that we are a part of? What type of care does a financialized world produce, through us, in this moment of actual raw need?

Let's imagine there is a person selling newspapers outside my local train station, and that I am an anti-debt activist focused on care and wealth redistribution. As I approach, I'm not sure what to do. They are afraid to look at me, but I am also afraid to look at them. They are asking for money because they need an indescribable form of help, which is any help besides money. I want nothing more than to help this person, but also I have no idea how to help them even though their hand is out. I put some coins in their hand.

I know that my change doesn't affect their situation. Nothing transforms and the person looks embarrassed. This potential connection is ruined because we both tacitly just want time to pass and for this difficult non-moment to be forgotten. I fear that they see me as money.

What if I cancelled my coffee date and sat down with them. What if they need more than I can comfortably give?

Why Is the Answer No?

To offer more than money in this situation requires a personal risk, not a social one. When I think about it theoretically, sharing substantial resources with a single stranger feels like losing what I have earned, instead of supporting the social body that the stranger and I are a part of. By tossing some change in their cup, I can perform care without doing it, and show that I am a good person (to myself and to anyone watching), but there is no precedent for how to give support to a stranger as if they are a member of my community or society.

By the time I was born, assigned American at birth,[3] financialization had acted upon my world in ways I could never unimagine. In my lifetime there was never any such thing as a welfare state, and even as a teenager I was keenly aware that institutions that used the word *care* always meant profit. I always assumed there would be no meaningful help available at an institutional level that could ever support me, this stranger, or anyone to thrive, no matter what the scale of our needs. And so looking at the silent request for money in the above scenarios is like looking at a little pothole in the street. When I look closer, I can see that the pothole leads to a huge underground cavity and the whole sidewalk is about to cave in. I realize that in my imagination, that hole can never be filled, and I feel so close to falling into it. There's a pang of personal responsibility. Oh wait—is that my mindfulness app? It says: "Live in the moment. Focus on your breathing. Imagine yourself sinking into the ground. There is nothing there. You are completely supported. Did you pay your student loans?" I throw my phone and it falls down a hole.

What's Down There?

Neglect of an unknowable scale. The stranger seeking money represents needs that are immeasurable, that our society will not fulfil. The cave gets deeper. So many people are in the same position as this person or worse, though we can't see them right now. The cave gets wider. This level of neglect has been developing for so long, even before 1973. I realize that the cave is actually everywhere underneath us, a big void. The earth has no core; it has been hollowed out and sold and made into a debtors' prison and condos. And soon we realize that what we are standing on is so fragile it can barely hold us up. To begin to address this scale would take much more than I can do in a day, between jobs. I would have to change my whole life, and that would not be enough. I would need to change my life, all my routines, and values, and I would need everyone to do it with me.[4] All our habits would have to change, to soften, and move to centre care. The economy would shift, hierarchies would end, men would be socialized differently, carceral systems would turn into places of intergenerational healing, or would not exist at all. I would need to walk differently, and to think differently, and to stop seeing myself as my main project. I would have to feel like a part of a social world that includes all the people seeking money as help. I turn my music up really loud. My mindfulness app reminds me that I am 70% water.

Care Is a Miracle

A teacher asks students in Chile how they care for water. "How do we care for water?" In [the Chilean province of] Petorca there was lots of water. Now most households only have water for a few hours a day. "We have to care for it, because it determines our future," says the teacher.[5]

There's something about having a resource that occurs naturally, a gift, that makes it hard to appreciate until it is almost gone. The fact that it is common (we are made of it; it is all over the planet) has something to do with a recurring hiccup in our valuation system: when we need it, we don't value it, but it is also worth more than money. I am talking about care, but I am also talking about water, two things that determine our ability to live. In Petorca there is and was plenty of water. But there was legislation that happened on my birthday in 1981 that privatized that water, and allowed it to become profitable and not common. This was a project related to the Chilean Miracle, or the financialization of Chile, when social goods were privatized, divided up into little bundles and sold on international markets. It means that now there is not enough water for children in schools to drink, while big agriculture has plenty.

The scarce water becomes politicized in the wrong way. Children are taught that it is their personal responsibility to care for the water by not wasting an extra drop. The future becomes the responsibility of individual children in Petorca who must carefully turn the tap off. Are children also taught about what happened in 1981, and why there is no water? Children are taking responsibility for a water crisis caused in part by American imperialism, organized to test out financialization by "Chicago Boys". Is it a miracle?

What Is a Miracle?

The birth of the thing we call financialization is sometimes called a miracle. It began in 1973 when the US academic mercenary Milton Friedman went to Chile. Many internet neoliberals describe the time after this visit as the Miracle of Chile.[6] In 1970, 20% of Chile's population lived in poverty, and at the end of this miracle, poverty levels are said to have at least doubled. The president, Pinochet, was in power after a successful military coup to dismantle the former socialist era of former leader Allende, and this new economic system was delivered with the force of a military junta, causing danger and extreme trauma.

In 1990, the year Pinochet left office, Milton Friedman coined the phrase "The Miracle of Chile". What does it take to see a golden glow around a growing GDP while a military state takes over, all social services are privatized for the small wealthy elite, half the population is unemployed, and the military enacts extreme violence on the poor? I am really interested in the collective imagination necessary to see a miracle where there is actually social death.

Dying for Coffee

Sometimes I feel like I live a double life, between two dimensions. In dimension number 1, which takes place in Berlin, I drink flat whites to accelerate the inertia, and things are kind of fine. I adapt to my conditions like everyone does, but the conditions are somewhat stable, or I don't really notice them. I live a life where I am valued for my small contributions (of chaos and honesty) to places where capitalism usually wouldn't let them live. But dimension number 2 is a place I can only touch when I first wake up or when I slow down, though it is always underneath everything. It is one of huge existential dread, where pipelines are being attacked in the ocean as acts of war, where whole countries are flooded and washed away, where thousands of people are currently in the Mediterranean on ships that have nowhere to land, where places I have lived may be swallowed in fire. These parallel dimensions feel like they are two parallel horizontal lines moving closer to each other. In my imagination, when these two lines cross where I am, the fears that I have been cultivating will be more real than the current flat white dimension is right now. I don't know what to do when that intersection happens. I don't know what to do until that intersection happens. There may not be any care infrastructure left to deal with the large-scale harms

Figure 8.1 This photograph is from an exhibition of new works by Cassie Thornton, Anna Ihle, and Germain Ngoma. *To Break Up with Forms* was curated by Martina Petrelli for the Nitja Centre for Contemporary Art in October 2023. The work described below is by Cassie Thornton. This is a photograph of a Collective Psychic Timeline installed in a window. This timeline shows the (green) Flat White Dimension being overtaken by the (red) Demons Coming Out of the Sidewalk Dimension as we move forward in linear time, from left to right. (*Source*: Nitja Centre for Contemporary Art/Tor Simen Ulstein; reprinted with permission.)

that are taking place in most people's lives. For some of us, this is not the first time. There is so much to care about, but it also feels like there is nowhere to put that care.

Notes

1 Emma Dowling, *The Care Crisis* (London: Verso, 2021).
2 Genevieve Vaughan, *The Gift Economy*, 2023, http://gift-economy.com/.
3 Stella Lawson, "Astrology Session with Stella the Witch", astrology reading, 6 January 2023, Zoom.

4   Carolyn Pedwell, *Revolutionary Routines: The Habits of Social Transformation* (Montreal: McGill-Queen's University Press, 2021).

5   Ben Derico and Jocelyn Tabancay Duffy, "In Chile, Even Water Is Privatized: The New Constitution Would Change That", *The Intercept*, 12 August 2022, https://theintercept.com/2022/08/12/chile-drought-water-constitution/.

6   Alex Kaiser, "The Fall of Chile", *Cato Journal*, Cato Institute, 2020, www.cato.org/cato-journal/fall-2020/fall-chile.

China | Giulia Dal Maso

Capture, Death, (Divination), Gold, Interest, (Supply)

The arrival of finance capital in China turned out to be a "red swan" that quickly challenged most conventional models of economic and political change. After a complicated histori-cal trajectory in which colonial financial capital shook up the activities of the widespread network of local informal banks (*qianzhuang*, often translated as "money shops") during the second half of the nineteenth century, Chinese domestic finance remained subservient to the global development of modern capitalism. With China's "open door" at the beginning of the twenty-first century, however, the arrival of capital was "utterly different from that of a century earlier because this time global capital entered by invitation".[1] The establishment of the two stock markets in Shanghai (in 1990) and Shenzhen (in 2004) marked the prelude of the country's path to becom-ing a potentially global financial hegemon.[2]

Chinese financialization was unprecedented. Financial capital operations were unleashed in a country where private property had been abolished for almost half a century and the nationalization of the means of production had granted the state the status of defender and guarantor of the people. Finance quickly shed the old order, reshuffling the terms of the social and political legitimacy of the party state. It was not a smooth process. The value of money in China had been mar-ginal and subordinated to a socialist economic order where economic activities were organized through central planning and controlled prices. Rather abruptly, finance quickly gained popularity and became a powerful tool that succeeded in its scope of financializing en masse what were previously financially passive subjects.

Unlike in the West, finance capital was not unleashed in China because of capital's quest for new ways of valorization after declining industrial profits. Operating outside China's socialist legal system, the launch of Special Economic Zones (SEZs) in the southern Chinese coastal area attracted foreign direct investment in a huge manufacturing power that redefined the country's industrial relations within the world system. China famously became the "factory of the world". However, its initial role in the global chains of production was rapidly reshaped. The abundance of surplus capital was promptly put in motion through an almighty financial complex, opened and coordinated by the state to align with global capitalist transformation.

The opening of capital markets in the mid-nineties by Deng Xiaoping not only followed the principles that economic reforms had to be undertaken by "crossing the river by feeling for the stones". Continuing the Chinese historical trajectory of selectively both rejecting and absorbing foreign colonial knowledge and categories, the country remained immune to the Western orthodoxy of a division between the market and the state. This unique pattern saw the restructuring of its State-Owned Enterprises (SOEs) into shareholding corporations through the making of a state-controlled stock market as a new redistributive fulcrum. In this transition common people, including many workers and peasants, lost their labour and social rights. To make up for this cost, they were "invited" to invest their initially meagre savings in the shares of their previous employers.

People's increasing acquaintance with financial logic thus became linked to the expectation that the state provided them returns through its own artefact: the stock market. In China many people resorted to the stock market to make up for income losses caused by system reforms that left them in a precarious social and economic situation. This state-led "socialization of finance" made post-socialist China the country with the highest number of petty amateur investors in the world, amounting to almost 200 million, including precarious workers, housewives, and retirees. In China, as in most other countries undergoing financialization, private savings were successfully converted into stocks.

The epitome of American financial capitalism, the stock market, was implanted in China as a two-faced Janus, both creator and creature. On the one hand, it was a creator, because it generated *ex nihilo* an apparatus of regulatory bodies and an infrastructure that tied China's financial system to the world. A major impetus for Chinese state capital to "go global" through the circulation of Chinese state capital in global markets was a higher return on investment. To this end, the state equipped itself with state-owned financial intermediaries including Sovereign Wealth Funds (SWFs), government guided funds, portfolio investments, and state-owned banks, whose practices were geared to service the accelerated and transnational circulation of state capital. On the other hand, it was a creature, because it implied the risks and uncertainties of a changing relationship with the previous form of sovereignty. The state had to prove its accountability not only to its people but also to a global financial logic controlling the inflows of private capital through market-based mechanisms. This meant recalibrating state power with the inevitable risks and volatility posed by a global financial environment. China's financial apparatus, as a creature of the party hierarchy, started monitoring and steering financial actors and market participants to accomplish its own agenda.

This meant that the process of financialization became tightly linked to the pursuit of political objectives, including the management and control of the population. The population was asked to *jiefang* (free up) their minds, unleashing their individual capacity and desires, to no longer be dependent on the state. At the same time, however, they were asked to rely on "market" structures inextricably linked to the state's guidance. By organizing the relationship between the state and the multitude of investors, the stock market became a tool of *financial*-cum-*biopolitical* management. As a major owner and shareholder of the "market", the state engaged in a form of social engineering that managed the population, putting it in sync with China's reforms and economic objectives. A new contractual relationship, once based on wage labour, was gradually redefined through what Chinese people started calling a *gupiao re* (stock fever)—a feverish craving for stocks that seized the population.

The legacy of the socialist Chinese social contract was rewritten in a financial formula, akin to speculative politics, played out by investors and investees. In contrast to developed economies, where governments prioritize appeasing creditors in the form of investors over citizens' welfare, and view individuals and workers as investees, in the context of the Chinese stock market those roles are inverted. On the one hand, the state expects citizens to invest their money in state-owned SOEs to increase the value of its own assets, while, on the other hand, investors count on the state, as the planner and provider of financial opportunities, to guarantee a return on investment. This economic and political dependency has brought new imperatives based on financial expectations, managing to create new financial wealth from the general social orientation and cooperation of this multitude of investors. Partially vacating its function as primary employer, the state is now characterized by its ability to divert investors' money into state-owned assets and thus distribute capital according to its own plans.

Language and money, the building blocks of speculation, become the primary signifiers through which to project politically sanctioned images of a future otherwise feared and unknown. The state covers up growing inequality by channelling narratives of the past, of greater China, into the vision and imagination of a "Chinese dream", a "Chinese renaissance", and a "common prosperity". Meanwhile, the mass of investors enters this relationship conscious that what the state promises through this kind of evocation is a false and never realizable vision of the future.

As an illustration, the term *bailan*, meaning "let it rot", is a neologism coined by both workers and investors who are dissatisfied with the socio-political system. Stemming from a general feeling of exhaustion, and a feeling of being trapped, it opposes a national disciplining that seeks to subsume people's desires and creativity for the sake of national productivity. It conveys an anti-productivist attitude which, when applied to the market, invites small players to engage in investment practices that go against any economic rationale, especially the ones of big state-controlled players, which are also termed *dazhuang*, meaning "big usurer, usurer" (from the above-mentioned term for bank, *qianzhuang* or "money shop"). While denouncing the inequality between players on the stock exchange, this attitude characterizes small investors' irrational and herding behaviour, which by wanting to disturb and derail the moves of the big state-controlled players has become politically charged.

A further illustration is the term *jiucai* ("garlic chives"), which recently became a popular self-deprecating meme used by investors to describe their own tendency to persistently

throw cash at the markets to retrieve what they lost in a previous investment, never learning their lesson. Like garlic chives,
they sprout and regrow again after their stems are chopped off
to make dumplings. In this declination, investors' mass participation in the stock market redefines a new biopolitical dimension in which the investors become *jiucai*. Their role is no
longer confined to one of investors, but it is extended to that of
a multitude constantly trying to be a part of the winning, good,
and protected activities of the state, "but whose investments
are then consumed by the establishment".[3] In this dimension
the investors appear as cows, never tiring of being milked.
Converging the power of biology, economics, and politics into
the self, the *jiucai* meme defines the investors as subjects that
"put to work" their energy, bodies, and relational activities into
the web of national capital expansion, but which at the same
time reflect the production of cynical subjectivities, increasingly autonomous and disaffected by the state.

In the form of a paradox, Chinese mass financial mobiliza-
tion appeals to the state as the institution that allows investors
to get rich through means of financialization, but at the same
time, the investors develop an opportunistic attitude that
deliberately seeks to distance themselves from and obfuscate
their dependency on the state. What is striking in the Chinese
context is that the mounting widespread distrust and indigna-
tion towards the state does not seem to impact the financial
realms. Investors want the stock fever to continue. Such a relationship acquires a performative value, producing commu-
nally instituted rules of making sense of the future projected
by investors.

The stock market becomes a battleground where money
obliterates social relationships from their real contexts and
transforms them into "automated acts of enunciation that tend
towards themselves".[4] Under this new financialized contract,

it is increasingly money, upgraded to the rank of an absolute value, that is left to filter the relationship between the state and the population. For investors, the search for money hides the close relationship between the state and its creation (financialization), making this latter a sphere existing on its own terms. Financialization acquires an eschatological power, one which produces a very specific form of imagination binding the political end to the financial one, and which leaves the ends to finance themselves.

Notes

1   Leo Panitch and Sam Gindin, "The Integration of China into Global Capitalism", *International Critical Thought* 3, no. 2 (2013), 151.
2   Giovanni Arrighi, *Adam Smith in Beijing: Lineages of the Twenty-First Century* (London: Verso, 2007).
3   Laikwan Pang, "China's Post-Socialist Governmentality and the Garlic Chives Meme: Economic Sovereignty and Biopolitical Subjects", *Theory, Culture & Society* 39, no. 1 (2022), 83.
4   Franco "Bifo" Berardi, *Futurabilità* (Roma: Nero Edizioni, 2018), 233.

Comedy | Madeline Lane-McKinley

(Crisis), (Dystopia), **Fictions, Men, Utopia**

Fredric Jameson describes postmodernism's aesthetic relation to financialization as a "symptomatology of yet another
stage of abstraction" in capitalism's history. In a similar manner, comedy brings form, however fleetingly, to this terrain
of "unrepresentable symptoms".[1] Comedy is a web of desires,
anxieties, fears, pleasures, frustrations, furies, knotted up and
entangled in the ideological blockages and everyday miseries
of capitalist life. Comedy is a mess. And it articulates this world
as a mess.

Comedy also gets into trouble: "[T]he funny is always tripping over the not funny," Lauren Berlant and Sianne Ngai note,
"sometimes appearing identical to it".[2] Through troubles and
troubling, comedy expresses, like pus from some sublime and
gaping wound, the utopian, dystopian, and anti-utopian all at
once: a collective dream for the end of capitalism, always in
conflict with constraints of political imaginability, as a shared
dread for the end of the world.

In its most revolutionary capacity, comedy can insist: capitalist totality is such a joke.

Today, many anti-capitalist comedies—at least the most
conspicuous, if not heavy-handed—tend towards satire (e.g.
Succession), while being fundamentally quite earnest (and liberal) about the joke of capitalist totality and how to represent
it. The irony of these satires is how literal-minded they ask us
to be. But the possibilities of anti-capitalist comedy needn't
be reduced to a matter of solving the problem of abstraction
through representation, as Leigh Claire La Berge writes of
the financial scandal, "highly narrativized and conclusive".[3]

Driving so many contemporary satires is this desire for representation, so often fixated on scandal and corruption as modes of sense making, attempts to individuate and dramatize what exceeds perceptibility.

The joke is not just representational, but epistemological. That is, joking can make political contradictions thinkable. Jokes are modes of critical negation, as well as utopian experimentation—they are as much about interrogating the world as about unthinking it.

The empty promise of comedy, however, is escapism from a world of seemingly no escape. Adorno and Horkheimer saw in the culture industry a version of this ever-worsening dystopia, where "there is laughter because there is nothing to laugh about". In this hell, "fun is a medicinal bath," they quip, "which the entertainment industry never ceases to prescribe. It makes laughter the instrument for cheating happiness."[4] Comedy, it would seem, doles out mere temporary relief, anesthetizing us from pains otherwise unavoidable. By this logic, comedy can only make our dystopia appear more tolerable—heard with each laugh are echoes of a false utopia.

At the same time, Adorno and Horkheimer's critique of comedy is undeniably hilarious, riddled with zingers, banter, and vivid metaphors. What are we to make of the comedy at work in their critique? What do we do with this laughter?

"This is a laughter that can turn the laughter of the culture industry back on itself," Anca Parvulescu writes, marking out "another form of laughter, qualitatively different from that of the culture industry".[5] In Charlie Chaplin's comedy, Walter Benjamin hears this other kind of laughter as "the most revolutionary emotion of the masses",[6] and the experience of a "preemptive and healing outbreak of mass psychosis".[7] When we laugh during *Modern Times* (1936)—watching Chaplin's "Tramp" sabotage the assembly line, breaking apart the machinery of capitalist production along with its stronghold on reason—we catch glimpses of a not-quite world, not quite ours. Laughter is "potentially revolutionary the moment we know it intervenes within an already laughing Emerald City," Parvulescu insists—this laughter is both, indivisibly, "a medicinal bath ... and the echo of revolutionary noise".[8]

Revolutionary laughter demands revolutionary ways of listening. If we can't laugh, we don't want to be part of your revolution.

Of laughing together, Georges Bataille wrote that "we pass very abruptly, all of a sudden, from a world in which each thing is qualified, in which each thing is given in its stability", and we move into "a world in which our assurance is suddenly overthrown, in which we perceive that this assurance is deceptive, and where we believed that everything was strictly anticipated".[9]

To laugh at this world is not just to endure it but to make its preposterousness felt. Comedy might as well be science fiction.

Notes

1   Fredric Jameson, "Culture and Finance Capital", *Critical Inquiry* 24, no. 1 (1997), 252.
2   Lauren Berlant and Sianne Ngai, "Comedy Has Issues", *Critical Inquiry* 43, no. 2 (2017), 234.
3   Leigh Claire La Berge, *Scandals and Abstraction: Financial Fiction of the Long 1980s* (New York: Oxford University Press, 2015), 15.
4   Theodor W. Adorno and Max Horkheimer, *Dialectic of Enlightenment – Philosophical Fragments* (Stanford, CA: Stanford University Press, 2002), 112.
5   Anca Parvulescu, *Laughter: Notes on a Passion* (Cambridge, MA: MIT Press, 2010), 151.

6   Walter Benjamin, "Chaplin in Retrospect", in *The Work of Art in the Age of Its Technological Reproducibility, and Other Writings on Media* (Cambridge, MA: Belknap Press of Harvard University Press, 2008), 337.

7   Walter Benjamin, "The Work of Art in the Age of Its Technological Reproducibility", in *The Work of Art in the Age of Its Technological Reproducibility*, 38.

8   Parvulescu, *Laughter*, 154–155.

9   Georges Bataille, *The Unfinished System of Nonknowledge* (Minneapolis, MN: University of Minnesota Press, 2001), 135.

Commodity | Ursula Andkjær Olsen

Fictions, Gift, Gold, Luxury, Men, (Performativity), (Social Reproduction), Value

The point of purchase is a train you cannot get off, headed for the promised land. I dream I arrive at the most incredible bakery: a big—enormous, even—bright, high-ceilinged space painted in creamy colours and gold. And the display counters! So big is the bakery, in fact, you have to take a train to get around it—well, that's to say, at first I just stand there, overwhelmed, staring. Then I spot the croissants. A display counter filled with nothing but croissants, each decorated in its own colour: lavender, lilac, rose, violet. On closer reflection, it's as though each croissant is wearing its own coat of arms and hence its "own colours", also in the sense of wearing its country's colours. I find a saleswoman and ask her for a croissant, any croissant, maybe fuschia-coloured, maybe plum, and that's when suddenly this train pulls up, and I'm asked to climb aboard. Ordered to, in fact. I assume it's going to take me to my croissant. Or, I don't know what I'm thinking, but then I'm told—or rather, I'm not really told anything at all, but I realize the croissants are merely a SIGN. That is, by pointing to a croissant, selecting a particular croissant with a particular coat of arms, wearing its own colours, I am NOT purchasing this selected croissant, which is merely a sign of something else entirely, and it is this thing I have in fact purchased. Or asked for permission to purchase. And to which I am now headed, riding in a cream-coloured train trimmed with gold.

What the actual thing was I do not know.

ANALYSIS

What to make of this? Von Shop, the department stores, I am constantly led away from what I was intending to do. Perhaps some image analysis is necessary here. We have WOMB SYMBOLS, containers, PHALLUS SYMBOLS, towers, and long things in general, and PUSSY SYMBOLS, which are sort of … portals, various forms of portals.

I really like phallus symbols, towers, all kinds of towers; I don't get people who are against towers; no towers in the city, no towers on the horizon, no towers anywhere. But I'm equally wild about womb symbols: containers, boxes, chests, cases, diving bells, home, sweet home, all of it. And then pussy symbols, of course: the ultimate symbol of portals, symbol of transitions: doors, gates, portals that lead from one world to another. I'm also very fond of stairs. I've debated whether stairs belong to the portal department. Take escalators, for example: you go up or down, riding it, and are brought to another level. If you combine them, that is, you go up the stairs—through a "portal", so to speak—to get to the top of the tower. Maybe the phallus offers a nice view; I would think so.

The bakery is the epitome of a womb. Or maybe a breast—wait, I completely forgot the BREAST SYMBOLS—a breast full of model trains and croissants. Cream and gold … long chains of god-given gifts, flowing out across the world.

Translated by Jennifer Russell

Counterfeit | Jonas Eika

(Divination), (Faith), Flesh, Money, Organization, Sacrifice, Utopia

All Tits Are Real, All Money Is Fake, All Hail Satan

Peachlyfe[1]

Liège, Belgium, 1233

Their habit is simple, made of unbleached homespun. It falls loosely around their hips and shoulders, the outer veil billowing about the tightly fitting headpiece. It makes them look small and peculiar, Jacomyne thinks on their way to the market, like infants lost in their own swaddling—but also that the habit offers a sanctuary, a warm and shadowy space between skin and fabric that is all one's own.

*

"Until the end of the twelfth century the noun *purgatorium* did not exist; *the* purgatory had not yet been born."[2] But then it was, in a Christianized Europe where urban economies were rapidly growing, and monetary payments became increasingly common, both in everyday exchanges and when paying taxes and tithes. Before, the souls of the dead had gone directly to heaven or hell, but now, when neither the Church nor feudal lords nor burghers could remain unsullied by money, *an intermediate place* was required. A purifying fire which would allow ordinary sinners to enter heaven before the last judgement. For the poor and the outcast, and for all who harboured hopes of the imminent coming of heaven on earth, purgatory was bad news: redemption, once attained by living as Jesus and the apostles had *in* the world—that is, by selling one's possessions and holding everything in common—could now be attained after death, through repentance and intercessory prayers. Something about money required a third place, an intermediate time, a deferral of the coming of the Messiah.

*

They walk down Jacob's Stairway, 324 steps, past the Franciscans' herb gardens, growing behind walls on small terraces, and through town. The streets are dim, the morning still damp on the cobblestones. A dark, pungent smell emanates from a newly tarred wooden shed, somewhat out of place among all the mud-built houses. Men pass by them; craftsmen, beggars, and weavers, but also a few nobles and merchants who aren't usually up at this hour. Some step aside with their head bowed and hands devoutly on their chest; others stare suspiciously, but all add to Jacomyne's unease, her feeling of always being an exception: neither married nor cloistered, spiritual in the world; as a beguine you live the life of angels here in the flesh.

She sighs and tries to recover some semblance of calm. She thinks of their visit to Eve the Anchoress at dawn. When they told her of their longing for the Eucharist, for receiving it more often, Eve went over to her chest in the corner and returned with a thin, whitish-brown linen cloth. The piece of cloth she said was Saint Veronica's veil. That is, the True

Face of Jesus. That is, the veil Veronica had used to wipe the blood and sweat from Christ's face when he walked the Via Dolorosa; Jacomyne ached to touch it. It didn't matter that Eve had obtained the cloth by leaving it on her own face all day and all night one Good Friday—this was how she had channelled Jesus through herself, into the fabric. She unfolded it and held it up in her cell, behind the thick wooden shutters tilted sideways in the window opening. A brownish imprint on the cloth, the traces of two tired eyes and a half-open mouth ...

*

"You cannot serve God and mammon." "It is easier for a camel to pass through the eye of a needle than for a rich man to enter the kingdom of God." And so on. What is it exactly about money that is incompatible with redemption? What was it about the dissemination of money that made purgatory necessary? For theologians in the twelfth century, the problem seemed to be money's severance of value from the material world. While land was something in and of itself and required labour and cultivation to yield crop, money was pure method of payment that could self-replicate through loans, unconstrained by the hours of the earth and the body.[3] From the outset, it was this slippage towards immateriality that made money threatening—a process of abstraction that did of course accelerate through the centuries, from the implementation of paper money to modern financialization, but which was perhaps already intuited and feared back then, in the twelfth century. Meanwhile, partly as a reaction to the proliferation of money and the Church's accumulation of it, there was a burgeoning of new religious movements based on a simple principle: *imatitio*, imitating

Jesus and the apostles, following their example and repeating it, varying it, copying it ...

*

At the marketplace, after they have laid out their woollen goods and legumes on the cart, Jacomyne's father suddenly approaches them.

"Honourable beguines of the House of Saint Catherine," he says, hinting at a bow, and then stopping a few steps from their stall and looking at Jacomyne. "Honourable daughter, how good it is to see you."

Now he smiles, moved, but also hesitant, his posture slightly stooped. His small, firm cheeks are moving beneath his dark beard, his dark, flickering eyes.

"And I am glad to see you," says Jacomyne neutrally.

He nods and looks at her with his mouth half-open in question, as if suddenly unsure whether he can speak to her now she has renounced everything and gone halfway into the next world. She clears her throat; she must try: "I cannot help but worry about your business affairs."

He looks at her in surprise. "But there's nothing to worry about?"

"Yes, for you are trading in money and committing usury!"

"But, my dear," he says, sighing, "it isn't possible to trade anything without money anymore. And what's so bad about lending a little to men in need? My interests are lower than most."

"But what you are earning money on," says Jacomyne, "is nevertheless time, which belongs to God."

He sucks in his lips, looking offended. And yet there is something, an uncertainty or anguish, she senses, that makes him reply instead of simply silencing her: what about the risk he runs when lending money? Or when he brings back wool and dye all the way from England because the weavers here in town are running out?

Jacomyne nods; she knows he is risking something. But does he not *expect* to be repaid, just as Luke cautions against in his gospel?

No, he says, raising his voice: he does not expect, he *hopes*. Just as she ought to hope he is able to forget her behaviour here today. Besides, he gives plenty of alms.

Jacomyne feels her courage dry up like clay in her throat. An old, heavy silence beneath his reproachful gaze. Behind him, a few of the other market-goers have stopped to listen. Nearby, the farmers' children play with the dogs that have pulled their carts here. A group of Franciscan friars walk about barefooted with their begging bowls, appealing most adamantly to the merchants: "Brother Francis once belonged among your ranks." Jacomyne breathes in and thinks of Veronica's veil. How Eve laid it out in her cell, and each of them in turn was permitted to step up to the shutters, as close as possible. Jacomyne closed her eyes and felt her lips tingle. A slight contraction between her legs, an urge to get past those shutters. To feel the True Face of Christ against her own. His beautiful face against hers. His strong face against her weak one, her inadequate and wretched one. ... She thought of the veil, how it imitated Jesus when he wiped his face with it. How Veronica, out of kindness, the only thing she had to give, made an imprint and carried him with her, onwards down a side street to Via Dolorosa. And then she envisioned that street, narrow and lined with small doors, winding its way through time. All of the saints were standing on that street, each of them imitating another who was imitating someone who had, at some point, imitated Jesus. Jesus, who was imitating his mother when he said: "This is my body." But not as a son, just as Jacomyne did not feel like a daughter or a bride to him. She was a sister, just as he was a sister, which is to say: beside.

*

Theresa Hak Kyung Cha: "God who has made me in His Own Likeness. In His Own Image in His Own Resemblance, in His Own Copy, in His Own Counterfeit Presentment, in His Duplicate, in His Own Reproduction, in His Cast, in His Carbon, His Image and His Mirror. Pleasure in the image pleasure in the copy pleasure in the projection of likeness pleasure in the repetition."[4]

*

Somewhere right beside me, always present, always possible to imitate, thinks Jacomyne and looks back up at her father. She lifts her chin, draws herself up and feels the resolute calm of the Virgin Mary settle in her chest. And behind her, the other Saint Catherine sisters as a warm, steady presence at her back. "But why do you give alms, Father?"

He looks back at her, puzzled.

"You want me to go ahead of you. I am your daughter, the power is yours entirely, I have no power myself. And yet you want me to go ahead, out of this world and into the Lord God's—but now I ask you: why? What is it inside you that wishes to be with God? Who inside you wishes to give alms for the Lord's sake?"

He looks down at his shoes, his lips whirling around his face as though he were rinsing his mouth. "It is he who wishes to do good," he then says.

"Yes," says Jacomyne, and feels the words come to her in the same breath, "it is he who wishes to do good, but knows how hard it is to do it. And it is he who looks on, full of sorrow, while the sinner in you, the *usurer* in you, continues to charge interest and amass money."

"But I give plenty of alms!"

"Like washing a body that is rotten on the inside! Do you not still own what you let go of? Is one not still rich when one can afford to give away?"

Her father opens his mouth, insulted but at a loss, and she feels it too. He has lost touch with the temper, the hot-headedness with which he usually sets people straight. She continues: "Demons hide in the coin, Father. Money begets more money, like heretics that breed in the dark. Money is always in the dark, and it drags its servants down with it. But I know you wish to rise into the light."

Veni, Sancte Spiritus, someone behind him suddenly sings—an elderly man dressed in rags—at first cautiously, almost in jest, but then several others who have stopped to watch the scene start to sing along. Jacomyne tries to catch her father's eye. It's not too late, she says. *Veni, Sancte Spiritus*. He wants to set her free to approach God on his behalf, but why send a representative when he can walk the path himself? *Veni, Sancte Spiritus*. Instead of hoping she will get close enough to God to intercede and reduce his time in purgatory, why not walk the path himself? *Veni, Sancte Spiritus*. Now they're singing from the stalls as well, farmers and paupers, fisherwomen and petty craftsmen. "Instead of giving alms," Jacomyne continues, "in the hopes of buying indulgences for your riches, for all the mammon that grieves you so, the money that keeps you awake at night—how is it earned? In whose hands has it been? How much of God's time has it laid claim to? Instead of all that despair, day in and day out, why not give it all away? Once and for all?"

Translated by Jennifer Russell

Notes

1 Reprinted with permission of the artist.
2 Jacques Le Goff, *The Birth of Purgatory*, trans. Arthur Goldhammer (Chicago: University of Chicago, 1984).
3 Jacques Le Goff, *Your Money or Your Life: Economy and Religion in the Middle Ages*, trans. Patricia Ranum (New York: Zone Books, 1988).
4 Theresa Hak Kyung Cha, *Dictee* (Berkeley, CA: University of California Press, 2001), 17.

Credit | Michel Feher

Bookkeeping, (Hostile Takeover), **Iconomy, Interest, Liquidity,** (Risk), **Trust, Value**

Capitalism, it is generally assumed, runs on profit. Whatever the nature of their activity, both privately owned and publicly traded companies are expected to compensate their stockholders by extracting a net gain from the sale of the commodities they supply. The successful outcome of their pursuit is variously attributed to luck, entrepreneurial daring, technological innovation, efficient management, astute marketing, and rigorous budgeting—otherwise known as labour exploitation.

Whether the profit motive can contribute to collective welfare is of course a disputed issue, even among its apologists. Throughout the postwar era, Western governments, while committed to free enterprise, worried about the allocative properties of unbridled capitalism. Looking for a balance between the returns of private investments and the containment of inequalities, they relied on progressive taxes to redistribute resources, on social programmes to cover risks, and on financial regulations to discourage speculation.

At the time, the concerns of public officials were shared by the executives of large corporations, who engaged in balancing acts of their own. Seeing themselves as the legitimate representatives of the firm, corporate managers staked its growth on negotiated settlements between the conflicting demands of financial backers and labour providers. To broker such deals, they impressed upon both parties that their long-term interests called for patience and a sizeable proportion of retained earnings.

By the mid-1970s, however, the stagflation generated by floating currencies, volatile oil prices, and declining productivity rates exposed the wisdom of reining in the appetites of profit seekers to mounting scepticism. No longer sidelined by their neo-Keynesian colleagues, neoliberal economists challenged the assumption that governing a nation involved tinkering with market mechanisms to guarantee full employment and provide a sturdy safety net. Meanwhile, in business schools, like-minded scholars rejected the view that managing a corporation was about mediating between the expectations of its various stakeholders.

According to the new orthodoxy, corporate managers needed to be reminded that they were hired executives, paid to do the bidding of their employers who, as Milton Friedman remarked, generally want to "make as much money as possible while conforming to the basic rules of the society".[1] As for elected officials, instead of meddling with prices to sustain aggregate demand and tame capital markets, they were to secure an environment of free and fair competition where economic agents would be empowered to make their own choices and enjoy the product of their efforts without undue impediment, whether in the form of red tape or burdensome taxes.

Forwarded by the conservative revolution of the early 1980s, the neoliberal refashioning of corporate governance and public service dispelled all previous misgivings about the pursuit of profit. "The magic of the marketplace", Ronald Reagan marvelled, would not only reward hard work and bold initiatives but also cause prosperity to trickle down from visionary entrepreneurs to anyone seeking to emulate them.

Neoliberal path-breakers certainly recognized that the rising tide created by supply-side incentives and regulatory restraint could not lift all boats equally. Yet they professed that

getting rid of stultifying subsidies and addictive social benefits would not only enhance the profitability of businesses but
also awaken the entrepreneurial spirit dormant in every self-
employed, wage-earning, or even jobless person.

Forty years hence, preventions against fiscal redistribution, market regulations, and social programmes still suffuse
the choices of policymakers, while businesses continue to
view financial prowess as the yardstick of success. Frequent
crashes, soaring inequalities, and environmental disasters
notwithstanding, returns on capital have thus been able to
grow at a staggering rate in the last four decades. Is it then the
case that, more than ever, profits are the fuel of capitalism? The
record seems to show otherwise.

Achieved under Ronald Reagan's tenure, the re-education
of the American managerial class involved a combination of
sticks and carrots. On the one hand, the swift deregulation of
financial transactions acted as an efficient disciplining mechanism. Threatened by intruders who could leverage their
way in the capital of publicly traded companies and replace
underperforming officers, chief executives quickly learned
that keeping stock prices high was their best insurance against
hostile takeovers.

On the other hand, to help senior appointees shed their
old ways, boards of directors voted to increase the share of
variable income allotted to them—mainly in the form of stock
options. With their own welfare pegged to the market's view
of their performance, corporate managers could hardly fail to
identify with the wishes of liquidity providers.

Looming raiders and potential bonuses were meant to
remind CEOs that, in their updated job description, the cheer-
fulness of capital owners took precedence over the growth of
the output and the appeasement of employees. Yet to measure both the likelihood of a raid and the value of their stock

options, the pertinent metric was not the company's profit margin but the rating of its stock. What became known as the pursuit of shareholder value did not refer to free cash flow but to unrealized capital gain.

According to the promoters of the revamped corporate culture, extracting profits from a business and creating value for its shareholders amounted to the same thing. As they saw it, a highly regarded stock merely reflected the record of a healthy and profitable firm.

John Maynard Keynes, on the other hand, had emphasized the chasm between the entrepreneurial and speculative logics respectively presiding over the generation of income and the appreciation of assets. While the former involved "superior long-term forecasts of the probable yield of an investment over its whole life", the latter was essentially about "foreseeing changes in the conventional basis of valuation a short time ahead of the general public."[2]

Drawn by Keynes in his 1936 magnus opus, the distinction between "enterprise" and "speculation" brings in stark relief the unintended consequences of the neoliberal assault on the postwar order. Enticements such as tax rebates, market deregulations, and flexible compensations were meant to shake up an increasingly technocratic corporate world by reinstating the primacy of the profit motive. However, once persuaded to elect the standing of their company's share as their compass, business executives became less concerned with the profitability of commercial operations than with the creditworthiness of the stock.

Though thrilling investors is not incompatible with wooing consumers, the recent history of corporate governance indicates that the improvement of a firm's credit and the maximization of its profits call for different moves. Whether they involve taking on loans for the sake of sheltering dividend distribution from the vagaries of sales reports, using large portions of net revenues to purchase the company's own shares, or, better still, borrowing funds in order to engage in stock buybacks, the techniques purported to create value for the shareholders do not fit easily in the entrepreneurial mindset championed by neoliberal reformers.

Admittedly, the so-called best practices devised by the new breed of business executives did not prevent capital owners from making "as much money as possible" and even from bending "the basic rules of society" along the way. Nevertheless, the relentless pursuit of unrealized capital gain, over and above any form of actual revenues, scarcely stands as a minor deviation from the profit-seeking ways vaunted by neoliberal publicists, insofar as it has all but reversed the teleology of capitalist enterprise.

Raising capital used to represent a means to an end: bank loans, initial public offerings, corporate bonds, and contributions from venture capitalists enabled companies to buy the equipment and hire the people required by the production of commodities which would then be sold to consumers, hopefully for a profit. If the operation proved successful, investors would be likely to renew their trust and keep funding the firm, thereby upholding its good name. Credit thus figured in the process of conducting a profitable business both as a material condition (collected funds) and a moral consequence (reputation among funders).

Under the current mode of governance, however, the various components of the business plan—the choice of material and human resources, the volume, and even the nature of the product—are determined and tailored to retain shareholders and bring in new backers. Selling to customers is ultimately about attracting sponsors, not the other way round. Profits may contribute to and accrue from the appeal of a brand—though not necessarily, as attested by the success stories of many uni-corns. Yet they stand as no more than a contributing factor and a possible outcome of a business manager's primary mis-sion, which is to sustain the credit of the stock in the eyes of investors.

The ascendency of asset appreciation has not been limited to the private sector or even to institutions: in time, creditwor-thiness also became the leading concern of public officials and households.

Having reckoned that the improvement of their econo-mies' competitiveness was less about fostering growth than about luring liquidity handlers, business-friendly govern-ments were quick to introduce fiscal reforms and a regula-tory framework propitious to stock valorization. Faced with an ensuing loss of tax revenues, they then proceeded to slash social programmes and privatize public goods, but also to bor-row the funds they no longer collected from taxpayers.

Once dependent on the confidence of bond markets to carry out tasks previously financed through deficit spending, elected representatives started to regard the valuation of their nation's public debt as their main guideline. Eager to keep interest rates low, they refrained from letting citizens' demands get in the way of lenders' expectations. Their agendas, in other words, came to be crafted for the purpose of sustaining their credit in the eyes of bondholders.

Eventually, the tailoring of business plans and public budgets to the preferences of investors proved highly conse-quential not only for the material conditions of the popula-tions affected by it but also for their mindset. Confronted with a steady decline of stable jobs and unconditional benefits, households and individuals previously reliant on wage labour and its attendant guarantees were compelled to adopt a more speculative outlook, both as consumers seeking to acquire skills or durable goods and as producers trying to generate revenues from their work.

On the side of consumption, change came in the form of a swelling private debt. To stay in bondholders' good graces, elected officials increasingly chose to assume their obligations to their fellow citizens by helping them access commercial credit rather than by providing for their welfare on public funds.

Though private lenders still required collateral to risk their money, governments availed financial institutions and their prospective clients of a regulatory environment which made it possible to obtain loans even in the absence of sizeable possessions and wealthy guarantors. Aspiring debtors could now borrow against the estimated worth of what they wanted to acquire—a home or a college degree—and a good "credit score" encapsulating their reputation for reliability (largely earned by repaying previous loans). Creditworthiness thus imposed itself as the privileged pathway to homeownership, higher education, and, in some cases, day-to-day survival.

On the side of production, the salient factor of change was the casualization of work. Worried about the negative impact of hefty payrolls on shareholder value, large businesses consistently shed in-house labour performed by fully employed workers, opting instead to outsource or subcontract a number of tasks as well as to multiply short-term hiring and unpaid internships.

For jobseekers, adapting to precarity involved a perspectival shift. Whether applying to project-based and other temporary positions or turning to independent contracting and gig work, they discovered that their lot hinged less on negotiations over the price of their commodified labour than on speculations about the value of their human capital. With collectively bargained salaries and secure employment on the wane, it was now incumbent on them to cultivate their professional appeal and, for that purpose, to assemble a portfolio of appreciable assets, ranging from sought after proficiencies and appealing social connections to displays of unlimited availability and flexibility.

As had been the case with corporations and governments, credit, understood as a protean ability to reassure lenders, sway recruiters, and attract patrons, imposed itself as the prevailing concern of private citizens. Neoliberal social engineers had imagined that cutting taxes, eliminating subsidies, privatizing public goods, and deregulating financial transactions would turn entitled technocrats and over-protected wage earners into self-reliant and price-alert entrepreneurs equipped to budget their satisfaction. What their reforms seem to have delivered, however, is a world of asset-gathering and rating-obsessed speculators whose main preoccupation is to leverage their appreciation.

Whether the credit motive is better suited to foster collective prosperity than the profit motive is open for debate. Yet given the shape of our brave new capitalism, it is a question that begs to be addressed in its own terms.

Notes

1   Milton Friedman, "The Social Responsibility of Business Is to Increase Its Profits", *New York Times Magazine*, 13 September 1970, 17.
2   John Maynard Keynes, *The General Theory of Employment, Interest and Money* (1936) (London and Basingstoke: Macmillan Press, 1973), 154.

Cynicism | Arne De Boever

Animals, (Art), Death, Mapping, Men, (Trader), Void, (Whiteness)

When Gordon Gekko rhapsodizes about greed in Oliver Stone's film *Wall Street* (1987), he calls it good and right—but he does not call it beautiful. Unlike fascism, which as per Walter Benjamin's analysis at the end of his essay on "The Work of Art in the Era of Mechanical Reproduction" aestheticizes politics, neoliberalism has no truck with beauty. Benjamin recalls Filippo Marinetti's manifesto which states that "war is beautiful".[1] If Gekko delivers a manifesto for neoliberalism, it's worth noting that it contains no parallel claim about greed.

Perhaps that is partly why scholars have had some difficulty pinning down what Walter Benn Michaels has dubbed "neoliberal aesthetics".[2] It's not that such an aesthetics cannot be found—there is some very interesting work that has been done in this area (by Alberto Toscano and Jeffrey Kinkle, who are working after Fredric Jameson[3]). There is also the argument (for example, in Sarah Brouillette's work after Eve Chiapello and Luc Boltanski) that neoliberalism has learned a thing or two from the arts, as is evident from the creative economy in which the artist becomes the model of the flexible worker.[4] The issue is, rather, that the "rendering aesthetic" that Benjamin talks about in his analysis of fascism is not part of neoliberalism's operations—it does not seek to render beautiful. And so any talk about beauty in relation to neoliberalism will ultimately always only be dealing with a foreign element, something that is brought to neoliberalism from the outside. (Consider, as a comment on this, how in Bret Easton Ellis's

American Psycho, Patrick Bateman's David Onica is hung "upside down".[5])

Aesthetics is eliminated in neoliberalism by profit. Economics does not only eliminate *homo politicus*, as Wendy Brown (after Michel Foucault) has argued, but *homo aestheticus* as well.[6] In the neoliberal novel, for example, art is typically only present as a marker of profit (look at how much profit I have made!), or at best as an instrument for generating it (this goes against the core of the modern understanding of art as purposiveness without purpose which, when rephrased as a categorical imperative—never use art as a means towards an end—also reveals its moral purchase). To read art in the neoliberal novel as a marker of cultural capital, even with the acknowledgement that it is a fake marker, would be naïve. An outgrowth of Marcel Duchamp's intervention in the aesthetic—which enforced a shift from asking "is it beautiful?" to asking "is it art?"[7]—art under neoliberalism is determined by the question "is it value?" This is art as investment or financial instrument, for example a hedging strategy against market losses (as in Isaac Julien's video installation *Playtime* from 2014). A neoliberal will happily destroy any work of art out of greed: witness how the company Injective Protocol burnt the British art vandal Banksy's work *Morons (White)* (from 2006) in order to turn the work into a non-fungible token or NFT. Fascism—perhaps due to Adolf Hitler's personal history as a failed painter—was pickier, and it may be the centrality of aesthetics to its operations (noted by scholars like Tobin Siebers, among others) that in part explains its continued appeal (to some) under what, after Grégoire Chamayou, one may call contemporary authoritarian neoliberal conditions.[8] At least fascism still has something to call beautiful, however fucked up that something may be. This also reveals to us the dubiousness of beauty. It's worth recalling the Trump administration's effort to "Make Federal Buildings Beautiful Again".

The lack of beauty in neoliberalism is an indicator of its to-the-bone cynicism. A cynic believes that people are motivated solely by self-interest. Cynicism has become (as per multiple analyses, most notably perhaps that of Peter Sloterdijk in *Critique of Cynical Reason* from 1987) widespread in Western societies and beyond after the failure of 1968, and with the start of the neoliberal era in the early 1970s (even if it has its roots at least two decades before that). This is also the era that gives us conceptual art, which deals in a new kind of abstraction that can only with difficulty still be called "aesthetic". Conceptual art is closer, rather, to the abstractions of finance (from collateralized debt obligations to the already mentioned NFTs)— Patrick Bateman as an "idea", as Ellis's novel has it. Mary Harron's film *American Psycho* (2000) perceptively has what seems like an aesthetic description of Bateman's morning routine early in the novel culminate in a passage taken from much later in the novel, in which Bateman is described as "some kind of abstraction".[9] The point, as I see it, is that Bateman is precisely *not* an aesthetic—it's not about him being beautiful.

With capitalism having entered the phase of what Robert Brenner has shown to be its "long downturn", self-interest— already a core feature of capitalism and its cynical "extortion of surplus labor"[10]—took on the added urgency of despair: let *me* at least get rich quick while the global economy crashes. Thus, we reached the apex of cynicism: *fiat meum lucrum— pereat mundus* (let there be profit for me—even if the world perishes). The end of the world is easier to imagine than the end of my own profit. Contemporary cynicism is a philosophy rooted in a notion of the human being as motivated in the final instance by self-profit. This notion progressively took on validity during capitalism's long downturn which, pace Gordon

Gekko, opened up an evolutionary perspective in which only the fittest can survive.

When Gekko casts neoliberalism in evolutionary terms, he makes it sound natural, but taking our cue from Patrick Bateman, it may be more correct to refer to neoliberalism as conceptual. As the art dealer and curator Jeffrey Deitch points out in an essay for his curatorial project *Post Human* from 1992, we have moved from "the 'Me' decade" of "self awareness and self-improvement in the 1970s" to the decade of "self-image and self-indulgence in the 1980s", which both "demonstrated the intense interest in redefining and perhaps reformulating society's definition of the self". After this period of what Deitch calls the "disintegration of the self", a new period is opening up that is "conceptual" and about the "reconstruction of the self".[11] Deitch's account is one of subject formation and has the value of showing, as others have also done, how neoliberalism is about the production of subjectivity—in this case a subjectivity that is no longer, as Jason Read's analysis, for example, has shown, the classical self-interested liberal subject "focused on exchange" (think Adam Smith, for example) but a neoliberal *homo economicus* whose way of life is driven by "competition" and, ultimately, the self-interested motivation to survive.[12] The culture has abundantly testified to this, from *The Hunger Games* (2012) to *Squid Game* (2021). The popularity of such films and television series is an indicator of cynicism's grip on society.

In times like this, it is perhaps good to remember, with Sloterdijk, that there used to be a cynic—called *kynic*, in Sloterdijk's book—who "farts, shits, pisses, masturbates on the street, before the eyes of the Athenian market".[13] This is the *kynic* from ancient Athens, Diogenes, nicknamed "the Dog", "kunos", by Plato (whose discourse Diogenes called "a waste of time")[14]—hence the words "cynic" and "cynicism".

To capitalism and finance's bestiary of the bull and the bear and the cynicism they have produced, let's add the dog as a counter-figure who, before the eyes of the market—the *polis*'s space of appearance—takes a piss. This seems particularly appropriate given that Diogenes Laertius's account of Diogenes in his *Lives of the Eminent Philosophers* begins with the peculiar story of how Diogenes, or perhaps his father, or perhaps Diogenes on behalf of his father, restamped his local coinage after receiving an oracle, and was banished as a consequence of this adulteration—a finance-related exile that stands at the beginning of his life as a philosopher. Originally someone who messes with currency, then, Diogenes the *kynic* proposes a way of life, an ethics, that through ascetic training leads to virtue in accordance with nature. From this position, Diogenes relentlessly practised *parrhesia* or free speech (he deemed "freedom of speech" to be "the most beautiful thing in the world")[15] and criticized how those around him were living. When Alexander the Great proposed to Diogenes that he ask him "whatever you desire", Diogenes told him to "move—you're blocking my sun" (my translation). While Diogenes's way of life certainly has a focus on the self, it is far removed from neoliberal self-profit—from a subject understood as a competitive *homo economicus*—that is at the root of contemporary cynicism. A place in the sun is all Diogenes desires.

How to play out this *kynicism* against cynicism, as Sloterdijk some time ago already asked? "The Enlightenment"—inevitably caught up, Sloterdijk shows, in the development of contemporary cynicism—may have some role to assume when it comes to answering that question. If the consequence of contemporary cynicism is the kind of attitude that simply accepts, cynically, that "there is no alternative" (to quote Margaret Thatcher), the Enlightenment in Michel Foucault's interpretation tells us that it could always be otherwise. Whereas

Immanuel Kant at the end of the day told us to "obey" after "arguing all you please", Foucault's interest was to turn this position into a transgressive critique—into a critique that would exceed the limits of its operation. This entailed an experimental work on oneself as a free being that, in a critical project that seeks to disconnect the growth of our capabilities from the intensification of power relations, opens up "the possibility of no longer being, doing, or thinking what we are, do, or think"; thus, he writes, "we are always in the position of beginning again".[16] To identify such a position with the neoliberal production of subjectivity as some who characterize Foucault's late work as neoliberal have done is, in my view, to confuse the form with the content: it is not because both neoliberalism and Foucault are interested in the production of subjectivity that the content of the subjectivities they envision is the same. Certainly, the plasticity of the subject itself is not neoliberal; that would be so only for an approach that confuses plasticity with flexibility, something against which Catherine Malabou in her anti-cynical manifesto *What Should We Do with Our Brain?* (worth reading next to Sloterdijk's "Rules for the Human Zoo"[17]) already warned us: unlike the flexible subject modelled on the artistic worker, the plastic subject does not stretch infinitely. It breaks; it has the revolutionary capacity to explode. That is the political meaning of Malabou's debt to Karl Marx, specifically to Marx's sentence that "human beings make their own history, but they do not make it just as they please".[18] The sentence negotiates between a cynical attitude that would focus on the second half of the sentence and conclude that at the end of the day, self-profit determines everything, and a *kynical* belief in human beings' emancipatory power to actually make history, and thus bring into the world an alternative. At times, power makes this difficult to see. It should move and get out of our sun.

The *kynic*, then, with a doggedness that was born out of a currency fuck-up, gives it to the neoliberals straight, pissing before the eyes of the market and carving out a way of life that is not focused on self-profit. The *kynic* believes that human beings are not only economic beings engaged in competition. To those who say there is no alternative, the *kynic* responds with a bark that, given the proper conditions, which are in part of our own making, may become a bite. This, too, may not be beautiful—but perhaps that's just as well.

Notes

1   Walter Benjamin, "The Work of Art in the Era of Mechanical Reproduction", in *Illuminations: Essays and Reflections*, ed. Hannah Arendt, trans. Harry Zohn (New York: Schocken Books, 1969), 241.

2   Walter Benn Michaels, "Neoliberal Aesthetics: Fried, Rancière, and the Form of the Photograph", *Non-site.org*, 25 January 2011, https://nonsite.org/neoliberal-aesthetics-fried-ranciere-and-the-form-of-the-photograph/.

3   Jeff Kinkle and Alberto Toscano, *Cartographies of the Absolute* (Winchester: Zero Books, 2015).

4   Sarah Brouillette, *Literature and the Creative Economy* (Stanford: Stanford University Press, 2014); Luc Boltanski and Eve Chiapello (eds), *The New Spirit of Capitalism*, trans. Gregory Elliott (London: Verso, 2005.

5   Bret Easton Ellis, *American Psycho* (New York: Vintage, 1992), 244.

6   Wendy Brown, *Undoing the Demos: Neoliberalism's Stealth Revolution* (New York: Zone Books, 2015).

7   See Thierry de Duve, *Kant after Duchamp* (Cambridge, MA: MIT, 1998).

8   Tobin Siebers, *Disability Aesthetics* (Ann Arbor, MI: University of Michigan Press, 2010); Grégoire Chamayou, *The Ungovernable Society: A Genealogy of Authoritarian Liberalism*, trans. Andrew Brown (Cambridge, MA: Polity, 2021).

9   Ellis, *American Psycho*, 376.

10   Gilles Deleuze and Félix Guattari, *Anti-Oedipus: Capitalism and Schizophrenia*, trans. Robert Hurley, Mark Seem, and Helen R. Lane (Minneapolis, MN: University of Minnesota Press, 2003), 255.

11   Jeffrey Deitch, *Post Human* (Athens: Cantz/Deste Foundation for Contemporary Art, 1992).

12   Jason Read, "A Genealogy of Homo-Economicus: Neoliberalism and the Production of Subjectivity", *Foucault Studies* 6 (2009), 25–36.

13   Peter Sloterdijk, *Critique of Cynical Reason*, trans. Michael Eldred (Minneapolis, MN: University of Minnesota Press, 1987), 103.

14   Diogenes Laertius, *Lives of the Eminent Philosophers*, ed. James Miller, trans. Pamela Mensch (Oxford: Oxford University Press, 2018), 270.

15   Ibid., 291.

16   Michel Foucault, "What Is Enlightenment?" in *The Politics of Truth*, ed. Sylvère Lotringer, trans. Lysa Hochroth and Catherine Porter (Los Angeles, CA: Semiotext(e), 2007), 114–115.

17   Peter Sloterdijk, "Rules for the Human Zoo: A Response to the Letter on Humanism", *Environment and Planning D: Society and Space* 27, no. 1 (2009), 12–28.

18   Karl Marx, *The Eighteenth Brumaire of Louis Bonaparte*, trans. Daniel De Leon (New York: International Publishers, 1998), 15; Catherine Malabou, *What Should We Do with Our Brain?*, trans. Sebastian Rand (New York: Fordham, 2008).

D

Death | Srinath Mogeri

Care, China, Cynicism, (Health),
Interest, Money, (Pandemic), **Void**

You're listening to RFHK, Hong Kong's favorite radio station. Time now for a virus update, brought to you by Bank of Eternity. Ten days after the outbreak, the death toll is nearly five hundred, most of them in East Kowloon. But worryingly, cases are also being reported in the west, as well as Mong Kok, Yau Ma Tei, and Tuen Mun. It seems no part of the city is safe. The government's advising us to stay at home. But tell me, if you don't go to work, how are you expected to feed your family? With one in three cases proving fatal and no cure in sight, survival is purely a lottery. So what are you supposed to do? The only thing you can do is hope for the best and prepare for the worst. Should the unthinkable happen, you'll be glad to know that you can enjoy the same lifestyle in the next life that you do in this one. For just three thousand dollars! It's like you've never died at all. How, you ask? Call 1 800 IMMORTAL now or visit BankofEternity.co.hk. Eternal happiness for just three thousand dollars. That number again, 1 800 IMMORTAL.

Hi there. In today's Bank of Eternity virus update, the Department of Health has announced they've identified the index patient: a farmer from Guangzhou who came to the city on business and stayed in a hotel in Central. He died a few days later, but not before infecting other hotel guests. That, my dear friends, is how this whole damn thing started. Now, if this piece of information is supposed to make us feel better, I'm afraid it isn't working. In just three weeks, since the arrival of the farmer, the virus has claimed over a thousand lives. If this continues, ten percent of the population will be wiped out by the end of the year. We can only hope that's not going to happen. But with the virus spreading at an alarming rate, the smart thing to do is protect yourself for any eventuality. With an Afterlife Dollar account, should the unthinkable occur, you'll be able to enjoy the same lifestyle in the next life that you do in this one. And for a limited time, we're giving ten percent off on purchases over three thousand dollars, plus a free H5N1 coronavirus survival pack, designed by renowned healthcare experts. Call 1 800 IMMORTAL now or visit BankofEternity. co.hk. Eternal happiness for just three thousand dollars. That number again, 1 800 IMMORTAL.

Debt | Marina Vishmidt

Animals, Capitalocene, Care, Disruption, Flesh, Interest, Leverage, Liability, Property, Rollover, Speculation, The University

When considering finance from an aesthetic perspective, or a problem for aesthetics, debt soon emerges as a preeminent object of inquiry. The reason for that is that aesthetics is defined by experience, sensory experience to be precise, and debt is the main channel by which financial abstraction manifests as experience in an individual, group, or collective life. Not only experience as something that happens, or that can be grasped, but also as a tangible absence of the means of life. Debt is both how you lose and a tangible path by which to make good the loss. How to acquire objects—and the experiences they can offer—or acquire them once again. It is both the clarity of the feeling of ownership and the transience of this ownership, its perforation by the priorities of banks, payment schedules, credit cards, APRs. But also, bailiffs, credit scores, even incarceration—debt is not just the aesthetics of possession and loss, spread out over a period or a life as shackled temporality, it is also the materiality of violence in the processes that sanction individuals and collectives for non-payment, that dispossess lives, projects, homes, institutions. Starting from scratch. It is not necessarily about a financialized self if that is taken to mean an ideological construct, even one of materialized ideology ("indebted man"). It is more a structural adaptation, an imperative to survive, and often the imperative to cloak that survival in a material glaze over a precarity that is general but is experienced as keenly personal and catastrophic.

Debt is the medium of transience because it is the medium of ownership in such a landscape, and the other way round. Ownership and debt are two sides of the same coin for those who have little or nothing in reserve, which is to say most of us. But if we follow this trajectory to aesthetics as a specific type of experience associated with specific cultural, or more narrowly artistic, objects or ecologies, then the analysis of debt can go a number of ways. In line with the outlook of this query, it is generative to think the registration of debt in contemporary art in relation to form and crisis—the crisis of comprehending, through praxis or critique, the shattering effect of finance as it not only reshapes but inhabits and then fully supplants the "real". We could then say that it is precisely the ecological crisis of the world being consumed by finance capital, treated as expendable waste, which features this dynamic today. Then the question of aesthetics arises from the experience of living in a world riven by important contradictions and counter-influences, yet a seemingly clear trajectory towards escalating endings. This is the aesthetics of totality, or even totalization as a process rather than some conceptual object; there is not much difference in where this is going, aside from a processual understanding allowing for struggle, counter-planning, antagonism, a level of both contingency and social determinacy that doesn't come into focus with anything so mystical as just objects, or just relations.

Decadence | Signe Leth Gammelgaard

Flesh, Gift, Gold, Period

The last decades of the nineteenth century in key respects mirror the changes that have occurred in our own time in the past fifty years: a rapid financial expansion, high economic inequality, a shifting of the world power centres, and recurring economic crashes during what is now termed the "long depression" from 1873 to 1896. This period, however, also saw the emergence of a new literary and proto-modernist movement: the Decadence.

The term "decadence" of course denotes much more that this specific movement, and the literary style from the late nineteenth century has various precursors and stylistic inspirations; in particular, it shares traits with the Roman decadence. However, the nineteenth-century movement of Decadence in France and Britain is especially interesting in the context of finance: it occurs in a relatively recent period that resembles our current times, and the conception of a decaying civilization takes a rather different form in this period than it did during the waning of the Roman empire. At this point the French and British empires were not yet in acute decline, and the nineteenth-century Decadence has often been interpreted as a critique of modernity as such rather than an expression of imperial or economic decline.[1] However, a view upon the concurrent developments tells a more precise story, namely one in which financialization entails a deferral between signifiers in the form of various kinds of money, and the material world, where money becomes overabundant and growth in the financial sphere outweighs growth in the real economy. A similar change in the relationship between the signifiers of words and the material world can be observed in the decadent aesthetics, which, furthermore, present a response or "compensation" for this deferral.

The key work in decadent literature from this period is Joris-Karl Huysmans's *À rebours*, a fairly strange novel about the various sensuous and aesthetic pleasures of the protagonist, Jean Des Esseintes. This book, frequently termed a manifesto for decadence, was published in 1884, and Huysmans developed the decadent aesthetic in opposition to naturalism, Émile Zola's style in particular. He wanted a new style, a break with the conventions of both realism and naturalism, and *À rebours* became the foremost expression of these new ideas. The novel has been described as having no plot, and the majority of the text outlines the various sensory experiences of Des Essientes, whether it is how he decorates his lodgings, how he wallows in ancient, decadent literature, how he indulges in exquisite scents or tastes, or how he observes the characteristics of gemstones or flowers. As such, the text presents an extreme form of hedonism and a distinct focus on the experience of the senses. The novel does have some kind of a plot, however, namely the gradual withering away of Des Esseintes's body and mind. Furthermore, throughout the text runs a strong note of apathy, pessimism, and weariness of life as well as of other human beings, and the book ends on a sombre note, concluding that even "the ancient hope" can no longer provide any form of light or consolation.[2] Similar to other key decadent works, moreover, like Octave Mirbeau's *Le Jardin des supplices* or *Les Affaires sont les affaires*, or, more famously, Oscar Wilde's *The Picture of Dorian Gray*, *À rebours* describes a societal state of affairs corrupted through and through by the chasing of profit: people lie, merchants cheat, churches dilute the wine and the hosts to save money. Every group and every class have lost their sense of moral value, and society is now dictated by the rule of money, the "caliphate of the counter", as Huysmans terms it in *À rebours*.[3]

However, these tirades against the general corruption of society take place chiefly in the first and the last chapter, while the main part of the text concerns the aesthetic experiences. One of the central chapters narrates Des Esseintes's acquisition of hothouse flowers. These flowers embody succinctly the decadent aesthetics, and they connote a crisis of representation in more than one way: on the one hand, they are described with imagery of decaying corpses, illness, and death, that is, imagery of disintegration and fragmentation. This imagery, furthermore, is also used in a chapter of the novel where Des Esseintes indulges in the Roman literary decadence and portrays the language of the period as a "completely rotted corpse, its limbs falling off, dripping with pus, and preserving, in the total corruption of its body, barely a few firm parts".[4]

On the other hand, the flowers convey a crisis of representation in their function as symbols. As flowers are usually understood as symbolic expressions, they work well to underline changes in the symbolic function of language. For Des Esseintes, the language of flowers no longer exists, red roses do not signify love, nor lilies purity; in Huysmans's own later commentary, these flowers are "mute" or "aphonic".[5] Thus, the hothouse flowers that he buys signify, if anything, a loss of symbolic meaning. First, they portray a muddling of the distinction between natural and artificial. In a brilliant convolution that is also a key decadent feature, these hothouse flowers are real organic flowers that are mimicking Des Esseintes's previous pastime of artificial flowers made by gum, paper, and cloth, which in turn tried to imitate organic flowers. This process in itself would seem to indicate a problem in the representative function. But further, when Des Esseintes looks at the flowers, all he sees is decaying flesh:

> they simulated the appearance of fake skin scored by artificial veins; and the majority, as though eaten away by syphilis and leprosy, exhibited livid flesh marbled with roseola and damasked with dartres; others were the bright pink of scars that are healing, or the browning tint of scabs in the process of forming; others were blistering from cautery or puffing up from burns; still others revealed hairy skins pitted by ulcers and embossed with chancres.[6]

Thus, to the extent that Des Esseintes interprets and associates, he does so based on the very looks of the flowers, not on a symbolically informed societal meaning.

In Roland Barthes's short essay "L'Effet de reel", he outlines an aesthetic process that is very similar, though Barthes denotes this process as the central identifier of realism rather than decadence. In effect, it describes the dissolution of representation in modernity, the "disintegration of the sign" in Barthes's own phrasing.[7] He argues that the literary device of a mute or "useless" detail, of details in the narrative that do not have a symbolic, plot-related, or explanatory function, instead functions merely to signify reality, a reality that does not give way to the process of symbolization. More specifically, he analyzes the semiotics of this effect: "the 'concrete detail' is constituted by the direct collusion of a referent and a signifier; the signified is expelled from the sign, and with it, of course, the possibility of developing a form of the signified, i.e., narrative structure itself".[8] What is lost, then, is the semiotic category of the signified, which is, in turn, the very meaning of the sign. In Ferdinand de Saussure's original schematics, the signified is the mental concept that is invoked by a signifier, for instance a word, and thus the meaning that we ascribe in adherence to a social convention. While this explains the linguistic phenomenon, in the decadent works the reality effect is taken very far, and it functions to illustrate not only a "mute" material world but a downright loss of meaning, social and existential as well as linguistic. As such, the intense focus on sensory experiences and hedonism in the works emerges as a desperate attempt to feel, to reawaken the lethargic body, and to reinvent meaning as direct sensation, as sense.

If the proto-modernist aesthetics of decadence register and respond to a loss of social and existential meaning, the question remains of what brought about this loss of meaning in the first place. Rather than the standard invocation of "modernity", "industrialization", "alienation", or "capitalism", this can be linked to the specific phases of capitalism that experience intense growth of the financial sector. Various scholars have outlined both historical and theoretical parallels between the representative systems of money and of language, and the work of Mary Poovey in particular indicates that, historically, crises of representation in literary language can be understood as responses to problems in the representative function of money, specifically that economic events like crises, booms, or busts could generate anxieties in the population as to the nature of representation and the foundation on which money rests.[9] The final decades of the nineteenth century saw a number of such events, like the crash of the Union Générale bank in 1882, which functions as a model for Zola's depiction of a bubble economy in *L'Argent*, or like the long depression which entailed stalling growth, low interest rates, and ruthless price competition. According to the philosopher Jean-Joseph Goux, in these years the stock exchange took on an importance that would turn it into a thought paradigm affecting economic theory, literature, and morals.[10] Moreover, the onset of Decadence occurs almost simultaneously to a shift in capitalism noted by Giovanni Arrighi in his Braudel-based model of cycles of accumulation. At this point, then, what is called the British cycle reaches its point of maturity and becomes dominated by financial investments rather than growth in the real economy. Tellingly, such a shift towards finance figures as a sign of decline of a specific period of capitalist expansion, thus indicating economic and imperial decadence if not an absolute fall.[11]

Goux associates the new literary aesthetics of the late nineteenth century with the increased importance of the financial sphere and the disappearance of a universal equivalent in a Marxist sense.[12] Though such an equivalent in practice has been precious metals throughout various parts of history, these metals function, according to Marx, as a stand-in for the real universal equivalent, namely labour, which can only be conceived in an abstract manner, as a fraction of the total socially necessary labour time to reproduce a given society.[13] And productive labour is precisely what is lost in an economy dominated by financial growth, banking, and lending. Therefore, the concept of value can no longer be fixed to an underlying entity, value becomes equal to price, and it is determined solely by the fluctuations of supply and demand, scarcity and hype; in a sense, this means that the signified of money, its societal meaning, is lost too. The change in conceptions of value in this period can be traced in the paradigm shift of economic theory called the marginal revolution in the 1870s. Contrary to the earlier political economy, value no longer hinges on labour but instead on "marginal utility", in effect on supply and demand.

The parallel between finance economies and decadent aesthetics emerges, then, through the appearance of a lost signified in both cases. Words and things no longer evoke symbolic meanings but must instead be sensed directly, appreciated for the mere appearance or the sensory qualities. And money, in all its forms, is no longer fixed by any stable category, can no longer be understood as a mediator of a shared societal wealth, but fluctuates more or less arbitrarily according to the whims and fads of the market economy. Money becomes a means of manipulation and speculation, subject to an almost magic form of growth. Understood in this way, the decadent works appear as a literary form that shows how the world of finance can alter our perception of reality, of materiality, and of societal meaning. When money ceases to mediate value in a meaningful way, the experience of society as a coherent whole begins to disintegrate, and so does its representative language.

Notes

1   Jane Desmarais, "Decadence and the Critique of Modernity", in *Decadence and Literature*, ed. David Weir and Jane Desmarais (Cambridge: Cambridge University Press, 2019), 98, https://doi.org/10.1017/9781108550826.007.

2   J.-K. Huysmans, *Against Nature*, trans. Margaret Mauldon, (Oxford and New York: Oxford University Press, 2009), 181.

3   Huysmans, *Against Nature*, 129.

4   Theophile Gautier, *The Works of Theophile Gautier, Vol. 23, Art and Criticism: The Magic Hat* (New York: George D. Sproul, 1908), 38–42, http://archive.org/details/worksoftheophile028595mbp; Paul Bourget, "The Example of Baudelaire", trans. Nancy O'Connor, *New England Review (1990-)* 30, no. 2 (2009), 98; David Weir, *Decadence and the Making of Modernism* (Amherst: University of Massachusetts Press, 1995), 88–89.

5   Huysmans, *Against Nature*, 31.

6   J.-K. Huysmans, "Appendix: Preface 'Written Twenty Years after the Novel'", in *Against Nature*, 190; Robert Ziegler, "Huysmans's Flowers", *Romance Quarterly* 62, no. 1 (2 January 2015), 50–57, https://doi.org/10.1080/08831157.2015.970115; Suzanne Braswell, "Mallarmé, Huysmans, and the Poetics of Hothouse Blooms", *French Forum* 38, no. 1/2 (2013), 69–87.

7   Huysmans, *Against Nature*, 74.

8   Roland Barthes, "The Reality Effect", in *The Novel: An Anthology of Criticism and Theory, 1900-2000*, ed. Dorothy J. Hale (Malden, MA: Blackwell Publishing Ltd, 2006), 234.

9   Ibid., 234.

10   Mary Poovey, *Genres of the Credit Economy, Mediating Value in Eighteenth- and Nineteenth-Century Britain* (Chicago, IL: University of Chicago Press, 2008), 5–6.

11   Giovanni Arrighi, *The Long Twentieth Century: Money, Power, and the Origins of Our Times*, second edn (London and New York: Verso, 2010), 6; Fernand Braudel, *The Perspective of the World: Civilization and Capitalism, 15th–18th Century*, Vol. 3 (London: Collins, 1984), 246.

12   Jean-Joseph Goux, *The Coiners of Language*, trans. Jennifer Curtis Gage, Vol. 16 (Norman, OK: University of Oklahoma Press, 1994).

13   Karl Marx and Friedrich Engels, *Marx & Engels, Collected Works. Volume 35. Karl Marx – Capital Volume I* (London: Lawrence & Wishart, 1996), 46–51, 76–81, 99–102.

Disruption | Sarah Brouillette

(Borders), (Data), **Debt**, (Dystopia), (Future), **Mapping**, **Men**, (Platform), **The University**, **Work**

Disruption is an ideological formation: a desperate obfuscation of a brutality that is patently obvious, perhaps providing ameliorative balm to the brutalizers but not fooling many other people. The concept is strongly associated with the influential work of management theorist Clayton Christensen, a Professor at the Harvard Business School, that esteemed site for production of research explaining how to maximize returns for corporate shareholders and minimize labour costs. Christensen uses the word in concert with innovation: a *disruptive innovation*, for the point of disruption is that if you do not innovate you will fail. A disruptive innovation is a threat, precisely one posed to a company by a competitor that is "bringing to market a product or service that is not as good as the best traditional offerings but is more affordable and easier to use".[1] Disruption is something to fear; you must disrupt or be disrupted. Yet cognizing the threat posed by a newer version—Uber disrupting the taxi industry, Wattpad disrupting publishing, non-fungible tokens disrupting the art world—comes as well with a romantic hacker aura of rebellion, which helps support the idea that the old offering should be glad to remake itself to ensure it can compete in conditions controlled by the new player.

The idealization of corporate disruption is indivisible from today's university. The university is where those who then and now celebrate disruption's beautiful potentials have been trained and supported, and one of the sites where its tendencies were first developed and realized in the form of justifications for restructuring in the wake of dramatic withdrawals of public funding. The theory of disruptive innovation could even be said to be the contemporary university's own managerial self-theorization; the theory adores a conflation of the higher education sector itself with other kinds of business, advocating for the rightful treatment of the university as just another corporation that must embrace disruption or die. Grounded in a fear-engendering threat of closure and bankruptcy, pushed by profit-seeking private companies, universities' embrace of disruption requires and cultivates uncertainty and unease.

In higher education, disruption's lodestar is EdTech. When Christensen co-wrote his book about disrupting the university in 2011, he was already promoting online learning as light from the future. EdTech entrepreneurs have been competing to claim the crown as the source of innovations most disruptive of the old models of face-to-face learning, most able to ensure that digital technology is central to every learning experience. They have received deep support from governments such as that of the province of Ontario, which mandates that all post-secondary students must be provided some learning experiences that are primarily digital, and which requires every university programme to offer some kind of "experiential learning"—usually a Trojan horse for course designs that are digitally intensive. The conditions of the pandemic have only intensified these tendencies, while amplifying the sense of risk if one refuses to adapt, given the sheer numbers of closures of departments and programmes over the past few years. From where I write in Canada, EdTech is now a billion-dollar industry, with universal platforms and learning management systems, from Zoom to Brightspace (D2L) to Google Classroom and Microsoft Teams all competing for our attention, supplemented by more targeted applications such as Top Hat, Turnitin, Perusal, Kahoot, and Proctor U.

Writing from the UK, Will Davies notes that these platforms have been "creeping into English schools for some years", as state spending per pupil has been falling precipitously: "As budgets are squeezed, schools are understandably tempted by products and services that promise to improve 'learning outcomes' without additional staff."[2] The temptation is heightened by the management idea that universities are in dramatic crisis because their models of delivery of learning have become far too expensive, due in no small part to high faculty salaries and small class sizes. What is papered over are the deleterious effects of decades of government defunding, never mind its relation to the general downturn in labour productivity and capitalist dynamism that has been producing our indebted austerity-era governments which prioritize spending not on education but on debt financing, natural disaster response, and policing and border patrol to discipline rising rates of "surplus humanity". The resulting deteriorating education system is, then, ripe for corporations to step in and position themselves as our salvation, leaving us with little choice but to accept the university's transformation via "privatization, profit generation, and marketization of students".[3]

This marketization partakes of the global phenomenon of expanding labour informality: the contemporary university has reoriented its priorities to train students for fitful "flexible" work in and out of formal employment, and to monetize their non-work student activity by contracting with EdTech companies that track and sort data, such that their time in school becomes its own kind of subemployment. School becomes time spent on activities that generate revenue for EdTech capitalists—activity compelled by the need to earn a degree, or to avoid having to try to enter into other forms of employment which would leave one prey to student loan debt collectors.

Though some EdTech disruptions may appear gimmicky— the interactive whiteboard, the MOOC, the clicker—the general environment fostering EdTech innovation depends upon decades of accrual of experiences, values, and affects, shaped by that underlying "constancy of crisis rhetoric" which makes technological solutionism so tempting.[4] EdTech takes advantage of a student body that is itself uncertain and anxious, increasingly inclined to take STEM courses that have been construed as better preparation for the job market—STEM courses being better suited to online learning platforms, which excel where there is content delivery with little interpretation, debate, or discussion, with testing that can be assessed automatically or by underpaid graders. "The cognitive skills that can be trained in this way are the ones computers themselves excel at: pattern recognition and computation," Davies writes.[5]

When students have massive loans to pay off after graduation, shouldering the burden of covering rising tuition rates that attended the decline in public funding, this further recommends that practical considerations trump everything. This depends in turn upon a decades-long campaign to undermine humanistic study, not least through imputing to it an impracticality, as though a STEM degree is a straight path to wealth and a History degree takes you nowhere—flying in the face of what we know about the relatively small size of the STEM labour force compared to other sectors.[6] EdTech disruption foments the cultivation of a calculus that worried students have learned from a young age, involving carefully devising plans to parcel out their time, fitting in snippets of schoolwork where possible, skipping what can be skipped, speeding up lectures, and playing their captions to maximize efficient absorption. EdTech assumes also that student engagement will be hard to elicit, that attention will be divided among open tabs, social media, competing alerts calling for your attention and response. It assumes that, as Moore, Jayme, and Black write, all students have secure reliable access to the internet, have devices that support the latest technologies, with the newest software installed, have already been exposed to all the "technological aptitude" they would need to learn successfully, and have the digital literacy that would protect them from some of the risks that come with online learning.[7]

EdTech disruption also participates in the downsizing of university employment by attempting to offer the same content to more people, and by having content produced in packages that can be administered by contingent faculty, or by administrators not trained in education at all, ideally paid a fraction of what a tenured employee earns. It participates in linking university education to customer convenience and content delivery. As Matt Seybold recently wrote of one EdTech grifter's vision of the future of education, it "combines mostly automated and 'self-guided' remote asynchronous coursework with 'applied assessments' that require 'learners' to pay for the opportunity to donate their labor to businesses who rebrand entry-level drudgery as cutting-edge training".[8] It in turn assumes a faculty willing to participate in an "audit and surveillance culture",[9] by providing means to track students' levels of attendance and "engagement" with course materials. As part of its data capture efforts, EdTech embraces gamified learning, rewarding students for active participation, continuously appealing to them to push a button, to select an onscreen response, to indicate true or false, agree or disagree; "pupils are guided and assessed continuously," Davies writes. "When one task is completed correctly, the next begins."[10]

Jesse Stommel, a scholar of critical digital pedagogy, reports that during a 2019 investor conference, the then CEO of Instructure, which makes the Canvas learning management system, bragged about their "growth initiative focused on analytics, data science, and artificial intelligence", claiming: "We have the most comprehensive database on the educational experience in the globe. [...] No one else has those data assets at their fingertips to be able to develop those algorithms and predictive models."[11] This language critiques itself: students are little more than "data assets". Much like the activities of people doing microwork online, or any of us merely filling in the CAPTCHA we encounter when asked to prove we aren't robots, student activities in class aid in processes of machine learning and AI development. Not exactly work, but not quite not work either. EdTech features functionality designed to track when students have logged in and accessed materials and how much time they have spent doing so. Moore, Jayme, and Black describe this as encouraging an "insidious managerialism, built directly into the technology", which "positions teaching as the regulation of students".[12] In the process it acclimates students to the kind of button-pushing tech training and connection mediated via online life—let's call it unity in separation—that so many will eventually find themselves immersed in for work or to supplement stagnant wages in other jobs.[13]

None of the discourse associating EdTech's disruptions with liberation from the constraints of the classroom has to be convincing to anyone. We need not accept the delimitation of our capacities and curiosities for the material compulsions towards EdTech to be effective. The point of describing disruption as an ideological formation is precisely to emphasize how thin the veneer is that it places over the uglier reality that more and more people, already drawn into market dependence, are struggling to find a reliable income to support themselves in a marketized life, and that the fate of the contemporary university reflects these conditions utterly. As Seybold writes, EdTech's rationalization perhaps "reassures people whose income depends on the next round of venture funding that they belong to a cadre of rescuing angels", with those they "intend to disenfranchise" cast as "Luddites, obstructing student access to 'the future of work' ".

My friend and fellow English professor Derek Nystrom tweeted recently that he: "Taught [Lauren Berlant's] Cruel Optimism today & when I said that one fantasy of the good life was that working hard in uni guarantees a well-paying job after graduation, a student wrote in the chat 'sir all due respect most of us are getting B.A.s in English, there is no delusion of a paying job.'"[14] People still enroll in humanities courses, not despite but perhaps because of their stony reckoning with the limitations of the conception of education as the conduit to workplace skills and successful employment. In a crisis of futurity, does it really matter if you take Science or English, Engineering or History? Who believes in these good life fantasies anymore? And who sees in the language of disruption anything more than a comforting mystique for those steering this ship towards oblivion? Pointing out what the language so badly hides is one means, insufficient and inadequate, of critiquing the underlying system that occasions it, with an eye to the broader struggle to overcome all that.

Notes

1 Clayton M. Christensen and Henry J. Eyring, *The Innovative University: Changing the DNA of Higher Education from the Inside Out* (New York: Wiley, 2011), xxiv.

2 Will Davies, "How Many Words Does It Take to Make a Mistake?", *London Review of Books* 44, no. 4 (24 February 2022), www.lrb.co.uk/the-paper/v44/n04/william-davies/how-many-words-does-it-take-to-make-a-mistake.

3   Shannon Dawn Maree Moore, Bruno De Oliveira Jayme, and Joanna Black, "Disaster Capitalism, Rampant EdTech Opportunism, and the Advancement of Online Learning in the Era of COVID19", *Critical Education* 12, no. 2 (January 2021), 4.

4   Ibid., 8.

5   Davies, "How Many Words".

6   On the valorization of STEM-based education as workplace "skills", see Daniel Greene, "The Access Doctrine", *Logic* 13 (17 May 2021), https://logicmag.io/distribution/the-access-doctrine/.

7   Moore, Jayme, and Black, "Disaster Capitalism", 14.

8   Matt Seybold, "Jason Wingard's EdTech Griftopia", *Los Angeles Review of Books* (23 February 2023), https://lareviewofbooks.org/article/jason-wingards-edtech-griftopia/.

9   Moore, Jayme, and Black, "Disaster Capitalism", 6.

10 Davies, "How Many Words".

11 Jesse Stommel, "Love and Other Data Assets", 11 May 2020, www.jessestommel.com/love-and-other-data-assets/.

12 Moore, Jayme, and Black, "Disaster Capitalism", 6.

13 On "unity in separation", see "A History of Separation", *Endnotes* 4 (2015), https://endnotes.org.uk/issues/4/en/endnotes-preface.

14 Derek Nystrom (@dereknystrom1), Twitter, 22 February 2022, 2:43 p.m., https://twitter.com/dereknystrom1/status/1496209011779248131.

E

Enclosure

Equity

Extraction

Extraction | Nicholas Alan Huber

Animals, (Assets), (Body), (Borders), **Capitalocene, Capture,** (Faith)**, Flesh, Gold,** (Health)**, The Invisible Hand, Mapping, Migration, Property, Value**

When my teeth ache—and they do ache, now, with some regularity—I dream of selling them. I pull one out, find its price, create a bidding war with any luck. Victor Hugo, *Les Miserables*, Fantine at the dentist: two gold napoleons for a pair! Accounted for in the ledgers of George Washington, great American slaver, is the "purchase" of "nine teeth" from "Negroes",[1] though we the auditors are left to assume that this is an extraction for the Founding Father's own prosthetic dentures. Imagine entering such a storied transactional history! A secondary exchange could arise, a derivatives of extraction, trades on the market price of bicuspids, on the maturation of wisdom teeth. I have an intact and very symmetrical juvenile canine, a pristinely extracted image file of which could revolutionize non-fungible tokens. I dream, I speculate, my teeth ache. I worry about the overhead.

Let's imagine a particular tooth, and let it be a great big one, a massive asset, not the kind of penny stock that fills my own gums. And beautiful! Gilded, even: a gilded molar the size, let's say, of a cow. An absolute unit. Gilded meaning papered over with gold, a thing that glitters thinly above the entrance to a San Francisco dentist's office. Frank Norris's dentist protagonist, McTeague, a bullish man who worked the Big Dipper mine, a man with the hands for pulling something out of something.

Keynes wished that "economists could manage to get themselves thought of as humble, competent people on a level with dentists".[2] The American Dental Association's *Glossary of Dental Clinical Terms* features an entry, below "incision" and "drainage and incisor", for "indigent". Read: "Those individuals whose income falls below the poverty line as defined by the federal Office of Management and Budget (OMB)."[3] Keynes need only have reversed his wish, to have hoped for dentists who become economists.

They say the market is a hand that can't be seen, as if to reassure us, as if a hand does not grip and seize, does not strangle, as if we ourselves have not been grabbed, throttled, leveraged, stood on our heads, our lunch money and its referent culled by the gravitational force of rent, fees, compound rates, and the bonds of wages. As if the hand were an open palm, an offering.

McTeague (1899): around our "bull-like" dentist, an ecosystem of grotesque racial caricatures all tearing things out to mass or circulate. They hoard, they mudlark, they speculate, their teeth ache. There's Zerkow and Maria–Miranda–Macapa (M-M-M, money-money-money) and their junk fetish, their gilded tableware. There's Marcus Schouler: *shuler*, schooled by McTeague and schools him, schools as in "cheats"; the shark, the cardsharp, who gets the dentist disbarred, whose cuffed corpse roots McTeague to the Death Valley sands, extraction impossible.

Greed (1924), von Stroheim's adaptation with Gibson Gowland as McTeague, dentist. They say Gowland was a prospector in the colonies. Diamonds. Martín Arboleda's planetary mine in orbit[4]: oil, gas, coal, copper, bauxite, lithium, nickel, cobalt. Data, labour, interest, fee. Castoreum, rennet, carmine, collagen, milk, blood, placenta. Extract, from the Latin: *drag out of.*

They say that capital is like a vampire, dead labour with two long cuspids, and teeth at the throat of living labour; it breaks flesh, draws, mines, sucks, drags out of, and lives, newly blooded. But living labour is not human tissue: these find themselves opposed in circulation, commodities farmed from the human animal, the abstract, and the concrete. The wonder of finance is its graft, its having unearthed mechanisms which grasp and throttle and clench the tissue and the labour in relation: go to work across a border to pick fruit that will be gilded by dyes, to pull nickel from the earth to get the money to carry across a border to pay to have a tooth plucked, bloody and wet, at a discount that will leave you enough to make a payment on the phone you used to record the whole thing, upload, monetize, speculate, teeth aching, worrying about the overhead. A tourism of extraction, a dental machinery, a systemic mastication.

The teeth of humans, dog teeth, the teeth of elk and of dolphins: a cross-species history of the money form, a means of payment, a means of settling accounts.

It's 2016 and we stand shabby in a clean administrative office building holding signs, chattering. Among them: "DENTAL CARE FOR UNIVERSITY WORKERS". As the celebrated provost flees the scene, we are greeted instead by strangers in tailored suits. Pearly Whites. Someone asks us what we want. We do not say we want to drag out of this place what it has dragged out of us and more. We do not say we know about the cuspids. We say we want to go to the dentist. We say we want to get our teeth cleaned, adjusted, excised, assessed, ~~appraised~~. Pearly Whites opens his mouth to deliver the corporate prayer, *oremus*: "Cost-benefit analysis!"

They say they'll drag it out of us.

Pascal says, more or less: kneel down, rinse and spit, and you will believe.

Notes

1 The George Washington Financial Papers Project, "Ledger B, 1772–1793: p. 179, Credit", http://financial.gwpapers.org/?q=content/ledger-b-1772-1793-pg179. Also "George Washington's Dentures FAQ", *The Digital Encyclopedia of George Washington*, www.mountvernon.org/george-washington/health/teeth/.

2 John Maynard Keynes, "Economic Possibilities for Our Grandchildren", in *Essays in Persuasion* (New York: Norton, 1963), 358–373.

3 www.ada.org/en/publications/cdt/glossary-of-dental-clinical-terms.

4 Martín Arboleda, *Planetary Mine: Territories of Extraction under Late Capitalism* (London and New York: Verso, 2020).

F

Fictions | Jens Beckert

Comedy, Commodity, Flesh, (Future), Speculation, Trust

All financial investments are directed towards the future. By lending money or buying stakes in a company, capital is put at risk in the hope that it will generate interest or dividends and that the asset can be sold with a profit at a later point in time. The time frame of this future can be milliseconds or years. Elaborate models of finance economics, due diligence, and artificial intelligence are applied to help investors to understand the risks of their investments and lead them to engagements that will not disappoint them. The future orientation of the economy makes expectations become central. What is the epistemological status of the expectations on which actors in financial markets base their decisions?

They are fictional.

In the 1930s, John Maynard Keynes shattered the belief that future yields in financial markets could be fully calculated. Expectations, Keynes wrote, "cannot be uniquely correct, since our existing knowledge does not provide a sufficient basis for a calculated mathematical expectation. In point of fact all sorts of considerations enter into the market valuation which are in no way relevant to the prospective yield."[1] The reason for this is that we cannot foresee the future. The economic, political, and social contexts that shape the valuation of assets in financial markets are so complex that market development cannot be predicted with any certainty. Novelty, a prime feature of capitalist economies, implies that actors often can't know what features the world will have in the future. Who, in 2001, would have thought that social networks and smartphones would shape our lives as profoundly as they do today and that Apple, Google, Amazon, and Facebook would be the most valuable companies in the world? Who would have predicted that in 2020 economic activities would globally slow down because of a pandemic? Who can anticipate the next financial crisis?

The world of financial markets is a world of fundamental uncertainty.[2] It is a world of novelty. It is a world in which information from the past is an unreliable guide for the future. Despite this uncertainty, actors need to form expectations about the future and make decisions based on the assessments they arrive at. Since there are no future facts, these assessments of the future cannot be (probabilistic) representations of the future. But what are they?

Under conditions of uncertainty, expectations are contingent images of the future, imaginaries on how the future will unfold and which courses of action and decisions will lead to the imagined outcome. We envision the world in the grammatical form of an accomplished future, as a present that has already occurred, and then decide as if this imagined future was the future that is actually going to occur. In their doings actors combine facts with imaginaries and present them as narratives, thus forming "fictional expectations",[3] which then guide their actions. The imagined futures are turned into stories which serve as "placeholders",[4] enabling actors to make decisions as if the future would unfold in a specific way.

The representation of the world in the mode of an as-if, however, is precisely what fictional texts are also doing. Novels and literary fictions are based on the author pretending as if a course of events occurred as described. It is true for both decisions under conditions of uncertainty and literary fictions: authors and readers have a "broken relationship to reality".[5] Two important differences nevertheless remain. First, in a fictional text the author deliberately creates a world that is not entirely factual, though it typically entails many facts that are true outside the fictional world. When assessing a financial future, actors want to anticipate a future reality as closely as they can, but they are limited due to uncertainty. Fictions are relevant in the economy not because political and economic actors like to engage in fantasies but because the future is only accessible in the mode as-if. Second, fictional accounts in the financial world are (or at least should be) continuously scrutinized for indications that they are wrong and adjusted accordingly. Not every story achieves credibility. Nor is the credibility of a story eternal. When reading fiction, by contrast, we don't ask the author to correct his narrative when we find a statement to contradict known facts. But in the end it remains true: as future facts cannot exist and as the future is open, expectations can only be statements about future states of the world which pretend to represent a future present. To influence decisions, they don't need to be true but need to appear credible to the decision maker putting assets at risk or liquidating them.

One might argue that the term fictional expectations is a pleonasm, since all expectations have to be fictional as they relate to the future. But this is not the case. Fictional expectations are connected with the condition of uncertainty in the sense of Frank Knight. When you roll a die, to expect that the probability of getting a four is one in six is not a fictional expectation. When life insurances calculate premiums, they do this grounded in probability calculations based on a large number of people insured, not based on speculations about the life expectancy of an individual. When financial markets, however, expect that we will be chauffeured by self-driving cars in ten years, this is a fictional expectation.

The notion of fictional expectations challenges the theory of rational expectations, the most influential theory of macroeconomics during the last half century.[6] I argue against this theory that expectations are not determined by the optimal use of all information available. Nor do expectations of actors correspond to a prevailing economic model which simply reflects fundamental data accurately. The financial market bubbles that have burst in the last few decades show this not to be true.[7] Instead, the notion of fictional expectations builds a bridge between social and cultural sciences. To understand expectations, how they are formed, how they persuade, and why they fail, it is worthwhile taking a look at the disciplines developing theories on fictions, namely cultural sciences and, in particular, literary studies.

The dynamic of modern economic systems significantly depends on whether financial investors bet on an unpredictable future. Start-up companies begin with a new business idea. If financial investors decide to fund a start-up business, they are convinced by a story about the business's future. Only years later will the investors know if the business has become successful and the narrative has come true. The decision, however, must be taken in the present.[8]

The imagination of worlds that do not exist but are yet to unfold shows the unique human ability to create fictions, which is perhaps the most fundamental human ability. It shows the creativity in our doings, which has been the backdrop of capitalism's enormous growth dynamic since its very beginnings. Yet, it creates new challenges too, one being the vulnerability of economic systems because their development relies not least on the credibility of stories.

The future orientation of the economy thus makes possible both the phenomenal economic growth and the economic crises that have recurred since the expansion of capitalist markets. Crises emerge when stories found to be credible suddenly become discredited. Markets no longer believe in the rising value of Dutch tulip bulbs or the repayment of Greek state debt. A failed investment destroys capital which might possibly have enabled a groundbreaking innovation elsewhere. Whatever the outcome will be, expectations contribute to the formation of the future. They steer resources, drive innovations, and destroy capital.

When resources are steered by imagined futures, narratives can also be used strategically to achieve objectives. This can contribute to stabilizing the economy, for instance to prevent currency crises, when political actors "guarantee" bank deposits or currencies in public speeches. The American President Roosevelt as well as the President of the European Central Bank, Mario Draghi, managed to end financial crises by doing so: "Believe me, it will be enough," Draghi stated in 2012[9] and thus caused a turnaround in the European sovereign debt crisis by shifting the imagined futures of financial markets.

The technologies of forecasting and creating credible stories about future developments can also be used to push particularistic political, ideological, and economic interests.[10] The technological visions currently propagated by a handful of protagonists in Silicon Valley go along with models of society that are not the subject of a broader social debate. They could nevertheless come true, not by democratic decision making but through the financial investments in the propagated technologies. A recent possible example for this is Mark Zuckerberg's vision of a "metaverse". This shows there is a politics of expectations.[11] Exercising control over our imaginaries of the future is an important instrument of power in shaping the future—this is true historically and today.

Capitalism is characterized by expansion. This originally meant the geographical spread of capitalism to all regions of the world. It also meant that markets expand into more and more spheres of social life. Yet, another form of capitalism's expansion is that it makes the future available for profit making in the present. This form of expansion relies on the central human faculty of imagination and the ability to create fictional worlds.[12] Contrary to the geographical and substantial expansion of capitalism, it has no natural boundary.

Notes

1 John Maynard Keynes, *The General Theory of Employment, Interest, and Money* (London: Macmillan, 1964 (1936)), 152.
2 Frank H. Knight, *Risk, Uncertainty, and Profit* (Mineola, NY: Dover Publications, 2006 (1921)).
3 Jens Beckert, *Imagined Futures: Fictional Expectations and Capitalist Dynamics* (Cambridge, MA: Harvard University Press, 2016).
4 Annelise Riles, "Collateral Expertise: Legal Knowledge in the Global Financial Markets", *Current Anthropology* 51, no. 6 (2010), 795–818.
5 Anna Burgdorf, "Virtualität und Fiktionalität: Überlegungen zur Finanzwelt als 'Vorstellungsraum'", in *Finanzen und Fiktionen*, ed. Christine Künzel and Dirk Hempel (Frankfurt: Campus Verlag, 2011).
6 Eugene F. Fama, "Random Walks in Stock Market Prices", *Financial Analysts Journal* 21, no. 5 (1965), 55–59.
7 Jens Beckert and Richard Bronk (eds), *Uncertain Futures: Imaginaries, Narratives, and Calculation in the Economy* (Oxford: Oxford University Press, 2018).
8 Liliana Doganova, "Discounting and the Making of the Future: On Uncertainty in Forest Management and Drug Development", in Beckert and Bronk, *Uncertain Futures*, 278–297; Neil Aaron Thompson and Orla Byrne, "Imagining Futures: Theorizing the Practical Knowledge of Future-Making", *Organization Studies* 43, no. 2 (1 November 2021), doi:10.1177/01708406211053222.
9 "Verbatim of the Remarks Made by Mario Draghi: Speech by Mario Draghi, President of the European Central Bank at the Global Investment Conference in London 26 July 2012", European Central Bank, www.ecb.europa.eu/press/key/date/2012/html/sp120726.en.html.

10   Jenny Andersson, *The Future of the World: Futurology, Futurists, and the Struggle for the Post-Cold War Imagination* (Oxford: Oxford University Press, 2018); Jens Beckert, "The Exhausted Futures of Neoliberalism: From Promissory Legitimacy to Social Anomy", *Journal of Cultural Economy* 13 (2019), 318–330, doi:10.1080/17530350.2019.1574867.

11   Beckert, *Imagined Futures.*

12   Wolfgang Iser, *The Fictive and the Imaginary: Charting Literary Anthropology* (Baltimore: Johns Hopkins University Press, 1993).

Flesh | Kara Keeling

Animals, (Body)**,** (Bondage)**, Capture, Counterfeit, Debt, Decadence, Extraction, Fictions,** (Materiality)**, Property,** (Violence)**,** (Water)

The three theses on flesh and the aesthetics of finance that follow are an opening to what could be a much longer meditation on the topic.[1]

Thesis I

A distinction must be made between "flesh" and "the body". In 1987, as part of a theory of the gender dynamics of the system of chattel slavery in the Americas, Hortense J. Spillers wrote:

I would make a distinction in this case between "body" and "flesh" and impose that distinction as the central one between captive and liberated subject-positions. In that sense, before the "body" there is the "flesh", that zero degree of social conceptualization that does not escape concealment under the brush of discourse, or the reflexes of iconography. Even though the European hegemonies stole bodies—some of them female—out of West African communities in concert with the African "middleman", we regard this human and social irreparability as high crimes against the flesh, as the person of African females and African males registered the wounding. If we think of the "flesh" as a primary narrative, then we mean its seared, divided, ripped-apartness, riveted to the ship's hole, fallen, or "escaped" overboard.[2]

For Spillers, the "flesh" is an aesthetic category fundamental to the enslavement of Africans in the Americas; she posits that we might think of it as "a primary narrative". If this is true, what kind of narrative is the "flesh"? What stories is "flesh" capable of telling? How might we describe its aesthetic form(s)? Spillers posits "a kind of hieroglyphics of the flesh". The hieroglyphs are undecipherable, "hidden to the cultural seeing by skin color". They are "vestibular" to culture, in the "pre-view" of a colonized North America. The "flesh" tells tales of visceral violence that attended chattel slavery. In that context "flesh" is a narrative genre unto itself.

In Spillers's account, the genre's origin is chattel slavery in North America. As an aesthetic form, "flesh" is "lexical", and, therefore, fundamentally social. "The body" can be read as a cultural text legible to those habituated to and disciplined by the various institutions of the culture in which the body appears to anchor a particular "subject-position". Social, economic, and political systems work in and through bodies they make legible according to the logics of those systems. An antechamber to culture, "flesh" expresses the irreparably social innards of culture. It is a lexicon of desire, pleasure, and other, often violent, drives. It is a social medium.

What relationship does this flesh and the stories it can tell have to the aesthetics of finance?

Thesis II

A social medium, a reservoir for culture that is never fully emptied into culture, "flesh" cannot be owned; therefore, "flesh" marks a limiting case of finance's capacity to order things according to its needs for profit. Famously, Shylock, in William Shakespeare's *The Merchant of Venice*, demanded a pound of Antonio's flesh as payment if Antonio defaults on a loan of three thousand ducats. About this arrangement, Shylock explains: "A pound of man's flesh taken from a man/ Is not so estimable, profitable neither, /As flesh of muttons, beefs, or goats. I say."[3] According to the anti-Semitic logic of Shakespeare's text, Shylock wants Antonio's flesh out of revenge for Antonio's anti-Semitism. It could be said Shylock wants to collect Antonio's flesh simply for his own incalculable and cruel pleasure. In the end, Antonio's flesh could not be owned because it could not be easily extracted either from Antonio's blood or Antonio's organs to which the pound of flesh is connected. In the twenty-first century, a pound of human flesh still may be worthless, but "the hieroglyphics of the flesh" continue to record the often irrational and libidinal social excesses of finance's drives.

Thesis III

The stories told through the genre that is "flesh" are as incalculable as the bodies on which human flesh hangs. Yet, each story is part of a collective, social, and visceral store of perceptions and ways of knowing that cannot be parsed completely into "culture" or "knowledge". The "hieroglyphics of the flesh" persist, stubbornly material, yet anarchic. Owned by nobody and by everybody, they accrue wealth beyond measure.

Notes

1   The author would like to thank the participants in the Montalvo Lucas Artists Residency on "Underworlding" and Jennifer Wild for comments on and conversations about this essay.
2   Hortense J. Spillers, "Mama's Baby, Papa's Maybe: An American Grammar Book", *Diacritics* 17, no. 2 (1987), 67.
3   William Shakespeare, *The Merchant of Venice* (New Delhi: Delhi Open Books, 2020), 20.

G

Gaming

Gift

Gold

Gaming | Stephanie Boluk and Patrick LeMieux

(Algorithm), (Platform), Sacrifice, Value, Work

When we first moved to Oakland, pinball was still illegal. At the time, public establishments like the Pacific Pinball Museum had to register as non-profits and charge visitors a flat fee for unlimited play rather than let money enter a machine.[1] Across the US, public ordinances and municipal codes regulate coin slots, tilt sensors, persistent scoreboards, and electromechanical flippers in an attempt to delineate between gambling and gaming, chance and skill. Whether considering sponsorships in professional sports or betting on the stock market, the relationship between games and finance is not clear-cut—particularly in an era of what Susan Strange has called "casino capitalism".[2] Philosophers of play like Johan Huizinga have long described games as "magic circles" or "temporary worlds within the ordinary world, dedicated to the performance of an act apart" in which money can pop the bubble and spoil the game. Working in reverse, the application of games and gambling to the world of finance questions and destabilizes the authority of financial instruments. Huizinga notes: "[t]he gambler at the roulette table will readily concede that he is playing; the stockjobber will not", and, in the case of life insurance, "betting on future eventualities of a non-economic nature ... were repeatedly proscribed as illegal games of chance".[3] From betting on bagatelle and bingo to payouts from pinball and pachinko, financial aesthetics (and finance more generally) underwrites both the definition and practices of gaming.[4]

When Montague Redgrave submitted a patent for "Improved Bagatelle" in 1871, he proposed miniaturizing the popular eighteenth-century billiards mod, tilting the table, and replacing the cue with a spring-loaded plunger in order to create "an amusing game of skill ... that may be introduced into the social and family circles".[5] In these games a marble or ball bearing is launched up into a wooden playfield filled with pins or nails upon which the ball bounces haphazardly into various baskets, holes, or drains worth a certain amount of points. But, especially after Prohibition in 1920, glass-topped and coin-operated tabletop bagatelle machines like David Gottlieb's *Baffle Ball* (1931) and Bally's eponymous *Ballyhoo* (1932) were often used for penny gambling at speakeasies (and are rumoured to be part of Al Capone's vast money laundering schemes in 1920s Chicago alongside literal coin-operated laundry machines).[6] Despite emerging alongside the first slot machines, electromechanical pinball that included actuated bumpers like Bally's *Bumper* (1937) often contained small placards stating "A SKILL GAME FOR AMUSEMENT ONLY" and "PLAYERS WILL REFRAIN FROM GAMBLING" in an attempt to disavow their Prohibition-era association with gambling (see Figure 22.1). Further emphasizing this split, in 1947 Gottlieb famously added user-operated flippers to his *Humpty Dumpty* pinball machine to try and redefine pinball as a game and not a gamble.

All the king's horses and all the king's men—or rather, all the backbox pin-up girls rendered by Roy Parker and all the playfield ramps and rails designed by Harry Mabs—tried to put pinball together again with *Humpty Dumpty*, a "game of skill and timing" featuring "unique flipper action enabl[ling] the player to send balls zooming from bottom right back to top of playing field, whizzing and bounding around for super-high scoring!"[7] These electromechanical machines

Figure 22.1 Bally's *Bumper* (1937) transformed the playfield by adding electromechanical bumpers instead of Bagatelle's typical pins (left). The machines included warnings about the difference between gaming and gambling (right).

aimed to re-signify the meaning of pinball with all the insistence of Lewis Carroll's Humpty Dumpty in *Through the Looking-Glass* petulantly arguing "[w]hen *I* use a word ... it means just what I choose it to mean—neither more nor less".[8] Yet, while the manufacturers claimed pinball was merely a *game*, many from the broader public were as sceptical as Alice when it came to categorizing these devices: "[t]he question is ... whether you *can* make words mean so many different things".[9] Despite attempts to draw distinct boundaries between *gaming* and *gambling*, the two practices are deeply entwined in a way that goes back to their earliest usage in the English language.

Falling further down the etymological rabbit hole, at one point in time, gambling and gaming were synonymous with one another. According to the *Oxford English Dictionary*, the earliest recorded uses of *game* going back to ninth-century Old English had numerous meanings such as "[a]musement, sport, fun; pleasure, enjoyment" and "[a]n activity or diversion

Figure 22.2   An advert for *Humpty Dumpty* in *The Coin Machine Journal* focuses on its "sensational player-controlled flipper bumpers" and "super sensitive control buttons on both sides" which would transform a gamble into "a game of skill and timing". (*Source: The Coin Machine Journal*, 62; reprinted with permission.)

of the nature of or having the form of a contest or competition, governed by rules of play, according to which victory or success may be achieved through skill, strength, or good luck".[10] One notable usage of *game* or its derivative *gaming* was specifically in reference to games of chance: "[t]he action or practice of playing games, as cards, dice, etc., for stakes". This particular usage appears to have taken on a life of its own and developed an identity separate from other forms of gaming that, at least in English, became a new word. By the fifteenth century, the terms *gaming* and *gamer* had linguistically evolved into *gambling* and *gambler*. Whether this emerged as an early form of

Thieves' Cant or simply as slang in English city streets, terms in reference to games of chance played for money (whose early instances in writing were almost exclusively pejorative), a category of play deemed illicit, were bracketed off into their own unique word. By the twentieth century, this linguistic bifurcation only intensified as games moved from being folk practices to industrial products. Suddenly, play became enclosed within consumer products, players were bifurcated into demographic categories, and *gaming* and *gambling* started to mean different things.

The first use of *gamer* as an identity category to refer to players of board games was highly divorced from "unliefull gamer" of the fifteenth century in which *gamer* was used mostly to refer to gamblers. As many casino and gambling organizations have noted, although gaming and gambling are often used interchangeably to describe the same practices, they clearly do not have the same moral coding. In their linguistic analysis, Ashlee Humphreys and Kathryn Latour demonstrate how the application of the terms *game* and *gambling* shifts perception from whether practices are considered legitimate or a form of entertainment rather than associated with crime and immoral activity even when those terms are used to describe the same activities.[11] These categories extend into the academic research, as *game studies* and *gambling studies* mostly exist as two solitudes. After surveying the literature of these two fields, Sebastian Deterding and a panel of scholars at the Digital Games Research Association concluded: "[t]his distinction between gaming and gambling is being reproduced not only in law and everyday practice, but also in scholarship".[12] But after the bifurcation of *gaming* and *gambling* in the late nineteenth and early twentieth centuries, perhaps these practices were beginning to re-coalesce around their shared etymological roots.

The standard legal definitions of gambling typically identify three components—the presence of chance, a prize to be won, and consideration in the sense of something of value being wagered on an uncertain outcome. Returning to Huizinga, in 1938 he wrote on the etymological connection between *wager* and *wage* as well as *prize* and *price*:

Every game has its stake. It can be of material or symbolical value, but also ideal. The stake can be a gold cup or a jewel or a king's daughter or a shilling; the life of the player or the welfare of the whole tribe. It can be a prize or a "gage". This is a most significant word ... It is very curious how the words "prize", "price" and "praise" all derive more or less directly from the Latin *pretium* but develop in different directions. *Pretium* arose originally in the sphere of exchange and valuation, and presupposed a counter-value. Now while *price* remains bound to the sphere of economics, *prize* moves into that of play and competition, and *praise* acquires the exclusive signification of the Latin *laus* ... What is equally curious is to see how the word *wage*, originally identical with *gage* in the sense of a symbol of challenge, moves in the reverse direction of *pretium*—i.e. from the playsphere to the economic sphere and becomes a synonym for "salary" or "earnings." We do not play for wages, we work for them.[13]

In his examination of two of the three standard elements of gambling, he remarks on how the meaning of *wage* in reference to payment for services rendered emerges out of the Old French term *gage*, which could mean two things: it can refer to the money or object bet on something with an uncertain outcome as well as the prize won in a contest. As *wage* took on a new meaning in reference to a fixed salary and earnings as a product of one's labour, Huizinga culminates his analysis by noting that now "we do not play for wages, we work for them". But in the post-2008 information economy, it would seem that this concept of wage has been turned on its head and is reverting back to the original etymological origins—a bet with an uncertain outcome.

Back in Oakland, since the 1930s public ordinances required pinball machines to have persistent scoreboards and static prices[14] until Oakland city council staff discovered what appeared to be anachronisms in the gambling bylaws in the summer of 2014. At the time, the Public Safety Commission chaired by Noel Gallo was seeking to regulate another legal grey area: internet sweepstake casinos. Specifically, as Gregory Minor from the Nuance Abatement Division of the City Administrator's office argued on 24 June, "operators across the country ... are exploiting ambiguity in gambling laws and operating facilities in which theoretically the public was paying for 'internet time' but were using these machines to operate ... [what are] essentially slot machines under California Penal Code".[15] Proprietors of Fruitvale internet cafés argued that payments were for internet time, that there was no actual insertion of money into machines, and the games were predetermined by the computer programmer so there was no element of chance—an unlikely site for ontological explorations of the nature of random number generation. While debating the ambiguity between gaming and gambling based on the distinction between chance and skill, Minor also noted: "while we're at it, we're already looking at the gambling section, there is an outdated provision related to pinball which prohibited certain kinds of pinball machines that are no longer an issue so we went ahead and suggested editing that out of the gambling section". These minor edits[16] were accompanied by both national and international news coverage proclaiming: "Jackpot! Oakland decriminalizing pinball machines" and "Huge Tournament Celebrates End of Oakland's Bizarre 80-Year Pinball Ban".[17] Meanwhile, with or without the internet sweepstakes café, folks in Oakland continue to gamble with the gig economy: from Lyft ride-shares and Airbnb rentals to WeWork co-working spaces and Lime scooter pick-ups (when they aren't hurled into Lake Merritt). In the twenty-first century, our games are always gambles and our wages are also wagers.

After the US housing bubble and the global financial crisis, and with the emergence of the gig economy, crypto assets, and platform capital in the last decade, gaming and gambling technically and aesthetically converge in what Randy Martin calls the "financialization of daily life".[18] Credit card points and frequent flyer miles make a game of measuring and rewarding past purchases; Uber Quests and Lyft Challenges offer bonus incentives for reaching ride-share goals; Airbnb and WeWork gamble on the future value of real estate; and NFT markets and GameStop stocks encourage people to played with life savings during the pandemic. Meanwhile, cosmetic items and loot boxes in video games reward casual play; millions of dollars of online betting and grey-market gambling accompany esports spectatorship; and YouTube and Twitch transform games into a platform for harnessing and monetizing attention. Nowhere is the precarity and casualization of labour more evident than in the movement from the gamification of work in the 2010s to the gamblification of work today. Gamble, game, gamble. Wager, wage, wager. The meaning of *gaming* and *gambling* oscillates over time. From the financialization of everyday life to the gamification and gamblification of daily work, in the twenty-first century the games we play are not simple stand-ins or allegories of financial precarity but serve as technical platforms that simultaneously anticipate and enact the larger conditions of contemporary capitalism.

Notes

1   Carolyn Jones, "Jackpot! Oakland decriminalizing pinball machines", *SFGate*, 20 June 2014, www.sfgate.com/bayarea/article/Jackpot-Oakland-decriminalizing-pinball-machines-5565613.php.

2   Susan Strange, *Casino Capitalism* (Manchester: Manchester University Press, 1997).

3   Johan Huizinga, *Homo Ludens: A Study of the Play-Element in Culture* (London: Routledge and Kegan Paul, 1949), 53.

4   For an excellent history of pinball, from electromechanical to solid-state machines, see Christopher DeLeon, "Arcade-Style Game Design: Postwar Pinball and the Golden Age of Coin-Op Videogames" (Atlanta, GA: Georgia Institute of Technology, May 2012). And for a discussion of pinball's relation to gambling, see Carly A. Kocurek, *Coin-Operated Americans: Rebooting Boyhood at the Video Game Arcade* (Minneapolis, MN: University of Minnesota Press, 2015).

5   Montague Redgrave, "Improvement in Bagatelles", United States Patent No. 115,357, United States Patent Office (Alexandria, VA, 1871).

6   Kocurek, *Coin-Operated Americans*, 90.

7   "Humpty Dumpty", *The Coin Machine Journal* (December 1947), 62.

8   Lewis Carroll, *Alice's Adventures in Wonderland and Through the Looking-Glass* (New York: Oxford University Press), 191.

9   Ibid.

10 "game, n." OED Online (March 2022), www.oed.com/view/Entry/76466.

11 Ashlee Humphreys and Kathryn A. Latour, "Framing the Game: Assessing the Impact of Cultural Representations on Consumer Perceptions of Legitimacy", *Journal of Consumer Research* 40, no. 4. (2013), 773–795.

12 Sebastian Deterding, Faltin Karlsen, Joseph Macey, Torill Elvira Mortensen, Heather Wardle, and David Zendle, "The Convergence of Gaming and Gambling Research: What Can We Learn from Each Other", Proceedings of DiGRA (2020), 2.

13 Huizinga, *Homo Ludens*, 51.

14 Oakland municipal code "9.24.090 – Pinball machines" states "A. It is unlawful for any person to keep or use in any public

place any pinball machine equipped with any device which cancels and records the cancellation of free games won without the actual playing of said free games by the player", and "B. It is unlawful for any person to keep or use in any public place any pinball machine game which permits the insertion of more than one coin per game." Bay Area Pinball, "For Amusement Only: Strange Pinball Laws in Oakland", *The Pacific Pinball League*, 5 December 2010, https://pinballbayarea.com/2010/12/05/for-amusement-only-strange-pinball-laws-on-the-books-in-oakland/.

15 Oakland Public Safety Committee, "Public Safety Committee Meeting June 24, 2014", Oakland City Council, 24 June 2014, https://oakland.granicus.com/player/clip/1564.

16 Pun intended.

17 Jones, "Jackpot!"; Bo Moore, "Huge Tournament Celebrates End of Oakland's Bizarre 80-Year Pinball Ban", *Wired*, August 2014, www.wired.com/2014/08/oakland-pinball-tournament/.

18 Randy Martin, *The Financialization of Daily Life* (Philadelphia, PA: Temple University Press, 2002).

Gift | Hans Haacke

Commodity, Decadence, (Equity), Luxury

Figure 23.1 Hans Haacke, *Gift Horse*, Trafalgar Square—Fourth Plinth, period after 2015.

Figure 23.2   Hans Haacke, *Gift Horse*, Trafalgar Square—Fourth Plinth, period after 2015.

Gold | Joyce Goggin

(Art), China, Commodity, Decadence, Extraction

Bug, bullion, chrysography, coin, dust, filling, flake, halo, idol, jewellery, leaf, nugget, rush, shower, smith, standard ...

Gold is a precious metal and an element. A conductor of electricity, gold also has medicinal applications and is soluble in solution. Gold has been discovered around the globe and is mined, or "panned for", in rivers and streams in which gold nuggets and flakes are found.

In 1905, it was estimated that "all the gold in the world could be confined in a 10-metre cube (1000 cubic m.)", whereas in 1500 that same cube would have measured two metres (eight cubic metres).[1]

Of precious and semi-precious metals, gold occupies a unique place in aesthetics, economics, and culture. Contributing factors to gold's status and allure include its resistance to tarnish, its malleability, and its luminosity (like "a spontaneous light brought out for the underground world"[2]), qualities which make gold the most sought after, if not the rarest, of metals.

Minted as coin and bullion, gold has also served as a universal equivalent and a monetary standard against which commodities may be measured, as well as paper and other ephemeral monies.

Gold is both currency and commodity; hence, like the holy grail, gold is both symbol and thing.[3] Gold is also understood to have spiritual qualities, and all cultures have supposedly held gold in veneration and associated it with divinity.[4] For Freud the reasons for the special properties attributed to gold reside in the unconscious, where it is linked to defecation and faeces.

Gold modifies (i.e. gold bug) and decorates many things: its aesthetic qualities make it both precious and the material base for beautiful objects, i.e. jewellery. Gold has "its own economics as an artistic and industrial substance".[5]

Gold bug: particularly in the US in the nineteenth century. Gold bugs, advocates of the gold standard, held paper money in contempt as a licensed fraud.[6] Unlike their counterparts, the "paper money men", gold bugs believed that gold was the only "real money".[7]

Gold bullion: bars into which gold is worked as a standard measure. In the thirteenth century, "The money current among [the Russians] consists of gold rods about a half a foot in length and worth perhaps 5 gros sous apiece", and in China "they have gold in bars and weigh it out by saggi: and it is valued according to its weight".[8]

Gold chrysography: writing in gold suspended in solution, as in illuminated manuscripts, as the holy spirit or voice of God.

Gold coin: Herodotus attributed the kings of Lydia with the invention of minting coins of predetermined weight equal to their value; they were the first to use gold and silver coin in trade.[9] "[B]y the mid-thirteenth century gold minting [had] spread throughout the major cities and states" of Europe.[10] Geona: deniers d'or (1252); Florence: florins (1250); France: écus d'or (1266); Venice; ducats (1284). Flanders, Castile, Bohemia, and England began minting gold coins by the early fourteenth century.

Gold coins are an "internal participant in [their own] logical and semiological organization".[11] Gold minted into coin is both homogenous with itself (as gold) and heterogenous with itself (as numismatic sculpture or as money).[12] As numismatic sculpture, coins are also valued art objects and, beginning in the nineteenth century in the US, gold coins were often taken out of circulation to be gifted as beautiful objects, thus further complexifying the valuation of gold.[13] By 1914 "full weight" gold coins had already begun disappearing from circulation in many counties.[14]

From 1849 to 1855, "private gold coins were the main currency circulating in California"[15] and had completely dropped out of circulation as a currency after the 1930s. Gold coins are now purchased as collectors' items or used in jewellery making.

In Greek myth, Danaë is impregnated by Zeus in a shower of gold coins; hence gold as divinity transubstantiated. "[I]n myths, fairy tales and superstitions, in unconscious thinking, in dreams and in neuroses ... gold which

Figure 24.1   Title page from Pieter Langendijk's *Harlequin Stock-Jobber* (Arlequin Actions), a comic play satarizing the financial bubbles of 1720.

the devil gives his paramours turns into excrement ... and
everyone is familiar with the figure of the 'shitter of ducats' ... According to ancient Babylonian doctrine gold is 'the
faeces of Hell.'"[16] During the economic bubble of 1720, comic
prints circulated that reversed the myth of the shitter of ducats, depicting traders eating gold coins and shitting worthless shares.

Gold dust: Kara-jang: "In this province gold dust is found
in rivers, and gold in bigger nuggets in the lakes and moun-
tains. They have so much of it that they give a saggio of gold for
six of silver."[17] In 1278 Marco Polo recalls seeing "gold dust ...
recovered from sea water".[18] In early banking, gold coins were
often "sweated", "vigorously shaken in a pouch so that they hit

Figure 24.2   Show detail from the title page of *Harlequin Stock-Jobber*—a
projector being fed gold coins and excreting shares in the bubble of 1720.

and scraped against one another", leaving gold dust behind.[19] In legend, gold dust is akin to fairy dust, magic.

Gold filling: as early as the eleventh century, gold was used to fill and repair teeth because it is highly durable, polishes to a smooth surface, will not corrode, and its malleability makes it easy to work with. 1299: in the city of Vochan (Baoshan, Yunnan province), "they all have their teeth of gold—that is to say, every tooth is covered with gold".[20] Gold fell out of common use in dentistry in the 1980s due to prohibitive costs; hence, gold fillings and teeth now connote glamour and wealth.

Gold leaf: micro-thin sheets of hammered gold used for gilding various objects in order to impart luminosity. Used especially in objects of religious significance such as icons to symbolize the divine or the holy spirit.

Gold ground: in art history, a background of gold leaf. An aesthetic and technique used in various periods and places, such as in the first century AD in Roman mosaics for non-religious subjects. In early Christian art, gold ground connotes heaven, or a spiritual plane. Also prevalent in Byzantine art, icons, and illuminated manuscripts to connote holiness.

Gold idol: eleventh century, Ceylon, India: "when the king saw that his son was dead he had an image made in his likeness, all of gold and precious stones ... this was the first idol ever made by the idolaters and hence come all the idols in the world".[21]

Gold jewellery: known for its malleability and luminosity, gold lends itself to jewellery making. Here, gold's value as a metal and its aesthetic value merge. In the form of a wedding band, gold signifies the sanctity of marriage, purity, and permanence.

Gold rush: the emotional charge of gold and legendary fortunes to be made in the New World gave rise to a "rush" of emigrants from the East, Europe, and Australia to California, the Klondike, and Alaska. Gold was mined and nuggets and flakes were panned. The US gold-backed economy was both stimulated and destabilized by the great influx of gold during the rush years.[22] Gold and silver were also devalued in the sixteenth century due to enormous quantities imported into Spain and Portugal from their American colonies.[23]

Goldsmith: goldsmiths make precious objects such as jewellery from gold and silver, and functioned as early bankers or repositories for precious metals and gems for which receipts were issued. These receipts also circulated in trade and are known as an early form of paper money.[24]

Gold standard: based on the perceived relative scarcity of gold and its combined qualities as above, gold became a standard backing or guarantor for paper currency. History: "Socrates describes a substance—gold—that plays the same role as x. Gold has a universal nature that, like the sculptor's metal or the stamper's wax, can become something else and yet still remain itself", hence its use as a standard.[25]

In China in the thirteenth century: according to Marco Polo, the Great Khan "had money ... out of the bark of trees ... like sheets of cotton paper ... cut up into rectangles of various sizes" which corresponded to various weights in precious metals, i.e. "a silver groat of Venice" or "ten gold beznats", all as "authoritative as if they were made of pure gold or silver".[26]

From 1880 to 1914 gold was accepted as a universal standard for paper currencies. In the "volatile period following the American Gold Rush in 1849, and the Australian gold rush in 1851", during which gold production rose nearly ten times, a flexible gold standard and bimetallic systems were adopted.[27] The gold standard was abandoned for a fiat currency system after 1971.

In 2022, German artist Niclas Castello unveiled a hollow gold cube made of 186 kilograms of pure 24-karat gold, valued at $11.5 million, in Central Park. The sculpture was created to advertise the artist's new cryptocoin and related NFT. Castello: "Gold is a symbol of the sun, of light, of the good."[28] Castello's hollow gold cube—both art and commodity—is the gold standard for his cryptocoin currency, i.e. "this gold is but the money-form of those commodities themselves".[29] Castello's hollow cube, which is supposedly "beyond our world—intangible", is the symbolic standard for his likewise intangible NFT and cybercoin.

Notes

1 Pierre Vilar, *A History of Gold and Money 1450–1920*, trans. Judith White. (London and New York: Verso, 1984), 19.

2 Karl Marx, *A Contribution to the Critique of Political Economy* (New York: C.H. Kerr, 1859), 211.

3 Marc Shell, *Art & Money* (Chicago, IL: University of Chicago Press, 1995, 20.

4 Jack Weatherford, *The History of Money* (New York: Three Rivers Press, 1997), 26.

5 Vilar, *A History of Gold and Money*, 19.

6 John Kenneth Galbraith, *Money: Whence It Came, Where It Went* (Boston, MA, and New York: Houghton Mifflin, 1975), 93.

7 Brian Rotman, *Signifying Nothing: The Semiotics of Zero* (Palo Alto, CA: Stanford University Press, 1987), 50.

8 Marco Polo, *The Travels* (1299), trans. Ronald Latham (London: Penguin Classics, 1958), 176.

9 Galbraith, *Money*, 6.

10 Irene Finnel-Honigman, *A Cultural History of Finance* (New York and London: Routledge, 2010), 25.

11 Shell, *Art & Money*, 4.

12 Marc Shell, *The Economy of Literature* (Baltimore, MD: Johns Hopkins University Press, 1978), 53–54.

13 Viviana Zelizer, *The Social Meaning of Money: Pin Money, Paychecks, Poor Relief, and other Currencies* (Princeton, NJ: Princeton University Press, 1994), 107.

14 Eric Helleiner, *The Making of National Money: Territorial Currencies in Historical Perspective* (Itacha: Cornell University Press, 2003), 35.

15 Zelizer, *The Social Meaning of Money*, 15.

16 See Sigmund Freud, "Character and Anal Eroticism", 1908.

17 Polo, *The Travels*, 178.

18 Ibid., 249.

19 Weatherford, *The History of Money*, 129.

20 Polo, *The Travels*, 181.

21 Ibid., 283.

22 Galbraith, *Money*, 42.

23 Fernand Braudel, *A History of Civilizations*, trans. Richard Mayne (New York and London: Penguin, 1993), 418, 444; Weatherford, *The History of Money*, 100; Finnel-Honigman, A Cultural History of Finance, 37.

24 Mary Poovey, *Genres of the Credit Economy: Mediating Value in Eighteenth- and Nineteenth-Century Britain* (Chicago, IL: University of Chicago Press, 2008), 43.

25 Marc Shell, "The Ring of Gyges", *Mississippi Review* 17, no. 1/2, (1989), 54.

26 Polo, *The Travels*, 147.

27 Finel-Honigman, *A Cultural History of Finance*, 115.

28 www.ndtv.com/offbeat/why-a-gold-cube-worth-11-7-million-appeared-in-new-yorks-central-park-2748754.

29 Karl Marx, *Capital: A Critical Analysis of Capitalist Production*, Vol. I, trans. S. Moore and E. Aveling (London: Lawrence & Wishart, 1974), 72.

H

Health

HFT

Hostile Takeover

HFT | Gerald Nestler

(Algorithm), **Arbitrage**, (Data), (Derivatives),
The Pit, (Platform), **Speculation**

Data-driven technocapitalism mediates abundance in an obscure and asymmetrical fashion, producing precarity, inequality, and austerity for the vast majority.[1] In the microseconds of algorithmic trading, visibility collapses into immediacy, colonizing and exploiting the future at present. This asymmetry affects agency because those who master the resolution command a present that to everyone else is imperceptible future. Asymmetry is not accidental; it is fabricated infiltration, a product (unwittingly) consumed. As a result, technocapitalist resolution does not make us see and know; it makes us seen and known.

An aesthetics conducive to adequate forms of resistance would have to radically exceed and reform conventional frameworks of critique and dissent. We need to learn to sense anew, develop new senses, if we want to decipher the performative speech of technopower and nurture a new ecology of solidarity and care. Hence, establishing counter-visibility and cognition is a question of developing and performing resolution tools that deliver insight into a hidden "universe".

I propose a poietics of resolution to care for other sensibilities and to activate new forms of (political, cultural, economic, ecological) resistance against asymmetries of technocapitalist violence.[2] Resolution—an aesthetics ranging from perception, visualization, and cognition to knowledge production, problem solving, and decision making—is a conceptual template and toolbox against (black box) non-disclosure. In contrast to the passivity of transparency, poietics of resolution implicates a vast and adaptable array of agencies, able to access and unearth the manufactured "unknowns" of data-driven technocapitalism and disentangle hidden knowledge by enhancing resolution in the technological, legal, as well as social and political sense of the term.

A specific case in this regard is high-frequency trading (HFT) in financial markets. Surrounded by secrecy and privacy, HFT has flourished in obscurity, lacking resolution in the sense proposed above. What is the *aisthesis* of HFT, and how can it be perceived?

HFT trader Rishi Narang[3] defined the space as follows: "High-frequency traders (a) require a high-speed trading infrastructure, (b) have investment time horizons less than one day, and (c) generally try to end the day with no positions whatsoever." HFT is often depicted as a complex technological innovation, but its algorithms are more precise than complex because they need to boot quickly to capture tiny inefficiencies in bid-and-ask spreads.[4]

HFT started in the early 2000s and peaked around 2011. While some firms achieved immense market share in volume traded (e.g. up to 20% of US equities), the overall profit share was comparably small in relation to the whole of finance.

As part of the technocapitalist engine, exchanges compete for market share. When investment banks decided to trade on their own, partly due to what they perceived as a hostile exchange environment resulting from low-latency algorithmic trading, they set up dark pools (shadow banking). That allowed them to control the environment and stay below the radar of regulation. As a result, exchanges lost business to their opaque counterparts, and to recapture volume they incentivized HFT.

Also, regulation had unintended consequences: Reg NMS was introduced in 2005 to provide fairness and efficiency in an already automated financial ecosystem by ensuring orders were filled at the best price available, independent of the exchange traded. Unwittingly, Reg NMS provided HFT with a competitive edge on the level of low latency, but also led to collusion, abuse, and fraud. Apart from legal HFT tactics, like consolidated price feed exploitation or placing their systems near matching engines, exchanges protected HFTs against regulatory procedures with undisclosed order types (designed by HFTs because exchanges lacked the specialist knowledge and precision to make them work on a microsecond level). Incentives worked for both sides—HFTs need to trade high volumes to rake in profits, which benefits "their" exchanges' revenues, too.

HFT competition is a tech arms race towards a "natural" end: zero spread. In other words the efficient market hypothesis collapses in an environment where it becomes near impossible to detect inefficiencies and arbitrage opportunities to the point that profit cannot be made. How do players react when markets become pathologically efficient due to algorithmic trading, i.e. spreads tighten and profit margins approach near zero? And when there is no new class of algorithms that initiates a regime change? In other words, when technological innovation does not lead to competitive advantage and the rate of profit declines to unsustainable levels.

Following the HFT strategist and whistleblower Haim Bodek, people start to invent tricks to survive. One desperate approach, "regulation arbitrage", was the exploitation of loopholes and bugs in rules and regulations. That HFT firms have frequently been run by (SEC) lawyers, rather than quants, might thus come less as a surprise. Other black box tricks targeted exchange infrastructure bugs or attacks on the order book, e.g. "spam & cancel" (orders invisible in the order book, not illegal), "queue jumping (order types granting illegal top position), or "spoofing" and "momentum ignition" (orders not intended to be executed; illegal due to false appearance of supply and demand). The last resort for squeezing out profit is to manufacture fraud and collusion.

The main victims of these stealth features were mutual funds and investment banks. These abuses are still around and evidenced by repeated flash crashes. Evidently, the regulatory body, the US Securities and Exchange Commission (SEC), was incapable of erasing black box practices implemented for over a decade and, instead, achieved that practices must be disclosed. Now, at least you may know why you lose.

In proprietary financial systems, resolution enhanced to a degree that "everything is on the map" does not necessarily deliver full disclosure. The black box keeps us in the dark if the violence and those who exert it cannot be named and addressed from the outside. This also applies to resolution as a semantic and semiotic assemblage of tools against (black box) non-transparency, as described above. To come full circle, poietics of resolution includes an agent who complements, expands, and confirms findings. In other words, an agent who can make the black box speak from inside.

I call this agent a renegade—a figure that turns dissent into productive betrayal. A renegade could be whistleblowers who break loyalty and allegiance with their black box firm and/or system, expert witnesses who denounce systemic belief, or hackers who seek new and collective forms of engagement and empowerment. While she is stigmatized as a traitor, her exposure—inaccessible to algorithms; betrayal is a form of agency reserved to humans—produces public knowledge that destabilizes the technocapitalist discretion hegemony.

I conceive poietics of resolution as "making" access for collective knowledge and action—in other words, an activation of transparency. The resistance it offers, however, does not come without risk. Resolution, here, is not about probabilistic risk management. Instead, resolution points to an engagement with the sheer impossible—to risks experienced and lived. The renegade engages in a radical initiative full of ambivalence and vulnerability and is thus exposed to sheer limitless consequences. The ambivalence and perils of renegade counterperformativity surface in Haim Bodek's HFT whistleblower experience:

The whistleblower syndrome is kind of a pattern. The whistleblower says that "this is obviously wrong and I'm going to call it out" and then when I call it out everyone else is going to realize that it's wrong and it's just going to get fixed right away. What he doesn't realize is that everybody knows about it. ... you realize that that's what whistleblowing is—that you're making people go through the uncomfortable process of looking at themselves ... You're the guy pointing out the thing that no one wants to see, that everybody knows about. ... it's the same pattern over and over, where there's massive injustices no one wants to talk about and no one wants to admit vocally but everybody knows that's how things work. It doesn't change until the whistleblower does it.[5]

The renegade is not heroic but as ambiguous as the world she inhabits. In the midst of (fabricated) noise, the system accidentally yields information; exploiting the event of sectoral asymmetry resolves societal blindness. The renegade act—essentially a violation of custom, rule, or law—produces viable resolution materials across the semantic field of the term: visualization, discrimination, cognition, transparency, decision. Whatever the impulse, each act perforates an autonomy that is less and less conceded to natural persons. Hence, the renegade act reclaims autonomy from data-driven forms of capitalist sovereignty. That said, it does not constitute political autonomy with a capital A—an autonomy that bestows rights or vests powers. To the contrary, it constitutes an act that attracts serious consequences and might fail.

The renegade act of civil courage makes resolution possible in the first place because it brings compelling evidence to light that would otherwise remain hidden. Disengaging with capitalist infrastructure, the renegade's betrayal enters the realm of revolutionary negation by moving beyond critique and dissent. Here, poietics of resolution transforms into a possibility of politics bound to the urgency of civil support, a solidary environment. In this sense renegade activism is a call to emancipation that resists the false purity and determinacy of the technocapitalist doctrine.

Such renegade activism might seem at the margin of technocapitalism, but it is in fact right at its core, because it is an insurrection that holds the power to unlock the black box. It bears the potential to access knowledge and wealth, preempted by the capital–state nexus, finance conglomerates, and data platforms, as well as transform the acquiescent conditions of social automation and (digitized) labour. Renegade activism is a call to share the risk of insurrection in solidarity. It acknowledges the importance of acts that build alliances, collectives, and compositions against the violence of technocapitalist asymmetry.

Poietics of resolution recognizes that opaque asymmetries can be resolved by knowledge transpiring from inside the black box. It therefore proposes an aesthetics engaged in narrative instabilities that coagulate dissent into defection. And while the renegade act often starts from the perspective of an internal critique for improvement, its betrayal essentially constitutes a collapse of conventional frameworks of critique. It turns resistance into emancipatory insurrection.

Notes

1   Gerald Nestler, Christian Kloeckner, and Stefanie Mueller, "The Derivative Condition, an Aesthetics of Resolution, and the Figure of the Renegade: A Conversation", *Finance and Society* 4, no. 1 (2018), 126–143, http://financeandsociety.ed.ac.uk/article/view/2744.
2   Gerald Nestler, "Mayhem in Mahwah: The Case of the Flash Crash; Or, Forensic Re-Performance in Deep Time", in *Forensis: The Architecture of Public Truth* (Berlin: Sternberg Press, 2014), 125–148; Gerald Nestler, "Renegade Activism and the Artist-As-Collective", in Johnny Golding, Martin Reinhart, and Mattia Paganelli (eds), *Data Loam: Sometimes Hard, Usually Soft* (Berlin: De Gruyter, 2020), 426–449.
3   Rishi K. Narang, *Inside the Black Box: The Simple Truth about Quantitative Trading* (Hoboken, NJ: Wiley, 2013), 239.
4   Ibid., 260.
5   Gerald Nestler, "Contingent Ethics: Portrait of a Philosophy: Haim Bodek", series II, 2014, https://vimeo.com/channels/AoR, 33:46–36:42.

I

Iconomy

Insurance

Interest

The Invisible Hand

Iconomy | Peter Szendy

(Art), Credit, (Faith), Money

The neologism iconomy was coined in 1992 by Jean-Joseph Goux.[1] In a foundational move, he transposed to the domain of visual arts a number of insights from his previous work on the intertwined conceptualities of economics and language (or literature).

In his book published in 1973, *Symbolic Economies*, this transposition was already foreshadowed in the following terms:

Shortly after Saussure had declared that linguistic values ... had no foundation in nature, shortly after Wassily Kandinsky and Piet Mondrian had abandoned the search for direct empirical reference in order to espouse pure painting, the economic system dispensed with the gold standard, with the evident result of generalized floating.[2]

What Goux later described as Saussure's "'banking' theory of language"[3] thus had its equivalents in painting and in economics.

One has to look closely and critically at the birth of a concept that was to become increasingly important while it also underwent major transformations. Goux's notion of "pure painting", as opposed to "direct empirical reference", is dubious, as if one couldn't find figuration or mimetic gestures in so-called abstract art, for example in the representation of forces or processes rather than objects (balances or imbalances rather than "things"). But when Goux, in "Art and Money", coins the word iconomy, he rehearses an even more problematic view of "the history of Western currency" as the inexorable loss of its "materiality", of its "reassuring weight": once "shattered", money, he argues, has turned into mere "traces that refer to other traces", into "signs [that] point to other signs in an indefinite drift".[4] While money has undeniably undergone a process of dematerialization leading to the blockchains or digital currencies we witness today, one can wonder about Goux's conclusion, with its emphatic italicization: "*money no longer exists* (that is, real, authentic, absolute money that matches its imaginary construct)".[5]

This argument about money becoming immaterial and its ultimate disappearance confirms what Jacques Derrida suggested in a footnote dedicated to Goux the year before the publication of "Art and Money": "Does not this hypothesis," Derrida asked, "tend to naturalize and de-fictionalize gold-money, that is, to confirm an old and stable convention?"[6] There is an atmosphere of nostalgia—of lost origin—hovering around Goux's visual illustrations of what money supposedly was and is not anymore; commenting on a Dutch painting from 1539 by Marinus van Reymerswaele (*The Money Changer and His Wife*), he writes: "The reassuring, objective scales that measured the weight of gold to verify the value of a treasure has been replaced by another image of the banker ... at the keyboard of a computer."[7]

It is against the backdrop of this purported loss of foundation that the word iconomy was coined. What Goux defines as "the principle of 'iconomy'" (or "political 'iconomy'") is the following: "painting not only has monetary value, it is money".[8] But the apparent opposition between "to have" and "to be" shouldn't lead us astray: when Goux seemingly attributes to painting a monetary being, he only emphasizes the (relative) stability of painting's value as a substitute for the radically destabilized or unanchored values of immaterial currencies. In other words, painting is said to be money only because it is invested with the role of a new gold standard, because it vouches for money or stabilizes its fluctuations. Iconomy, then, is in no way synonymous here, as it will turn out to be in other approaches, with an ontological determination of the image itself by its general exchangeability.

These are the reasons why Goux's iconomy should be described, in a lexicon reminiscent of Georges Bataille, as a restricted iconomy:[9] 1) it presupposes that money had a solid origin and that it has lost it (rather than seeing gold itself as a sign, as a mark already caught in a network of traces of traces); 2) it focuses on painting, or art in general ("art objects, especially paintings", writes Goux), that is to say on a very specific and limited type of images; 3) it draws the consequence that these painted images are a substitute for a lost origin, i.e. that they can limit or halt the generalized deferral and drift of monetary signs in modern or contemporary economy. As opposed to this restricted iconomy, then, what would a general iconomy look like?

In its circulation after Goux, the iconomic concept has been increasingly applied to bearers of visual value that are only remotely related to painting or art objects. Indeed, in *Image, Icon, Economy*, her groundbreaking book on Byzantine iconoclasm published in 1996, Marie-José Mondzain takes a different and more capacious approach: without referring to Goux's newly coined portmanteau, she introduces the notion of "iconic economy", which she characterizes as the "organization, administration, and management of all visibilities".[10] When she focuses on numismatics, on the history of minting as an iconological battleground between iconophiles and iconoclasts (those who imprinted the image of Christ on their coins and, on the contrary, those who even went so far as to remove the cross), Mondzain suggests that image and money play similar roles as "fiduciary signs that incarnate ... the effects of faith and of credit".[11]

Now, on the one hand, this idea of an "iconic economy" has often been received in a way that loosens such a tight relation between images and monetary instruments: in 2007, in an article titled "Visual Empire", Susan Buck-Morss thus interprets Mondzain's notion of a management of the visible as an "iconomics of power", that is to say as control over "the visual economy of truth".[12] The icon in Goux's portmanteau, then, tends to sever its ties with its other half, with the economy, in order to become the object of a politics of truth telling. On the other hand, apparently without any explicit influence of Goux's or Mondzain's works, the word "iconomy" (or "iconomics") has made its way into the lexicon of finance, where it tends to lose its iconological dimension altogether: urbandictionary.com defines "iconomy" as an imaginary economy, where value doesn't match "the real economy" but multiplies "chaotically", as with the proliferation of derivatives. Other uses of the word seem only loosely related to images as such. Michael Kaplan thus understands "iconomics" as referring to a discourse about the market that relates to the market as an "indexical icon", a notion borrowed from Charles Sanders Pierce.[13]

Before Goux's coinage and Mondzain's expanded notion of iconic economy, Gilles Deleuze has offered the most capacious and at the same time most rigorous understanding of what we can, retrospectively, call iconomy. In a rarely commented on passage of *The Time-Image*, he wrote that "money is the reverse of all the images that the cinema shows and edits on the front",[14] a sentence that has to be read against the backdrop of the vastly expanded meaning acquired by cinema in Deleuze's thought. Indeed, if we remember that, in his first volume dedicated to film, Deleuze understood cinema as a synonym for the world or the universe ("the universe as cinema in itself"[15]), then the passage just quoted amounts to considering any image, inasmuch as it circulates, as the recto of a monetary verso that accounts not so much for its price or cost as for its ontological exchangeability.

It is precisely this Deleuzian idea of a structural and intimate relation between the image as such and money as the principle of universal exchange that has led me to offer the notion of a general iconomy: images, be they man-made or acheiropoietically produced by machines or "nature", are defined by their circulations, relations, metamorphoses into one another.[16] A relational, or, better, a differential concept of the image is what ultimately iconomy could mean.

The prefiguration of such a generalized iconomic perspective might already be found in Aby Warburg's work. The introduction he wrote for the unfinished project of his *Mnemosyne Atlas* gives only a very partial idea of the central role played by an economic lexicon in his iconological thought (I am thinking in particular of the metaphor of the "mint" that "coins" or "stamps" the "expressive values" in the history of art).[17] Indeed, Warburg's unpublished notes from 1927, titled *Allgemeine Ideen*, abound in iconomic formulations, for example when he speaks of a "savings bank [*Sparbank*] for energetic expressive values [*energetische Ausdruckswerte*]", or of the "exchange rate [*Kurwert*: also market value]" of gestural expressions as they are recorded—deposited—in images through time.[18]

Warburg's iconomic intuitions and Deleuze's iconomic theory *avant la lettre* have become more relevant than ever for today's digital images, with their metamorphic being or differential network: what Hito Steyerl has called a "poor image", i.e. a low-resolution digital duplicate, is essentially characterized by its instability, by its fluctuating nature ("it accelerates, it deteriorates", it is "an itinerant image ... squeezed through slow digital connections", it is "compressed", constantly "uploaded, downloaded, shared, reformatted").[19] But the contemporary Jpegs or GIFs or MP4s that feed the iconological traffic on social media (billions of images circulating each day, i.e. hundreds of thousands of images during the time it took you to read this sentence)[20] are only a particularly obvious illustration of the fact that images are (and have always been) "trans-formats": their consistence is their fast or slow transience between differential states (forms or formats), a metamorphosis sometimes so gradual (as when Goux's "art objects, especially paintings" start to decay) that they seem to be immobile and meant to last forever.[21]

Notes

1   Jean-Joseph Goux, "Art and Money: Toward a New 'Iconomy'", in *The Supermarket of Images*, ed. Peter Szendy, Emmanuel Alloa, and Marta Ponsa, trans. Deke Dusinberre (Paris: Gallimard-Jeu de Paume, 2020), 65–72.

2   Jean-Joseph Goux, *Symbolic Economies: After Marx and Freud*, trans. Jennifer Curtiss Gage (Ithaca, NY: Cornell University Press, 1990), 113.

3   Jean-Joseph Goux, *The Coiners of Language*, trans. Jennifer Curtiss Gage (Norman, OK: University of Oklahoma Press, 1994), 18.

4   Goux, "Art and Money", 66–68.

5   Ibid., 68.

6   Jacques Derrida, *Given Time: I. Counterfeit Money*, trans. Peggy Kamuf (Chicago, IL: University of Chicago Press, 1992), 110.

7   Goux, "Art and Money", 68.

8   Ibid., 70.

9   See Georges Bataille, *The Accursed Share: An Essay on General Economy*, trans. Robert Hurley (New York: Zone Books, 1988), 25.

10 Marie-José Mondzain, *Image, Icon, Economy: The Byzantine Origins of the Contemporary Imaginary*, trans. Rico Franses (Stanford, CA: Stanford University Press, 2005), 32, 34.

11   Ibid., 158.

12   Susan Buck-Morss, "Visual Empire", *Diacritics* 37, no. 2–3 (2007), 185. Without referring either to Goux or to Mondzain, Terry Smith analyses the visual coverage of 9/11 in terms of "the subtle power and the all-pervasiveness" of a "trafficking in images" that he calls "the iconomy"; see *The Architecture of Aftermath* (Chicago, IL: University of Chicago Press, 2006), 2.

13   See Michael Kaplan, "Iconomics: The Rhetoric of Speculation", *Public Culture* 15, no. 3 (2003), 479. Brazilian economist Gilson Schwartz offers another—somewhat hazy—notion of "iconomy" when he writes: "Iconomy shows us into an unprecedented universe: we are no longer dealing with the rules of 'household management' (or business, public accounts, etc.), but with the rules of icon management. The social networks produce reputation, affectivity, dialogs. This must be expressed, represented by icons; starting with an icon such as *like*, the quickest way to share contents in social networks. Thus, beyond price or pricing, we are entering a dimension of appreciation ... on the Internet, in this Iconomy, the *nomos* is defined by the icon, by something that is intangible, which is a visual, immaterial, real, and symbolic code at the same time." See Gilson Schwartz, "Iconomy, Cultural Diversity and Ludic Monetization on the Internet of Things", in *Diversity of Cultural Expressions in the Digital Era*, ed. Lilian Richieri Hanania and Anne-Thida Norodom (Buenos Aires: Teseo, 2016), 64.

14   Gilles Deleuze, *Cinema 2: The Time-Image*, trans. Hugh Tomlinson and Robert Galeta (Minneapolis, MN: University of Minnesota Press,1989), 77 (my emphasis). Translation modified.

15   Gilles Deleuze, *Cinema 1: The Movement-Image*, trans. Hugh Tomlinson and Barbara Habberjam (Minneapolis, MN: University of Minnesota Press, 1986), 59.

16   See Peter Szendy, *The Supermarket of the Visible: Toward a General Economy of Images*, trans. Jan Plug (New York: Fordham University Press, 2019); Peter Szendy, *Pour une écologie des images* (Paris: Minuit, 2021).

17   Aby Warburg, "The Absorption of the Expressive Values of the Past", trans. Matthew Rampley, *Art in Translation* 1, no. 2 (2009), 278–279.

18   See Christopher D. Johnson, *Memory, Metaphor, and Aby Warburg's Atlas of Images* (Ithaca, NY: Cornell University Press,

2012), 21, 149; Maud Hagelstein, *Origine et survivances des symboles: Warburg, Cassirer, Panofsky* (Hildesheim: Georg Olms, 2014), 64–65.

19   Hito Steyerl, "In Defense of the Poor Image", in *The Wretched of the Screen* (Berlin: Sternberg, 2012), 32.

20   In 2019 YouTube boasted on its official blog (blog.youtube/press) that there were more than 500 hours of video uploaded every minute, which means 720,000 hours a day, i.e. the equivalent of more than eighty years: more than a lifetime of images every day.

21   On images as "transformats", see Szendy, *Pour une écologie des images*, 20, 26.

Interest | Carmen Losmann

Bookkeeping, (Borders), **China, Credit, Death, Debt,** (Enclosure), (Land), **Mapping,** (Materiality), **Money,** (Oikonomia), **r>g,** (Social Reproduction)

Our economic system is structured in such a way that all goods and services are only produced if private companies expect to make a profit. What is too rarely put into context: because our modern money comes from debt, rising surplus on one hand requires a continuous growth in debt on the other hand. Interest is a key component in this circuit.

While developing the visual concept for the documentary *OECONOMIA*[1] and its exploration of the extent to which growing economic performance, growing debt, and growing inequality are related to each other, we tried to get hold of the ideology of capitalism in the aesthetics of its glamorous and stylish office worlds that we encountered in the economic centres of Germany. From this we developed five visual-aesthetic strands that characterize the film *OECONOMIA*.

1. Grid-Like Architectures Framing People

When we looked at the surfaces of the buildings, we discovered a grid-like world in which people acted small and inferior; above all, they seemed constrained by the frames, lines, and boxes that determined their range of motion. By placing our inner focus on the lines of these office architectures, the world showed itself to us as a giant maths book, and we concluded that the single rectangular sub-units can only relate to each other in a calculating way. All in all, we saw a world that seemed primarily concerned with calculating the profit rates of its actions.

2. Access and Restrictions

Moreover, in response to the question of what ideology is inscribed in the capitalist buildings, we revealed a powerful architecture of access and its restrictions. We observed at the entrances that the right of access to the office worlds and thus to both economic and social status was reserved for a certain type of person. To visually emphasize these structures of inclusion and exclusion, we directed our gaze into the in-between areas of this access-restricted world and deliberately shot images that featured cleaning and service staff. In looking at the architectures of power and their criteria of inclusion and exclusion, the gender, race, and class relations of our society shimmered back at us.

3. Apparent Transparency and Distorted Mirror Worlds

The building material we encountered was mainly glass surfaces that did not want to hide the view inside. We discovered a glass outer skin of the capitalist temple buildings, on which, despite their transparent, translucent material, a reflective, backward-looking mirror world appeared. So it was not so much a view of the inside of the buildings but rather a distorting duplication of the outside world. The reflective facades began to tell something else in it, and the fixed laws of the world around us seemed to blur in it.

4. Icons of Hypernaturality

In looking at the facade typologies, we found the recurring images of pristine natural landscapes remarkable. On walls, posters, and screens, vast forests, idyllic mountain landscapes, and deserted beaches beamed at us. So we were immediately confronted with the question of how to interpret this phenomenon—as a muralist attempt to iconically refute the nature-destroying side of the capitalist economy?

5. Neglected Spaces

And despite architectural efforts to make the world of capitalist centres appear in high-class splendour, we have encountered deviant images in the midst of this. Spaces that, for all their economic potency, reveal something of the neglect that the world of the permanent profit machine triggers in us humans.

The six selected stills from *OECONOMIA* are representative of the visual-aesthetic strands of the film outlined here, which are found and combined in the images in different ways.

Note

1   The director Carmen Losmann and the image designer Dirk Lütter developed the image concept for *OECONOMIA* (2020, 89 minutes) together. From the perspective of this collaboration, the text presented here is written in the "we" form.

Figure 27.1 a–f *OECONOMIA*, 2020, Petrolio/Lütter.

Figure 27.1 a–f (*Continued*)

The Invisible Hand | Hans Haacke

Extraction, Mont Pèlerin, Period

Figure 28.1 Hans Haacke: *Invisible Hand of the Market.* (X-Initiative, New York City, 2009)

Figure 28.2   Hans Haacke: *Invisible Hand of the Market.* (X-Initiative, New York City, 2009)

L

Ledger | Sarah Comyn

Bookkeeping, (Insurance), (Numbers), (Oikonomia)

Historically, and especially within literary fiction, the ledger can

Details	Debit	Credit
		balance,

but it can also

Details	Debit	Credit
	corrupt.	

The ledger

Details	Debit	Credit
itemizes		

not only accounts but also lives. Potentially a record of a life's expenditure and returns, the ledger is, as Adam Smyth has shown, a site of life writing.[1] Within the documents of household economies, the ledger can reveal

Details	Debit	Credit
	gendered spaces and knowledge,	
while also		providing testimony to the economic acuity and financial power of women, particularly in the early modern period.[2]

Details	Debit	Credit
The ledger		records facts

but it can also

Details	Debit	Credit
	keep ~~secrets.~~	
	As a site of duplication,	
the ledger is	re(-)	(+)iterative.
It repeats	(-) numbers	(+) numbers.
The ledger is also potentially		generative of knowledge
and it can	~~Repeat~~ revise.	

As a "system of writing" that contributes to the emergence of the "modern fact" in early modern Europe, the ledger with its double-entry bookkeeping has, according to Mary Poovey, both social and epistemological effects.[3] It is a record of expenditure and recompense that appears to promote accuracy and honesty. Opening their ledgers for public inspection, early modern merchants evidently declared the veracity and stability of their businesses and simultaneously transformed the domestic accounting of *oikonomia* to a system of publicly verifiable writing.[4] The ledger, thereby, became an increasingly necessary system of public credibility in a rapidly commercializing society.

Details	**Epistemological**	**Social**
The ledger is		representational
but it also seemingly binds	representative numbers to fact.	
Facts and numbers	become mutually constitutive,	
with the ledger conferring		"cultural authority"
	on numbers.[5]	
Facts can produce	new understandings of the world	
and simultaneously have		relational effects.

Details	Epistemological	Social
Money is legible.		
		"Money is gossip."[6]
	"Money is also epistemology."[7]	

Details	Epistemological	Social
The ledger can codify	knowledge, experience,	and narrative.

It asks to be read and judged.

Details	Social	Epistemological
And it, in turn, can reduce relation-ships to a	cost	benefit
	calculus.	
With the cipher [0=−1+1=0] as its symbol of	achieved equilibrium	
between	debts,	credits,
	income,	expenditure,

the ledger can perform a moral accountancy in literature. For nineteenth-century British novels—shaped as they were by the numerous financial crashes and insolvencies of the period—the ledger holds particular symbolic value. Being able to account for your household's finances lends you credibility, creditability, and a sense of moral virtue.[8] As is the case with Lucy Deane in George Eliot's *Mill on the Floss* (1860),[9] the balanced ledger comes to symbolize financial *and* moral rectitude: " 'Are you sure you won't do mischief, now?' he said, looking at her with delight. 'Yes, papa, quite sure. I'm very wise; I've got all your business talents. Didn't you admire my accompt-book, now, when I showed it you?' "[10]

Where the numbers do not balance, the ledger might indicate not only a moment of financial and epistemological crisis but social and moral crisis too. The ledger can therefore, as it does in Charles Dickens's *Little Dorrit* (1855–57) and *Great Expectations* (1860–61), register impending financial malfeasance, collapse, or disaster, as well as moral contamination. In *Little Dorrit*, the truth of Arthur Clennam's biological mother and the legacies of unpaid epistemological, social, financial, and moral debts lie hidden "among the old ledgers in the cellars",[11] which are described as having "as musty and corrupt a smell as if they were regularly balanced, in the dead small hours, by a nightly resurrection of old book-keepers".[12]

Unlike Lucy Deane, Pip from *Great Expectations* fails to keep accurate accounts of his expenses and instead

Details	Social	Epistemological
		moves his margins to accommodate his mounting debts.

Details	Social	Epistemological
This massaging of his economic margins has	social, as well as	epistemological effects.
"My business habits had one other bright feature, which I called	'l e a v i n g a M a r g i n.'"	"I had the highest opinion of the wisdom of this same Margin, but I am bound to acknowledge that on looking back, I deem it to have been an expensive device."[13]

The costs of Pip's margin include his affective betrayal of Joe and Biddy, the multiplication of Herbert Pocket's debts— "Herbert and I went on from bad to worse, in the way of increasing our debts, looking into our affairs, leaving Margins, and the like exemplary transactions"[14]—and the necessity of Joe paying off and forgiving not only Pip's financial and epistemological debts but his social debts, too:

"And when I say that I am going away within the hour, for I am soon going abroad, and that I shall never rest until I have worked for the money with which you have kept me out of prison, and have sent it to you, don't think, dear Joe and Biddy, that if I could repay it a thousand times over, I suppose I could cancel a farthing of the debt I owe you, or that I would do so if I could!"[15]

Pip's manipulation of his moral and financial ledger reveals, again, the autobiographical potential of the ledger, but also its epistemological fragility and the weight of its symbolic operation. Inviting inspection and requiring a reading audience for legitimacy,

Details	Epistemological	Social
the ledger oscillates continuously between	fact	fiction.

Notes

1   Adam Smyth, "Money, Accounting, and Life-Writing, 1600–1700: Balancing a Life", in *A History of English Autobiography*, ed. Adam Smyth (Cambridge: Cambridge University Press, 2016), 86–99.

2   See Smyth, "Money, Accounting, and Life-Writing"; Alexandra Shepard, "Crediting Women in Early Modern English Economy", *History Workshop Journal* 79, no. 1 (2015), 1–24.

3   Mary Poovey, *A History of the Modern Fact: Problems of Knowledge in the Sciences of Wealth and Society* (Chicago, IL: University of Chicago Press, 1998), 30.

4   Ibid., 36–41.

5   Ibid., 54.

6   Smyth, "Money, Accounting, and Life-Writing", 87.

7   Ibid.

8   See Katherine Fama, "Domestic Data and Feminist Momentum: The Narrative Accounting of Helen Stuart Campbell and Charlotte Perkins Gilman", *Studies in American Naturalism* 12, no. 1 (2017), 105–126.

9   George Eliot, *Mill on the Floss* (London and New York: Everyman's Library, 1908).

10   Ibid., 397.

11   Charles Dickens, *Little Dorrit* (Oxford: Oxford University Press, 2012), 764.

12   Ibid., 66.

13   Charles Dickens, *Great Expectations* (New York: W.W. Norton & Co, 1999), 211.

14   Ibid., 217.

15   Ibid., 354.

Leverage | Tom McCarthy

(Art), **Debt**, (Equity), (Hostile Takeover)

The use of debt to finance new investments; also the measure of a given company's debt–equity ratio. In British (rather than American) financial parlance, it's called *gearing*; in French, *levier*. The image, or conceit, is a mechanical one: a beam set atop a fulcrum, such that a large weight placed near the pivot point at one end can be lifted by a smaller weight placed at a greater distance from this point at the other. In German it's *Hebelwirkung*—same root as *Aufhebung*, central term in Hegel's thought system, a double-ended word meaning both "lifting up" and "cancelling" or "neutralising". Derrida, in a text on money and metaphysics, translates *Aufhebung* as *relève*, as in the substitution of one soldier or guardsman by another, a relief.[1]

Could leverage not also be said to name the basic work of literary language? "When a part so ptee does duty for the holos we soon grow to use of an allforabit," writes Joyce in *Finnegans Wake*.[2] Synecdoche, the *bit* doing the lift work for the *all*, *part* for the *holos*, is the essence of allegory and symbolization. Thus, an orange, being squeezed, raises the vision of an entire world undergoing "expression" (Ponge); thus, a red wheel barrow holds a vague, expansive "so much" else in pendant suspension all around it (Williams). Simile, conceit are acts of leverage. And so are metaphor—one thing standing for another thing, "carrying" it—and metonymy, a chain of signs each pointing to and working on the next so as to form an integrated system every part of which both receives its own force and value from *and* helps facilitate the general system's functioning. Money (paper representing gold, or invoking the wider realm of debt and credit in its networked generality) is itself both metaphor and metonym, of course. As such, it also serves as a useful metaphor for both. Of the long chain of links and substitutions built up over years by his neurotic Rat Man (rats—*Ratten*—borrowed money and payback instalments—*Raten*—gambling debts of his *Spielratte* father, the act of marriage—*heiraten*—and so on), Freud writes: "In his obsessional deliria he had coined himself a regular rat currency. Little by little he translated into this language the whole complex of money-interests which centred around his father's legacy to him."[3]

That psychoanalysis should be attuned to these connections and relations makes good sense. For Lacan, metaphor and metonymy (the terms with which he overwrites Freud's two main dream-work mechanisms, condensation and displacement) form the core of all psychic activity. His vision of the psyche is mechanical, or cybernetic: circuits, gears, and switches, drives and forces working on each other at a distance. It's all leverage.

Now I'm looking at a photograph, taken in 1958. A dinner party. Lacan's perched on the arm of a sofa. Counterbalancing him from the far arm is the painter Nina Lebel; between them, on the horizontal main stretch of the sofa, sit Max Ernst, Sylvia Lacan, Alexina Duchamp, and, centre and pivot point, her spouse Marcel. To the last named, economic mechanisms are no less important than they were to Sylvia's former husband Georges Bataille. Duchamp has even, back in 1924, turned leverage into an artwork, issuing "Roulette" bonds to fund an expedition to Monte Carlo, where he tried out a new gambling strategy of his devising. What's more, his understanding of the human body, movement, and desire are eminently mechanical. What is the figure of *Nu Descendant un Escalier* if not an action rendered as a set of joints and levers, their arcs and rotations? What is *La Mariée Mis a Nu par ces Célibataires, Même* if not life itself—existence, time, love, destiny—laid bare as a giant *Hebeltrieb*, a geared, cogged circuit in which moving parts work in proximity and at a distance to produce suspension, transposition, condensation, and displacement (gas to fluid, bottom left of lower pane to top right of upper)? The bachelors' gears grind, sending their seeds up through hinged scissors; the bride levitates above, *pendu femelle*, all shafts and cylinders and pedals. Is this *Aufhebung*, or an endless liveried procession, one uniform after the other, a *relève* that—self-willed, self-perpetuating maybe but never self-transcending or -redeeming—brings little or no relief? Duchamp's roulette system, by the way, was neither profitable nor ruinous: it broke even.

In a 1957 lecture titled "The Creative Act", Duchamp separates the process through which the aesthetic value of an artwork is established into two parts, two phases—rather like he does with the *Large Glass*. The first, that of the work's generation, involves a "subjective mechanism", a "chain of reactions" from which "a link is missing". This missing link, this gap, which represents the "arithmetical relation between the unexpressed but intended and the unintentionally expressed", he calls the "art coefficient"—a coefficient to which can be assigned a precise "digit". But it's not this coefficient, or its digit, that determines the ultimate value; it pertains to art in its "raw state" only. This is where the next phase kicks in: the eventual "refining" is effected in a second reaction or act of leverage, the "transference from the artist to the spectator". This second transference, Duchamp tells us, is of quite another order, bringing "the phenomenon of transmutation" into play: "through the change from inert matter into a work of art, an actual transubstantiation has taken place, and the role of the spectator is to determine the weight of the work on the aesthetic scale".[4] Is *this*, finally, *Aufhebung*? Magic? Metaphysics? Profit, at least? All that we can say for certain is that, set on the scale (*balance*), *pesé* or *pondéré*, it yields up a determined weight, a given measure.

Notes

1   Jacques Derrida, "White Mythology: Metaphor in the Text of Philosophy", in *Margins of Philosophy*, trans. Alan Bass (Chicago, IL: University of Chicago Press, 1982).
2   James Joyce, *Finnegans Wake* (London: Faber & Faber, 2002), 18–19.
3   Sigmund Freud, *Three Case Histories* (New York: Touchstone, 1996), 52.
4   Marcel Duchamp, "The Creative Act", *ARTnews*, June–July–August 1957), www.duchamparchives.org/pma/archive/component/ MDP_B017_F001_001/.

Liability | Annie Xibos Spencer

(Assets), **Debt,** (Faith), (Insurance), **Interest,**
(Risk), (Violence)

I

Creation: In the beginning God created an industrious farmer,
who turned Earth's abundance and his or someone's hard
work into loot, and a banker—a public servant. There was also
usury. The banker rented the farmer's money, and the first
liability was born. With it the banker shone the divine light
of benevolence, for a fee, on other industrious people who
wished to accumulate(/)loot.

Holy Trinity: Assets equal liabilities plus equity. The banker
alchemizes his liability into his exponentially greater assets
by lending it, producing exponentially more liabilities, other
people's debts. Banks make money by making debt. It is in
this way that all money, whether bullion or balance sheet, is
debt. Assets and liabilities are a unity, a circular-flow model,
an Ouroboros—Alpha to Omega and back again.

Acts of God: God created heaven and Earth, but who created
God? A farmer makes an initial deposit of money into the bank,
but who created the first money farmer? Like the first chick-
en's first egg and the first egg's first chicken, the initial deposit
materializes as if from thin air. It is simply spoken into being.

Feeding the Multitude: Through the miracle of fractional
reserve banking, two fish and seven loaves provide sustenance

for the masses. The masses express their gratitude in a stream of regular payments calculated as the initial principle plus compounding interest. They get the loot to cover their liabilities by turning more of Earth's riches combined with more of someone's labour into their assets.

Faith: When debts are money and money grows because debts grow, who or what backs any of it? A liability can be transmuted into assets only on the precondition that the newly minted debtors are a good investment. Only then are the resulting assets sanctified. The liability assets must appear to be unwavering—here today and here tomorrow. The banker must provide substance of things hoped for, evidence of things not seen.

Holy Communion: Faith in a sacred and symbolic abstraction must be enshrined with ritual consumption, something that can be guzzled, bitten off, and chewed on—wafers and wine, bodies and blood. Liabilities must be backed by *las venas abiertas*. Liquidity resides in a pound of flesh or a parcel of Earth.

Original Sin: The sorcery by which money farmers turn some into more hinges on this real base, that which is or can become possessed—a home, a kidney, a community, a country. It is in this way that private ownership is demonic. The reinvention of communal bounty into one person's wealth is nothing if not a fall from grace.

Revelation: If liabilities grow too large relative to assets, the individual or institutional debtor can't cash its checks. When leverage is exhausted, when liquidity runs dry, outstanding liabilities threaten solvency. Faith is shaken, and the investors make a run on the institution. Mass defection dismantles what once seemed all-powerful.

Confession: To avoid solvency problems, which is to say legitimacy problems, which is to say existential problems, the liability-holding entity must accumulate more assets or expunge some debts. Liabilities must be covered or covered up. It is in this way that the delicate balancing act between assets and liabilities is also a disappearing act.

II

Big Bang: One man's trash is another man's treasure. Trash a man and make him your treasure. Trash the land and make a buck selling the junk. Seize it, strip it, pump it, and dump it. The conditions for an ever-growing more reaches natural limits to the point of cataclysm, which is also productive. Liability: the compound growth of capital necessitates the compound growth of rates of ruin. The capacity to create ruin is the fertile loam that guarantees an abundant and proliferating money crop.

Black Hole: In a universe propelled by the collision of matter and money capital in pursuit of an ever-growing more, immense energy is expended defying detection, capturing light. Such mysterious forces of darkness are believed to be more powerful than the sun. The task before large liability-asset holders becomes the management of optics. The very threat of visibility is a liability. Institutions holding the most and most risky liabilities have the greatest incentive to obscure what is possessed, what is owed, and to whom. The phenomenon is not a conspiracy, but it does have an organizing principle: contain everything. Daphne Caruana Galizia was a liability. Her reporting shone light on the pervasiveness of immense hoards of hidden wealth and made visible that the assets of the Crowns and Cartels are essentially one and the same, tended and grown by the same money farmers. Her subsequent assassination was an off-balance sheet transaction. A car bomb is as effective a defence against volatile liabilities as any other act of regulatory arbitrage.

Spukhafte Fernwirkung: Investment in productive destruction pays dividends. In the instance of murdering dissidents and whistleblowers, it prevents runaway inflation in the number of others who might be inspired to the cause. Eager to avoid annihilation by defaulting on liabilities, the money-farming institutions not only engage in a ravenous effort to acquire more assets but also to acquire better means of securing the ones they have. Ostentatious displays of an institution's capacity to protect its assets is one way of bolstering staying power. But the ability to neutralize threats while remaining undetected is just as essential. The use and development of new tools for clandestine interference is a practice as old as money farming itself. It is evidence of the money farmers' often touted claim: the system promotes innovation. Novel and more efficient product lines provide more intelligent and more powerful means of covert obstruction and destruction—more bang for the buck. Stealth instruments for liability containment secure asset valuation and the appearance of ongoing creditworthiness, the paramount pageantry of here today, here tomorrow. Most significantly, this objective is critical for lenders of last resort, the most powerful money farming and liability-holding institutions, which often take the form of dominant nation-states or other kinds of imperial trading companies. Pegasus spyware achieves this objective. So do hypersonic weapons. When it comes to containing liabilities and preventing mass divestment or other kinds of secession, the capacity to search, locate, and destroy is the most supreme and liquid asset of all—the only thing better than money in the bank.

Liquidity | Christophe Hanna

Credit, Money, Trust

Liquidity: next week is Danièle's birthday; she will be eighty-one years old. Her friend Yvette, who participates in the same theatre workshop as us, decides to organize a collection. Yvette would like to be able to offer Danièle a plant for her garden thanks to the participation of all the actors: she asks for five euros from each one. Jean-Christophe, who leads the workshop, tries to temper: not all participants necessarily know Danièle well; each will do as they can ... Finally, it's Jacqueline who takes care of collecting the money because Yvette is not feeling very well. It's a rehearsal evening; there are ten people present including me and Jean-Christophe. I go on stage and ask each person how they keep their cash, if they have any on them now.

Marie is seventy-seven years old; she is a former gym teacher. In her youth Marie had money problems. Her parents helped her financially, as mine did for me when I was a student and even later, but they deposited amounts into my bank account (for example, the amount for the water bills). To Marie, her parents discreetly gave cash bills, as is done for New Year's gifts. It really helped her get her head above water. Now Marie always keeps cash on her. **She needs cash to do her everyday shopping, and tonight she has about sixty euros in bills on her.**

Marie has a first anecdote to tell us:

Marie's Anecdote: "Organizing a Collection Is Validating"

Marie: Throughout my professional life, I have had to organize collections. Towards the end of my career, it was most often for retirements of colleagues or deaths. People always give in these situations where the poverty of existence is so evident, the flatness of farewell speeches, these slideshows with the dead person's vacation photos: we compensate as best we can with this little personal something!

So, it's always validating to organize a collection and you shouldn't deprive yourself of doing it.

Jacqueline: It's true, I always do things **to validate myself**, let's be honest and say it, including collections.

Yvette: I agree ...

Marie: When I launch a collection, I always develop the same plan because it's the most effective:

1. I solicit members of a group while setting a desired amount. You should avoid receiving too small coins; that's why five euros seems like a good amount: it corresponds to a small bill, and the bill avoids getting lost in copper coins.
2. I pass the basket blindly, just as the collection at the end of mass.
3. Finally, I write small thank you messages for everyone.
4. Some people don't give in this way and that's sad, but

it's rare. Those who give well are always the same, it's not a matter of means.

Yvette: Who can't give five euros!!

Jean-Christophe: It's not that obvious! And in a group, there may be newcomers who don't know the person who benefits from the collection well; what sense would it make for them to give a fixed amount in advance?

Yvette is seventy-nine years old; she also uses a wallet that she normally has on her, but not tonight because it's bulky. Her wallet is normal, she claims, like the one in this vector drawing. She mainly takes it **for grocery shopping**.

Sandra is forty-six years old, and she is a special education teacher. She has a wallet that is actually just a card holder in which she puts everything she regularly needs for mechanical verifications: COVID pass, metro badge, entry badge. She has some money inside, a few coins **for tips, a few bills for the market**.

Sandra's Anecdote: "Sometimes You Can Be Surprised by What People Can Give"

It is not directly related to liquidity, but sometimes people surprise us with what they can give. Sandra has difficulty asking for money, but to finance her training as a specialized art therapist, she needed a sum that she was far from having: 3,600 euros. She then set up a fundraiser on the internet and to her great surprise, she quickly obtained the entire amount.

Marie then intervenes to repeat that there are people who give often, that it is their nature. She describes Suzanne, who gives in fundraisers and beyond. Suzanne is a tall woman with a severe face. She attaches importance to the value of work. She never complains, rarely asks for help. Her appearance is austere, yet she is endearing, with a very strong personality. She commands admiration and has many friends. **She gives generously to someone in need, but nothing to the lazy and the exploiters of situations.**

Chantal is sixty-eight years old and retired. Like

Yvette, she did not bring her wallet with her **as it is unnecessary at the theatre. But she is ready to describe it to us.**

Chantal's Anecdote: "If There Was No Market, She Wouldn't Use Coins Anymore"

The wallet is a kind of fanny pack like the ones athletes use when they run, as shown in this diagram: she only puts the minimum necessary in it. Chantal only uses it for shopping at the market. She fills it with a predetermined amount of cash, around sixty euros.

Jean-Christophe: But then, if there were no more markets, most of you wouldn't have a wallet anymore, it seems to me? And maybe you wouldn't even use cash anymore.

Yvette, Chantal, Sandra, Alix: say yes!

Alix is forty-seven years old and a documentary film-maker. Alix also has a very simple wallet, but in reality it is stuffed only with old credit card coupons.

Alix's Anecdote:
"A Ridiculous and Normally Embarrassing Thing"

Before, I used to balance my accounts the old-fashioned way by checking my bank statements, before we had online accounts. Now, I auto-matically store these receipts in my wallet until I realize it is too bulky to close, which can last for months, and then I keep the little papers on which I can write (which implies a very scrupulous sorting based on the content of the back of these papers), either for lists (I make a lot of lists) or to make bookmarks when I read books for work topics. Alix concludes that this is a ridiculous and nor-mally embarrassing thing.

Brigitte is fifty-five years old and a secretary. She has an even simpler wallet than Alix, a pocket without sec-tions with a zip in the middle. It is not filled much, a few red coins and three or four bills. She uses it to **launder money, more precisely to get rid of bills**.

Brigitte's Anecdote: "Never for Large Amounts"

I inherited an apartment in the south of France from my parents, she confides, but with my brother, in joint ownership. But her brother is scary: he doesn't pay anything and it's up to me to pay for everything: all the expenses, taxes, insurance ... I would like to sublet the apartment to be able to take care of all this with the rental income, but I cannot do it legally, I would have to agree with my brother ... So I am forced to sublet it secretly, to friends for vacations ... off the books. So I have a lot of cash to spend. For me, it's completely out of step as a thing: I always feel like a thief with all my bills when I pay in cash. Usually, I never pay for large amounts at once, but one day, at FNAC, I don't know what came over me, I cracked for an amplifier that I paid with my bills (I didn't have the amount in my account). For a while, I was

afraid; I thought: if I have a tax audit, this big bill in cash that comes out of nowhere will be noticed.

Jacqueline is seventy-eight years old and a retired medical professor; her wallet is the most rationalized: the central pocket that folds geometrically on itself contains the coins reserved for tips and also allows her to collect change; the side pocket contains bills for the market but **also those intended to reward people whose work has been particularly well done, to mark that the person has added something that is her own, and that she, Jacqueline, knows how to recognize**: this week a painter (a great job!), then a Christmas tree delivery man (young, starting his business!).

Jacqueline's Anecdote: "She Revived It in Two or Three Small Steps"

I went to the florist in my neighborhood, the one I always go to. I had the exact amount: sixty euros in ten and twenty bills. There was this plant that cost eighty euros, and it was a bit droopy. I said I was interested. When she saw the cash, my florist said, grabbing the pot, okay, I'll give it to you for sixty. She even revived the plant by giving a few cuts here and there.

There were some dead stems, yellowed leaves.

Jean-Christophe is fifty-five years old and an actor; like me, he hasn't used a wallet for a few years. Before, he kept quite a bit of money on him, bills—their presence against his chest reassured him. Sometimes he misses being able to give money directly in the street, but today he really only uses his card to pay.

Jean-Christophe also has an anecdote to tell:

Jean-Christophe's Anecdote: "It Can Be Difficult to Accept a Sum of Cash"

A few years ago, Jean-Christophe participated as an actor in a play about Simone Weil. The philosopher Simone Weil wrote about money. Her idea was that money should not be fetishized or accumulated, but should flow with as much fluidity as possible.

That's why the director had an idea that he proposed to the actors: at each performance, each of the eight actors would give a ten-euro bill to create a sum of money that would be given to a person chosen at random from the audience during the show.

The actors protested; they were already so poorly paid! To lose ten euros each evening on top of that! But on the day of the first performance, everyone ended up giving a bill.

Jean-Christophe was responsible for giving these eighty euros to a spectator during the show. He descended from the stage, walked in the dark among the stands, and in the second row, he saw a young man who looked modest. He said, "Here, this is for you. If you don't need it, give it to someone else", which was the formula that had been decided among the actors before the performance.

The young man seemed very embarrassed, took the wad of bills, looked at them, examined them for a moment, perhaps wondering if they were real bills. Then, with a gesture, he passed them to his neighbour on the right who didn't hesitate for a second before passing the money to a young woman just behind him.

It seems that until the end of the show, the wad of bills was passed among the audience like a hot potato. The curtain fell, half the audience left, and where did the eighty euros go? They looked for a while: a spectator in the back, in the eighth row, had left them on the ground under a seat.

The young man in the second row stayed for the discussion with the actors that took place after the play. He spoke up: for him, it was horrible to receive such a sum like that in front of everyone, to keep it for himself without any reason. Jean-Christophe later learned that the young man who said this was in a very precarious situation, almost homeless. At the end of the evening, very embarrassed, he finally accepted the money and left with it.

Yvette: I would have kept it without a problem!

Jacqueline: It reminds me of this story: one morning, I found a huge roll of bills on the ground in the street. I thought it was dirty money [for Jacqueline, a roll of bills necessarily meant dirty money]. I discreetly picked it up.

Then Jacqueline hesitated for a second: should she take it to the police station? Finally, **she preferred to give it to a "poor" person in her family**.

Translated by Torsten Andreasen

Luxury | Joseph Vogl

Commodity, (Equity), Gift, Money, Void

Since antiquity, the concept of luxury—its derivation from the Latin "*luxus*" (distorted) and the Greek "*λοξός*" (crooked, oblique) remains unclear—has involved an interplay of moral, economic, political, dietary, and aesthetic aspects, each with specific prioritizations and transformations of normative systems. It is discussed in connection with courtly splendour, status questions, private and public representation, referring to problems of value formation and wealth, and can serve as a guide for a history of the desiring subject. While Plato and Aristotle attributed luxury to a deviation from the precept of moderation and a dissolving force within the communities of *pólis* and *oikos*, in the concepts of the Greek-Roman Stoics, such as Seneca, it represents a disorganization of desires that demands a criticism of conduct and has both moral and medical implications. Moreover, the question of luxury permeates all areas of individual and public life, leading to the first debates on the connection between luxury, expenditure laws, and public order in Rome, for example, among Cicero or Horace. Insofar as this "luxury" also encompasses demonstrative consumption and splendour, it corresponds to the meaning of *luxuria* in rhetoric and poetics: as affected or obscene speech, as excessively embellished style or lost simplicity in verse form. Since the Patristic period, the New Testament's condemnation of debauchery and "luxurious" living has been added, marking a shift in emphasis. The objects of luxury and *luxuria* can now symbolize the worldliness of the world itself and, as a source of all the vices of the will, become a systematic item in Christian moral teaching: as the cause of the Fall, temptation of the flesh, and mortal sin.

Although scholastic versions of luxury continued into the modern era, new frames of reference become identifiable after the sixteenth century. In European legal history, this pertains, on the one hand, to a set of luxury regulations and policy rules that were intended to mark social distinctions and limit economically ruinous waste (while a "compulsion to luxury" applied to courtly representation). On the other hand, luxury is disqualified in mirrors for princes and government manuals, in political theory as well as in literature, as a disturbance of politically rational order and irrational social behaviour. By the seventeenth century at the latest, the concept of luxury dissociates itself from the realm of doctrines of virtue and *luxuria* and becomes the object of an economic-political intervention within the emerging field of political economy, negotiating questions of abundance and scarcity, natural and monetary resources, luxury patents, taxes, and tariffs.

Against this backdrop, an extensive debate on luxury developed in the eighteenth century. It found its focus in the economic and political discourse but spilled over into associated areas, including semiotic, aesthetic, and anthropological questions. The origins of this development can probably be traced back to Mandeville's *The Fable of the Bees* (1714). Here, "luxury" has become an economic functional term that opens two complementary but opposing perspectives. As an exponent of the superfluous, it represents the condition for trade, exchange, the circulation of wealth, and the progress of humanity as a whole, as seen in the works of Mandeville, Melon, Voltaire, or Saint-Lambert: "The superfluous, a very necessary thing."[1] Conversely, from the perspective of need and necessity, it must appear as a deviation from the natural measure. "Frivolous luxury"[2] designates those riches that do not find their reference in the satisfaction of needs, represented by useless goods and empty signifiers. Rousseau therefore situates luxury as the cause of inequality in general and opposes it with the rural economy of needs of Wolmar from the *Nouvelle Héloïse*. A similar ambiguity also characterizes the anthropological and aesthetic dimension of luxury. While on the one hand it represents the notorious thesis that private vices and the pursuit of luxury generate the common good, on the other hand it indicates a blurring of boundaries, assigning luxury an exposed position in the pathography of the eighteenth century. From the weakening of the physical and mental constitution to "literary luxury" and reading addiction, a line extends on to a "luxuriating" imagination, linking medical, psychological, and educational aspects. This suggests the notion of a "semiotic economy of luxury"[3] and leads to the discussion of the aesthetic. While luxury motivates the development or refinement of arts and taste, it also crosses the threshold to "excess", to illusions, to "exaggeration"[4] and "bad taste",[5] to the "luxuriance of the arts" and their "decline".[6] Finally, the appearance of the *Journal des Luxus und der Moden* (1787) marks a moment when an end to the luxury debates becomes apparent and the term itself opens up to the "amenities" of a bourgeois everyday culture.

While luxury survives as a spectacle of monstrous libertinage of the Ancien regime, as with Sade, the concept has largely become obsolete for the political economy of the nineteenth century and has given way to its historicization and sociologization. With it, social forms are now differentiated, cultural-historical collections are established, or a connection between way of life, structure of desire, and economic system is pursued, with which Werner Sombart, for example, explains the emergence of a capitalist culture. In parallel, the emerging discipline of sociology (with, among others, Gabriel Tarde, Max Weber, Thorstein Veblen, Marcel Mauss, Georg Simmel) pursues phenomena that—like prestige, ostentation, fashion, conspicuous consumption—cannot be subsumed under the principles of economic rationality and find their climax in theories of gift giving, sacrifice, and an-economic expenditure. The counterpart lies in literary and art-theoretical programmes that are dedicated to a paradoxical enjoyment of exchange value (such as in Baudelaire's *Rêve parisien*, 1857), a "luxury of destruction",[7] aesthetic distinction, or dandyism (such as with Joris-Karl Huysmans or Oscar Wilde). However, as luxury in the twentieth century allies itself with comfort, "a padding of existence that slightly swells beyond its frame",[8] or becomes synonymous with the "industrialization of pleasure",[9] it can now change its connotations, bid farewell to the "superfluous", and strive for the preservation of scarce resources, aiming for the "necessary".[10]

Translated by Torsten Andreasen

Notes

1   Voltaire, *Oeuvres complètes*, Vol. 10, ed. Louis Moland (Paris: 1877), 84.

2   See Anne Robert Jacques Turgot, *Écrits économiques* (Paris: Calmann-Lévy, 1970, 67.

3   Joseph Vogl, "Luxus", in *Ästhetische Grundbegriffe*, Vol. 3, ed. Karlheinz Barck, Martin Fontius, Dieter Schlenstedt, Burkhart Steinwachs, and Friedrich Wolfzettel (Stuttgart: J.B. Metzler Stuttgart, 2001), 702.

4   Immanuel Kant, *Werke in sechs Bänden*, Vol. 6, ed. Wilhelm Weischedel (Wiesbaden: Insel-Verlag, 1964), 578–579.

5   Jean-Jacques Rousseau, *Oeuvres complètes*, Vol. 4, ed. Bernard Gagnebin and Marcel Raymond (Paris: Bibliothèque de la Pléiade, 1969), 673.

6   Christoph Martin Wieland, *Sämmtliche Werke*, Vol. 7 (Leipzig: Göschen, 1853), 260.

7   Friedrich Nietzsche, *Sämtliche Werke: Kritische Studienausgabe*, Vol. 3, ed. Giorgio Colli and Mazzino Montinari (Berlin and New York: de Gruyter, 1988), 620.

8   Robert Musil, "Der Mann ohne Eigenschaften", in *Gesammelte Werke*, Vol. 1, ed. Adolf Frisé (Reinbek: Rowohlt, 1978), 1064.

9   Heiner Müller, "Ich wünsche mir Brecht in der Peep-Show. Betrachtungen zum Genuß", in *"Jenseits der Nation": Heiner Müller im Interview mit Frank M. Raddatz* (Berlin: Rotbuch Verlag, 1991), 65.

10 Hans Magnus Enzensberger, "Reminiszenzen an den Überfluß. Der alte und der neue Luxus", in *Der Spiegel 51* (1996), 117, www.spiegel.de/politik/reminiszenzen-an-den-ueberfluss-a-b81a742e-0002-0001-0000-000009134042.

M

Manhattan

Mapping

Materiality

Men

Migration

Money

Mont Pèlerin

Mapping | Laura Finch

(Colonialism), **Cynicism,** (Deindustrialization), **Disruption, Extraction,** (Future), **Interest,** (Land), **Money,** (Manhattan), **Property, Speculation,** (Whiteness)

Finance capital promises to work a kind of magic, namely to create value out of thin air. Marx's formula for finance, MM', is therefore a truncated version of the full formula for capital, MCM'. In finance, the commodity of labour power (C) drops out and "the social relation is consummated in the relation of a thing, of money, to itself. Instead of the actual transformation of money into capital, we see here only form without content."[1] While Marx makes clear that this is a sleight of hand, that the movement of money (MM') can never create value, a certain kind of unmoored abstraction has been credited to the working of finance capital, as if it truly creates value at a remove from the rest of the economy.

This idea of untethered abstraction has been central to theories of the aesthetic representation of finance. For example, in his work on culture and finance capital, Fredric Jameson claims that postmodernism is the representational correlate of finance. For Jameson, with financialization, "capital itself becomes free-floating. It separates from the concrete context of its productive geography … [becoming] a vast, worldwide, disembodied phantasmagoria."[2] Certainly, this unmoored postmodern aesthetic was front and centre in the global formation of Central Business Districts (CBDs) from the 1960s onwards. In these concentrated financial zones, the vertiginous skyscraper is barely anchored in place by a small grounded footprint, instead directing its energies into glass-ily vertiginous heights that have more in common with CBDs in other cities than with the city in which they are built. An illustration of this unmoored and abstract version of financial architecture can be seen in a 2007 advert for the *Financial Times*, which depicts a gleaming cityscape accompanied by the tagline "World Business. In one place." The image presents an amalgamation of buildings from financial centres around the world, lifted out of their concrete environs and arrayed together among their international peers.

Built within the globally homogeneous postmodern architectural style, these skyscrapers talk only to each other—money talking to money—and are not in relation to the cities they are located in.

However, what would a map of these CBDs look like if it didn't affirm the false appearance that these buildings create money out of thin air, the thin air of their vertiginous peaks, and instead showed how they drain wealth from the surrounding city by manipulating the inequitably valued land in urban centres? Rather than a phantasmagoric light touch, the financialization of the post-1970s US economy brought with it hugely disruptive urban restructuring in order to create CBDs. These material sites are not symbolic but were a wealth-generating project for banks, who leveraged cheap land in urban centres into highly valuable real estate.

Taking the example of the creation of the CBD in Lower Manhattan, this claiming of space by the financial sector can be seen through the archives of the planning committees who helped create this CBD in the 1960s and 1970s. As industrial demand decreased and the ports and industries in Lower Manhattan showed declining profits, land became increasingly available downtown. Coupled with this industrial decline, large urban centres in the US had been systemically emptied of white populations through the 1950s and 1960s in order to protect white people from the central blast radius of an imagined nuclear attack.[3] Often mislabelled as white flight, this is more accurately described as the federally bankrolled movement of white populations to the suburbs through the creation of suburban infrastructure, highways (accompanied by subsidies on gasoline[4]), and the Federal income tax deduction for home mortgage interest payments, which encouraged the construction of single-family houses in the suburbs, a move that Douglas Kelbaugh terms "the broadest and most expensive welfare program in the U.S.A".[5] As the white population moved to the suburbs, whiteness became further enmeshed with the idea of home ownership, while blackness became associated with the now devalued spaces of the inner city.

Writing of Manhattan in the 1960s, James Baldwin argued that this segregated cityscape was "pure heaven for financiers and speculators[, for] a ghetto is a great source of profit".[6] Into the now devalued space of Lower Manhattan bankers arrived: in 1957, Chase Manhattan built its new headquarters downtown. Determined to increase the value of his new property, Chairman and Chief Executive of Chase, David Rockefeller, spearheaded the creation of the Lower Manhattan Association (LMA), a planning committee tasked with cementing Lower Manhattan as a global centre of finance. In 1965, the LMA published a 450-page plan for Lower Manhattan, which set out to claim it as an "area of permanent value" (see Figure 34.1).

The image makes claims on the inner core of Lower Manhattan. Within this shaded area were a newly built and soon-to-be-built cluster of financial structures that were the centrepiece of the plan: the Chase Manhattan Bank headquarters (1961), the Home Insurance building (1965), the World Trade Center complex (1966), and the Jacob K. Javits Federal Office Building and Court of International Trade (1968). The

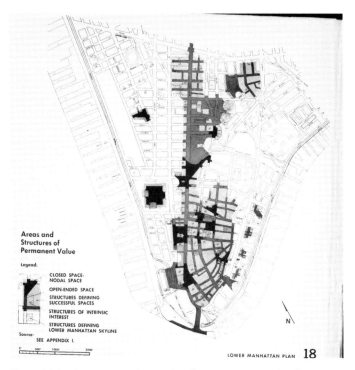

Figure 34.1   The Lower Manhattan Plan. (*source*: Internet Archive)

non-shaded areas now rendered non-valuable include ship-ping, marine supplies, fish and produce markets, warehouses, residential areas, textiles, machinery and hardware, and electronics.

Not only are the LMA's claims to value temporal—in perpetuity—but they were also spatially expanding (see Figure 34.2).

Figure 34.2 is an extraordinary series of historical slices showing the expansion of Manhattan since Dutch coloniz-ers genocidally cleared the Lenape from Mana-hatta in the

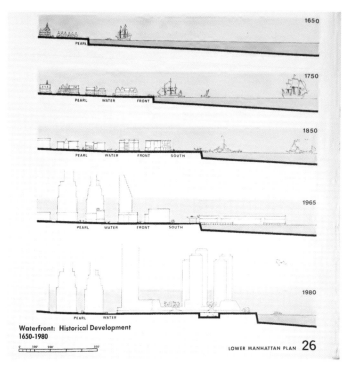

Waterfront: Historical Development
1650-1980

LOWER MANHATTAN PLAN 26

Figure 34.2 The Lower Manhattan Plan. (*source*: Internet Archive)

seventeenth century, through to the projected future expansion of the CBD by the 1980s. The image is a form of speculative map making and world building, a proleptic diagram for a future that the white business class wished to usher in. By enfolding the future into a mapping of the past, the expansion of the CBD is made to appear as inevitable as the "manifest destiny" of the theft of North America.

These maps from the LMA's plan show that the CBDs did not create wealth in Lower Manhattan but rather relied on the original and ongoing theft of Indigenous Land, and the ability to write off certain spaces—working-class spaces, black spaces—as worthless and therefore ripe for what is euphemistically called "urban redevelopment". The historical accretion of value to whiteness—whiteness as property, as Cheryl Harris has theorized—allowed bankers to capitalize on creating CBDs as high-value areas.[7] The architectural homogeneity of vertical CBDs across the globe enhances the illusion that value is being created in this phantasmagoric worldwide financial network, disconnected from the cities they are in. The maps from the LMA plan, however, reveal that these zones of skyscrapers and glass rest upon the racialized colonial valuation of space. They are, therefore, more accurate than any map or cultural representation of finance capital that remains enthralled to finance's own self-presentation as an unmoored abstraction.

Notes

1   Karl Marx and Friedrich Engels, *Capital: A Critique of Political Economy*, Vol. 3 (London: Lawrence & Wishart, 1972), 516.
2   Frederic Jameson, "Culture and Finance Capital", *Critical Inquiry* 24, no. 1 (1997), 251.
3   See Jessica Hurley, *Infrastructures of Apocalypse: American Literature and the Nuclear Complex* (Minneapolis, MN: Minnesota University Press, 2020).
4   John A. Powell, "Structural Racism and Spatial Jim Crow", in *The Black Metropolis in the Twenty-first Century: Race, Power, and Politics of Place*, ed. Robert D. Bullard (Lanham: Rowman & Littlefield Publishers, 2007), 41–66, 50–51.
5   Douglas Kelbaugh, *Repairing the American Metropolis: Common Place Revisited* (Washington, DC: University of Washington Press, 2002), 28.
6   James Baldwin, *The Evidence of Things Not Seen* (New York: H. Holt, 1995), 35. See also Katharyne Mitchell, "Pre-Black Futures", *Antipode* 41, no. s1 (2010), 239–261, for more on the production of "at risk" areas and populations as an avenue for speculative profit. See also Samuel R. Delany, *Times Square Red, Times*

Square Blue (New York: New York UP, 1999) for a case study of the creation of "risky" populations in order to allow for redevelopment in the service of tourism.

7   See Cheryl I. Harris, "Whiteness as Property", *Harvard Law Review* 106, no. 8 (1993), 1707–1791. See also Brenna Bhandar, *Colonial Lives of Property: Law, Land, and Racial Regimes of Ownership* (Durham and London: Duke University Press, 2018).

Men | Michelle Chihara

(Algorithm), **Amazon, Comedy, Commodity, Cynicism, Disruption,** (Pandemic)**, The Pit,** (Whiteness)

During the global pandemic in 2021, Elon Musk saw his net worth increase by $121 billion. The owner of the electric vehicle company Tesla and the space travel company SpaceX was named *TIME Magazine* Person of the Year—one of the richest men ever to have graced the planet.[1] One of a group of billionaires who did remarkably well during a time of global

Figure 35.1   Elon Musk, the entrepreneurial wiz, co-founder of PayPal and Zip2 and founder of SpaceX and now Tesla Motors. (*source*: photograph by JD Lasica, reproduced under Creative Commons Attribution 2.0 Generic Licence)

suffering, Musk became the richest and arguably the most famous. He tweeted with alacrity to his 78.8 million followers. Market activity seemed to follow him wherever he went.

In video interviews with *TIME*, Musk claimed expertise in production design, science, and the nature of money itself. Of money, he said: "There are very few people who understand it better than me." He implied that he and his sometimes girlfriend, the rock musician Grimes, were separated in part because of his intense devotion to unspecified work at the SpaceX campus. With two rockets standing unsubtly erect behind him, Musk told the interviewer: "there are hardly any women—well, there are some women here, but not many". If women were around, his masculine gaze could barely perceive them. "It's remote and we do technology," Musk explained. "It's a techno-monastery."

The *TIME* interview was arguably the peak of Musk's reputational climb as a particular genre of productive, and ostensibly apolitical, capitalist man. He performed a single-minded commitment to money, tech, and science that coincided, in his imagination, with the fact that the SpaceX campus was male-dominated. His was not the hypermasculinity of 1980s work-hard, play-hard, cocaine-and-hookers Wall Street, not the hypermasculinity of abstract finance. Instead, he spoke of an almost ascetic temple to the cult of "doing" technology. His was the supposedly concrete aspect of capital.[2] Musk justified his wealth to *TIME* by claiming the kind of masculinity that builds cars and rockets. He was a real man because he was rich and flew rockets; he worked hard at an innovative masculine space campus and was therefore wealthy.

Musk claimed the mantle of a visionary builder. In asserting his understanding of the nature of money, Musk referenced his position as a founder of PayPal, an early player in the market for facilitating payments online. But Musk was only a co-founder of that company, before being removed as its CEO.[3] After PayPal, Musk became a prominent booster of Doge Coin, a cryptocurrency that started as a prank. It was named after a meme about dogs. Musk has made money by boosting Doge, but he didn't invent it, nor design its affordances, just as he didn't invent online payments.

Neuralink is a company that Musk acquired in order to create implants that would link human brains directly to computers. The "Musk effect", as his influence on the markets is sometimes described, unquestionably helped a video of a monkey playing Pong with its brain go viral on YouTube.[4] However, Musk is also not a neuroscientist. While he did at one point claim sole publication credit for a Neuralink scientific paper, the basic invention that allowed the monkey to play brain-Pong preceded Neuralink's existence.[5] The reportedly brilliant Max Hodak, who co-founded the company with Musk, is a neuroscientist. He did run the Neuralink lab. But then he quit. Some journalists who cover gurus have compared Musk to a charismatic cult leader.[6]

Musk didn't change the nature of money and technology so much as his particular masculinist brand shaped the cultural landscape of what people imagined might become valuable. Musk has moved entire sectors in a different direction, primarily by drawing investment into his idea of the future. But with each new speculative wave in disparate technologies and ventures, especially after he bought a social media platform, it seemed to become less and less clear what Musk himself did.

Former employees at Neuralink, *Fortune Magazine* reported, said that Musk applies "relentless pressure and instills a culture of blame".[7] An investor friend suggested that Musk would be able to "solve for free speech" at Twitter.[8] However, a bet on a company of his was perhaps never a coherent bet on any one product or solution so much as it was a bet on his masculine vision.

Musk has always had too many unconventional ideas, too many technological and scientific pursuits, to be the primary subject driving sustained inquiry into the research behind any one of his projects. He is profoundly concerned with the possibility that artificial intelligence might take over the earth.[9] His fundamental plan for the future includes preparing for environmental collapse and super-robots. He supports direct democracy on Mars, but is not yet meaningfully closer to being able to move human society to space.[10] He has six children but regards babies as "eating and pooping machines", whom he can only interface with when they're older.[11] He does not do diapers. He "does" techno-monasticism.

When Musk presented himself to *TIME*, it was as a self-made genius with libertarian tendencies, the man who could disrupt, guide, and fund the way for the less manly eggheads across fields, claiming leadership in each discipline upon which he profited—neuroscience, space travel, the design of a complex production line—despite the depth of expertise that each required, but that Musk never seemed to value.

His leadership came from a petulant disruptive distance. When the progressive politician Elizabeth Warren pointed out that Musk evades income taxes, Musk called her a "Karen".[12] SpaceX is based on technologies created during the Cold War, in Russia and at NASA. Critics have repeatedly pointed out that the space programme was created with tax dollars— public funds built both NASA and the US research universities that undergird most scientific training. But Musk responded to Warren and her demand for accountability like a young boy sticking out his tongue.

The Musk effect gave him the ability to profit as the masculine presence behind technology that he didn't build. Even if he improved Teslas incrementally through his private guidance, as he claimed, he received government grants and relied directly and indirectly on the fruits of a public system.[13] SpaceX is majority-funded by NASA: it awarded the company a $2.9 billion contract in 2021 when SpaceX and Tesla had already received more than $8 million in government subsidies.[14] Musk has invented almost nothing. But through his aura, he enclosed and benefited from infrastructure made possible by generations of taxpayers.

That enclosure always included the sense that Musk was getting away with something. In his conflation of white masculinity with technoscience and disruption, it has generally behoved him to give regulators and politicians the middle finger. For a while he could position himself as a non-partisan trailblazer with no time for haters. In 2014, he told a reporter that he was a moderate, half Democrat and half Republican, "socially liberal and fiscally conservative", that favourite old chestnut of technocratic centrism. But the tech culture that Musk represents has long been associated with conservative missives like one from the Cato Institute touting the benefits of "permissionless innovation".[15]

In 2014, Cato argued that in order to foster widespread economic growth, policymakers and cultural norms needed to signal "a general acceptance of risk-taking". Musk's masculine persona performed a defiant "no" to rules and social mores, as evidence of risk taking, and his demeanour gained him credit with investors. The more Musk seemed to get away with petulant refusals—of the SEC's rules, of Alameda County's COVID restrictions, of labour laws, of the limits of biological science, of content moderation, of the idea that he might change a diaper—the more he didn't seem to need permission.

For a while Musk and his machines seemed to embody disruptive innovation. Tesla's operating cash flow was dwarfed by Amazon's—just under 3 billion to something more like 46 billion at time of writing. Yet Tesla's ticker value had increased almost every time they made a technology announcement. Even though other electronic vehicle companies entered the space and threatened to compete with Tesla based on the basis of "old-fashioned fundamentals of cash flow and valuation",[16] according to the markets, for a while it seemed that none of this mattered. Musk got much richer than Amazon's owner during the pandemic.

Tesla's wild valuation was due in part to an intricate web of financialized options built around it, a set of derivatives that reflect or refer to the company's basic stock price. In 2021, the *Financial Times* adopted a breathless tone to describe "the real importance and wider footprint of what might be called the 'Tesla-financial complex'"—"[A] vast, tangled web of dependent investment vehicles, corporate emulators and an enormous associated derivatives market of unparalleled breadth, depth and hyperactivity."[17]

The flabbergasting Tesla financial complex could be described as a market-based amplification of the Musk effect. This may be Musk's truest invention. Working just adjacent to the technical and scientific skills and accomplishments of the scientists and engineers he employs, Musk created a financial technology which magnifies investment in Tesla into endless levels of credit, a house of cards on the idea of the techno-monastery writ large.

It's important to point out that the stakes of the connection between Musk's white masculinity and finance are not about diversity in tech. The signals that Musk sends would land differently on the markets if emitted by a different body, but white masculinity is of course not sufficient to create his effect. Being a white dude is only one condition of possibility.

Musk never ran the labs or designed the production line, but he sold his own vision. As an obvious counterpoint, the female former billionaire Elizabeth Holmes also bullied scientists to bend reality to her will. She instilled a culture of blame and secrecy, while convincing venture capital that she was the future of medicine.[18] Like Musk, she may or may not have essentially believed that she could make her lies come true. But there are differences in their gendered self-presentations. From the beginning of her rise until her fall, Holmes claimed to have an invention which could do specific things. It could not do those things. Until that became clear, like Musk, she seemed to innovate without permission. Unlike Musk, she was never able to associate herself with functional rockets in space or cars on the roads. And unlike Musk, she was never petulant, mischievous, or obnoxious in public. Her thin, blonde, and respectful persona was heavily identified with the feminine version of productive capital, the body of her robotic machine.

A white man might have been less likely to be convicted than Holmes. But more than this, the Musk effect was built in part on the supposedly neutral authority automatically afforded to white masculinity. His social location allowed him to embody the promise of his many machines, to be many things to many people: a libertarian, a monk, and a reasonable progressive invested in a green future. His lucrative government contracts, his tax evasion, and his "quirkiness" all functioned to his advantage through the cultural formation that is his status as a man.

The cult of the disruptive founder is a feature of corporate governance in the twenty-first century, where capital searches the global financial system in search of the high yields that come with massive liquidity, through structures like the Tesla financial complex.[19] Liquidity demands speed. "Founders" with fast tech-based ideas wear their lack of (slow) scientific training as a badge of honour. Both Musk and Holmes dropped out of Stanford at different points and bragged about it. In the hustle culture dominated by the Musk effect, regulatory approval— like control groups, like scientific standards—is for normies.

In 2022, Musk outpaced Amazon founder Jeff Bezos by \$60 billion, and made a puerile joke about it.[20] Both men have been reported by ProPublica to pay very little federal income tax, percentage wise,[21] but this got less internet traction than their public sparring about whose space rocket was better. The men have gone to court over their entitlement to government contracts from NASA. When Bezos launched himself up in a remarkably priapic rocket, the world of the internet erupted into laddish jokes; both phallic rocket launches went through bouts of being mercilessly mocked. Folded into the jokes at Musk's expense have also been a series of issues about union busting, working conditions, safety concerns around Tesla's cars, documented use of child labour in the cobalt mines of Congo by Amnesty International, on top of violations of COVID policies during lockdown.[22] In the pissing contest between these two masculinities, the future could seem like a choice between two rockets, as if the winner might represent not the biggest ego but the machine most likely to solve the planet's problems.

But, of course, both rockets and both founders depend on the promise of unlimited growth. When Jeff Bezos was *TIME Magazine* Person of the Year in 1999, Amazon was on track to lose \$350 million in a calendar year. Then, the magazine asked, "[D]on't profits and losses matter anymore?" Bezos said yes. He insisted that his books, music, and video business would in fact be profitable by the end of 2000. Two decades later, still no profits. But Bezos's status was tarnished not by losses but by Musk's equally profitless rise, and his even more intense disregard for diapers, wages, regulators, and environmental consequences—*where we're going we don't need roads.*

In 2022, Tesla's sleek silhouettes and SpaceX's phallic tubes could still summon the promise of green technology and flying robot cars. Amazon's brand, haunted by the ghost of broken supply chains and hounded by unionizing warehouse workers, seemed to have fallen into the present. When he bought Twitter, Musk seemed to assume he could apply his effect to the platform. However, not only did he lack expertise in the algorithmic management of speech, but also, a website full of angry journalists, trolls, and memes can't be summoned to stand behind him like a tall silver rocket. He could no longer maintain the ostensibly apolitical stance of the manly avatar of productive technoscience. Musk veered sharply to the right and flirted publicly with right-wing conspiracy theories.[23]

At the level of global finance, the economy sometimes appears as a contest among men like these or as the search for a better visionary builder. But the idea that there is a difference between bad abstract finance and good productive capital, between men who build rockets and men who run media companies, or between Bezos and Musk—these are capital's illusions. The threats of man-made scarcity and male-dominated overaccumulation arise from the need for growth. Conflict and climate catastrophe are the hard limit to the dream of endless credit built on our belief in these men. Musk may try to sell the rockets back to us as weapons in the coming wars, the once and future man of the future.

Notes

1   Molly Ball, Jeffrey Kluger, and Alejandro de la Garza, "Person of the Year: Elon Musk", *TIME Magazine*, 13 December 2021, https://time.com/person-of-the-year-2021-elon-musk/.

2   Leigh Claire La Berge, *Scandals and Abstraction: Financial Fiction of the Long 1980s* (Oxford: Oxford University Press, 2015).

3   Raisa Bruner, "A Complete Timeline of Elon Musk's Business Endeavors", *Time.com*, 27 April 2022, https://time.com/6170834/elon-musk-business-timeline-twitter/.

4   "Monkey MindPong", YouTube, 3:27, 8 April 2021, https://youtu.be/rsCul1sp4hQ.

5   Elon Musk, "An Integrated Brain-Machine Interface Platform with Thousands of Channels (Preprint)", *Journal of Medical Internet Research* 21, no. 10 (2019), https://doi.org/10.2196/16194.

6   Christopher Kavanaugh and Matthew Browne, *Decoding the Gurus*, Episode 61, 29 December 2022, https://decoding-the-gurus.captivate.fm/episode/elon-musk-the-techno-shaman.

7   Jeremy Kahn and Jonathan Vanian, "Inside Neuralink, Elon Musk's Mysterious Brain Chip Startup: A Culture of Blame, Impossible Deadlines, and a Missing CEO", *Fortune Magazine*, 27 January 2022.

8   Vishwastam Shukla, Twitter, 25 April 2022, 11:53 a.m., https://twitter.com/vishwastam/status/1518664610705920000.

9   Daniel Oberhaus, "Explaining Roko's Basilisk, the Thought Experiment That Brought Elon Musk and Grimes Together", *Vice*, 8 May 2018, www.vice.com/en/article/evkgvz/what-is-rokos-basilisk-elon-musk-grimes.

10   Caroline Haskins, "Elon Musk Is Still Insisting Mars Will Be Settled in 2024 and Then Terraformed", *Vice*, 2 October 2017, www.vice.com/en/article/wjx7n9/elon-musk-is-still-insisting-mars-will-be-settled-in-2024-and-then-terraformed.

11   Maureen Dowd, "Elon Musk, Blasting off in Domestic Bliss", *The New York Times*, 25 July 2020.

12   Juliana Kaplan, "Elon Musk and Elizabeth Warren Have Traded Criticisms over Taxing the Ultra-Wealthy", *Business Insider*, 24 December 2021.

13   B. Garrett, M.D.L. Melo Zurita, and K. Iveson, "Boring Cities: The Privatisation of Subterranea", *City* 24, no. 1–2 (2020), 276–285.

14   Sissi Cao, "NASA and Military Contracts Make the Vast Majority of SpaceX's Revenue", *The Observer.com*, 23 October 2020.

15   Adam Thierer, "Embracing a Culture of Permissionless Innovation", *Cato Online Forum*, 17 November 2014, www.cato.org/cato-online-forum/embracing-culture-permissionless-innovation#.

16 Stephen Wilmot, "Jeep Maker Is No Tesla, and That's Suddenly OK", *Wall Street Journal*, 23 February 2022.

17 Robin Wigglesworth, "The 'Tesla-Financial Complex': How Carmaker Gained Influence over the Markets", *The Financial Times*, 22 November 2021.

18 John Carreyrou, *Bad Blood: Secrets and Lies in a Silicon Valley Startup* (New York: Knopf, 2018).

19 Bob Pisani, "Stock Buybacks Surge to $850 Billion in 2021, Setting New Record", *CNBC.com*, 30 December 2021, www.cnbc.com/video/2021/12/30/2021-sees-850-billion-in-stock-buybacks-setting-new-record.html.

20 Grace Kay, "Elon Musk Pokes Fun at Jeff Bezos with a Silver-Medal Emoji as the Gap between the Wealthiest Men in the World Widens", *Business Insider India*, 11 October 2021, www.businessinsider.in/tech/news/elon-musk-pokes-fun-at-jeff-bezos-with-a-silver-medal-emoji-as-the-gap-between-the-two-wealthiest-men-in-the-world-widens/articleshow/86942712.cms.

21 Jesse Eisinger, Jeff Ernsthausen, and Paul Kiel, "The Secret IRS Files: Trove of Never-Before-Seen Records Reveal How the Wealthiest Avoid Income Tax", *ProPublica.org*, 8 June 2021, www.propublica.org/article/the-secret-irs-files-trove-of-never-before-seen-records-reveal-how-the-wealthiest-avoid-income-tax.

22 Julia Carrie Wong, "Tesla Factory Workers Reveal Pain, Injury and Stress: 'Everything Feels Like the Future but Us'", *The Guardian*, 18 May 2017; Jeremy Owens, "Tesla, Elon Musk Found to Have Engaged in Unfair Labor Practices with Rules and Tweet", *MarketWatch.com*, 29 September 2019; "Electric cars: Running on Child Labour?", press release, AmnestyInternational.org, 30 September 2016.

23 Shirin Ghaffary, "Elon Musk Won't Stop Tweeting His Way into Trouble", *Vox.com*, 20 May 2023.

Migration | Jaime Acosta Gonzalez

(Abandonment), (Art), (Borders), **Capitalocene**, (Circulation), (Deindustrialization), (Logistics), (Violence), **Work**

Between 1986 and 1992 Brazilian photographer Sebastião Salgado embarked on a global project, *Workers: An Archaeology of the Industrial Age* (1993), which he considered a "homage to the working class around the world".[1] Composed of black and white portraits of the industrial proletariat, the project is a testimony to the resilience and unwavering spirit of the exploited masses, from shipbreakers in Bangladesh and oil workers in

Figure 36.1   Anthony Hernandez, *Landscapes for the Homeless #54*, 1989. (reprinted with permission of the artist)

Kuwait, to coal miners in India and agricultural workers in Rwanda. As Salgado intuitively understood, signalled by the subtitle of his work, he was documenting not only the plight of workers but a broader historical shift, or what he calls "the end of the first industrial revolution", an episode in the development of global capitalism that demanded attention.[2]

A few years later, Salgado produced a sequel to *Workers*, cementing Karl Marx's insight that to "be a productive worker is therefore not a piece of luck, but a misfortune".[3] Spanning seven years and thirty-five countries, *Migrations: Humanity in Transition* (2000) captures the harrowing journey of populations propelled into motion by political violence, environmental disaster, and economic crisis. The workers of the first project, bound however tenuously to the wage relation, reappear in *Migrations* as surplus populations on the move, expelled from the labour process and uprooted from their communities, condemned to "wander lost in the desert of structural unemployment", as Mike Davis usefully puts it.[4]

Salgado's projects represent both the profound suffering and quiet dignity of individuals pushed to the brink. As viewers, we are asked to locate the cruelty and catastrophe generated by shockwaves of economic and political tumult in the faces of its victims. Yet, as Susan Sontag notes, the sheer ubiquity and scale of his projects suggest that the suffering is "too vast, too irrevocable, too epic to be changed by any local political intervention".[5] What emerges for the beholder is a performative contradiction. While Salgado's pathos-laden photographs confront the viewer and compel them to intervene, they simultaneously produce a feeling of helplessness and inevitability. Salgado's attempt to mobilize outrage, engender sympathy, and prompt action is aided by his willingness to, in the words of T.J. Clark, "give a *face* to globalization".[6] "If we give a face to globalization," Clark continues, mirroring Salgado's intention, "we shall surely not be able to tolerate the look it gives us. We shall not be able to look it back, in the face. We shall be ashamed."[7]

In an age of dizzying abstraction, financialization, and speculation, Salgado's aesthetic and ethical engagement, predicated on establishing a sympathetic relation between the beholder and photographic subject, is worth interrogating for what it makes visible as much as for what it obscures. While Salgado's portraits, equal parts beautiful and devastating, highlight the faces of the dispossessed and dramatize their perseverance, they also make it difficult to register the broader economic and political forces responsible for their suffering, prompting Clark to ask: "could there be a photography of causes, not faces?"[8] Put another way, how can photography, in a moment of heightened abstraction, represent the world-historical transition Salgado intimates, from industrial to post-industrial, from employment to immiseration? Seemingly, photographers must go beyond representing the mass migration of people across the globe, since, as Brazilian critic Roberto Schwarz notes, "[o]nce reality has migrated into abstract economic functions, it can no longer be read in human faces."[9]

In the mid-1980s, roughly around the same time Salgado began his projects, Los Angeles-based photographer Anthony Hernandez stopped photographing people. Initially a self-taught photographer inspired by Edward Weston and Garry Winogrand, Hernandez shifted his aesthetic commitments and began refusing figuration altogether, focusing instead on the material traces left behind by vulnerable populations. This leap to abstraction, perhaps not accidentally, coincides with what geographer Edward Soja calls the "crisis-generated urban restructuring" of Los Angeles, which includes the globalization of California's economy and the emergence of the logistics sector and automation, as well as the widening chasm of income inequality and the increasing precarity of working people.[10]

Hernandez does not seek to dramatize human subjects or create affective attachments, departing from what Allan Sekula sardonically calls the "liberalism of the find-a-bum school of concerned photography".[11] A series of projects, including *Landscapes for the Homeless* (1988–91), *Waiting for Los Angeles* (1996–98), *Everything* (2003–04), and *Discarded* (2012–15), emerged from this new sensibility, representing processes of accumulation, displacement, and dispossession devoid of people, indexed only by destructive debris and ghostly demarcations. "The predominance of the abstract in modern art," Henri Lefebvre remarks, "accompanies the extension [and] unlimited power of money and capital, very abstract and terribly concrete at one and the same time."[12] In Hernandez's photography, abstraction measures the distance between the visible world, marked by detritus and disposability (the terribly concrete), and the imperceptible yet obdurate economic laws of motion that produce inequality and immiseration not as mere accidents but as a logical consequence of global capitalism's drive for profit.

When reality migrates into the abstract, photography must chase it.

Notes

1 Sebastião Salgado, *Migrations: The Work of Sebastião Salgado* (Berkeley, CA: Doreen B. Townsend Center for the Humanities, 2003), 2.
2 Ibid.
3 Karl Marx, *Capital: Volume 1: A Critique of Political Economy*, trans. Ben Fowkes (London and New York: Penguin Classics, 1992), 644.

4 Mike Davis, *Old Gods, New Enigmas: Marx's Lost Theory* (London: Verso, 2018), xvii.

5 Susan Sontag, *Regarding the Pain of Others* (New York: Picador, 2004), 79.

6 Salgado, *Migrations*, 24.

7 Ibid.

8 Ibid., 25.

9 Roberto Schwarz, "A Brazilian Breakthrough", *New Left Review*, 36 (December 2005), 91–107.

10 Edward W. Soja, *My Los Angeles: From Urban Restructuring to Regional Urbanization* (Berkeley, CA: University of California Press, 2014), 17.

11 Allan Sekula, "Dismantling Modernism, Reinventing Documentary (Notes on the Politics of Representation)", *Massachusetts Review* 19, no. 4 (1978), 859–883.

12 Henri Lefebvre, "The End of Modernity?", in *Key Writings*, ed. Stuart Elden, Eleonore Kofman, and Elizabeth Lebas (London: Continuum, 2017), 94.

Money | Phil Elverum

Counterfeit, Death, Iconomy, Interest, Liquidity, Luxury, Mapping, r>g, Trust, Void, Work

Contemplating death,

I scream to the stars at night

"Please give me money."

Mont Pèlerin | Quinn Slobodian, Ryan S. Jeffery, and Haruka Cheung

(Chicago), (Chile), (Dystopia), The Invisible Hand, Orthodoxy, Period, Utopia

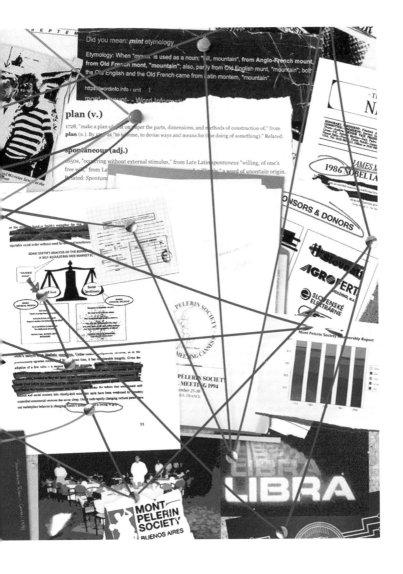

It is frequently observed that the mechanisms that govern global finance have a Rube Goldberg-like quality to them. Efforts to demystify the matrix of institutions, balance sheets, and financial instruments that we call an economy often veer towards madness or, at best, a never-ending detective caper that suggests a hidden world just beyond perceptibility. In attempting to understand how this separate dimension came into being, some scholars have turned to the more easily traceable realm of the written word: articles, conference proceedings, and books. A special role is played by an elite cadre who have gathered in the Mont Pelérin Society since 1947, a private debate club created by Friedrich Hayek and including neoliberal luminaries from Milton Friedman to James Buchanan.

While the scholarship on the Mont Pelerin Society often mirrors the sophistication of those who've gathered under its name, it is also stalked by its proximity to less credible methodologies' forms of conspiracy theorizing. Our contribution to the glossary plays with this proximity. In our montage, places like Hong Kong recall neoliberal templates for non-democratic capitalist governance, and the early arrival of think tankers in post-socialist Eastern Europe, where they pushed for maximal liberalization of capital flows, and minimal corporate and personal income taxes. The adepts of Mont Pelérin mark the space of the economy as an unknowable "catallaxy" beyond the ken of human knowledge. Yet every tack exposes a new node, and every string a geographical vector that might challenge this mysticism—perhaps quixotically but also persistently, seeking a pattern and a workable metaphor for the whole.

0

Occupation

Oil

Oikonomia

Organization

Orthodoxy

Occupation | Sadek Kessous

(Art), (Manhattan), (Struggle),
The University, Work

In a wildly misguided attempt to promote reskilling in cyber security, the UK government released an advertisement in October 2020 that showed a ballet dancer tying the ribbons of her pointe shoes. The caption read: "Fatima's next job could be in cyber. (she just doesn't know it yet)." The campaign made its cynical pseudo-feminism clear: a woman like "Fatima" (black? Muslim?) should be the enforcer of cyber security rather than a prospective security risk. By moving from ballet to "cyber", "Fatima" should step out of dance and into the modern economy. She was urged, in other words, to give up aesthetic pursuits and get a real occupation.

In an autumn nine years prior, another ballerina erupted into the political arena to entirely different effect. In its namesake magazine, the anti-capitalist media foundation Adbusters ran a poster depicting a ballerina perched on Wall Street's charging bull and flanked by protestors in clouds of smoke. In the image she is at ease, not slightly unsettled by dancing in the beating heart of global finance or in a maelstrom of civil unrest. Instead, her ambiguous call to #occupywallstreet—marked by the question "What is our one demand?"—comes from an artist protestor who uses her body deliberately, defiantly, and aesthetically to occupy spaces that are ostensibly hostile to her.

These two occupations reflect how, significantly, the word "occupation" is at odds with itself—semantically slipping between activity and work, between having and taking. Imagine a slogan: "Occupations against Occupations." Is this

Figure 39.1 One of the UK government's CyberFirst posters. (HM government, 2020; Crown copyright)

a piece of political spin, like that of the "Fatima" campaign, a catchphrase for work programmes that generate social "investment" among disaffected squatters? Or is it a demand to occupy workplaces and halt the vast millstone that grinds living activity into dead work? As one placard in Zuccotti Park jibed, "I LOST MY JOB BUT FOUND AN OCCUPATION." The occupation, then, is marked by contradictions. It is literal and ironic, material and abstract, conformist and dissident, individual and collective. The occupation is something that the body does and something that is done to the body.

The occupation has unique spatial logics: the buildings and institutions of the university create "students" as an occupational category, but when students stage an occupation of a university building, they assert contrarily that "WE ARE THE UNIVERSITY". Spaces shape bodies; bodies shape spaces. These contradictions are felt acutely under colonialism. There, the occupation is a means of domination and resistance. For the rebels in the 1916 Easter Rising, taking Dublin's General Post Office was an occupation against an occupation. It played out at the intersection of imperialism, militarism, finance, and representation.

The artworks that emerge from these contradictions are marked by struggle. Occupation aesthetics, then, is a

Figure 39.2   Occupy Wall Street poster, Adbusters, July 2011. (reprinted by permission of Adbusters Media Foundation)

dialectical aesthetics. Its struggles concern the material conditions that fix people singly in vocational-economic categories
and the same conditions that give rise to their violent overturn.
Its forms are contradictory: comic and serious, theatrical and
austere, optimistic and pessimistic. Like its subject matter,
occupation aesthetics takes enclosure as its theme: it resists
enclosure; it depicts enclosure. It does not possess singular intentions, objectives, or outcomes but instead embraces
plurality and a state of radical indeterminacy. Like "Fatima", it
does not fully comprehend the power of the professional occupation. Like the Occupy ballerina, it resists that power with an
unanswerable question: "What is our one demand?"

****

Christian Lorentzen offered one early definition of post-
Occupy aesthetics. He predicted that "in the fall of 2013 or
2014, if not before, we'll probably be reading a novel about
Occupy Wall Street", in which "you can bet the narrator will be
omniscient and the telling panoramic."[1] His claim drew on the
novels that rose to prominence immediately after the 2007–08
global financial crisis whose preoccupation with money was
expressed in realist modes. Unlike those fictions by Jonathan
Franzen, Don DeLillo, Jonathan Dee, Adam Haslett, and Alex
Preston, however, only a small number of Occupy texts have
hewed to this specification of omniscient panorama. Instead,
latter-day occupation aesthetics has favoured people to money
and energized incompleteness to stable holisms.

Magdaléna Platzová's *The Attempt* (2013/2016), for
instance, casts a wide narrative net that encompasses contemporary Eastern European academics and nineteenth-century
anarchists. But its transhistorical panorama collapses before
it can connect the history of Gilded Age industrialists and

immigrant anarchists to Occupy Wall Street. Platzová's protagonist hopes to uncover his relation to historic struggles but
manages only to add muddled scraps to a notebook. As he
despairs: "What's the use in pretending there's unity where
there isn't any? Why make things up? Why not let the individual fates rub up against one another as randomly as the
sheets of paper stuck into the blue notebook?"[2] Money and its
networks of power are as inscrutable as the history of radical
resistance that opposes them: a paradoxical cause for hope
and pessimism. As invoked by the novel's title, any attempt is
suspended permanently between success and failure. Caleb
Crain's *Overthrow* (2019) also bears some of the elements of
Lorentzen's prediction, particularly in the realist omniscience
of its free, indirect narration; yet Crain fixes his sights not on networks of finance but on a group of telepaths brought together
around the lower Manhattan encampment. *Overthrow*, then,
is less committed to tracing the destruction that lies in capital's
global wake and is more preoccupied by the possibilities of the
alternative forms of social connection that are immanent to
the occupation. Occupations are about people and the things
they do for and against the economy. As one Occupy placard
asserted, "WE ARE THE TRUE CURRENCY!" That is to say that
occupiers are not occupied merely by questions of money but
by the activity that sustains occupations in all their forms, from
professions to protests.

   In spite of this fact, fictions of #OWS have been largely
limited in the range of activities they have depicted. Instead
of proletarian labour, many of these fictions have, for better
or worse, foregrounded academic work. Both *The Attempt*
and *Overthrow* place university researchers at their centres.
Barbara Browning's *The Gift* (2017) turns on the thinly fic-
tionalized life of its academic author, figured as "Barbara
Andersen", as she participates in workshops, seminars, and

performances in Manhattan at the time of Occupy Wall Street. Ben Lerner's *10:04* (2014) discusses Occupy through a similar authorial avatar in "Ben", a college-educated novelist living in Manhattan during #OWS: he gives talks, takes up fellowships, and thinks cultural theory.

This emphasis on academia has linked occupation aesthetics to autofiction, a novelistic genre which deploys the authorial persona as a core fictive element. Small wonder perhaps, given that one of the outgrowths of #OWS were "Free Universities" that aimed to create spaces for the kinds of radical intellectual exchange that are hindered by a marketized higher education system. For these writer-academics, their professional occupations represent urgent zones of struggle. If the university has become the grand patron of literary production in the modern "program era"[3] and access to such patronage is linked largely to punishing indebtedness, then academia represents a key battleground—materially and intellectually—both for writers of the occupation and occupational writers. Rather than present easeful realisms that can open on to capital's global vistas without visible friction or effort, these writers resist presentations of intellectual labour as an abstract or autonomous activity by showing it as inextricable from academic systems of value production. For Browning, her income and relative wealth as an NYU associate professor is framed in direct relation to a performance artist friend whose MFA progress is measured in dollars paid: in one performance he announces: "I almost have my MFA. I'm twenty-four thousand four hundred and twenty-four dollars and eighty-four cents away."[4] In *10:04*, Lerner's narrator goes so far as to open the novel with a luxurious dinner scene as his agent details the "'strong six-figure' advance" he will receive for the book now in the reader's hands.[5]

The struggle over and within occupations persists in this reflexive representation of writerly academic labour. As Paul

Crosthwaite has noted, a quality of autofictions is what he terms their status as "market metafictions": examples of "fiction that self-consciously reflects upon its own marketability".[6] Writers foreground the economic logics that underpin their work and the effort required to bring it to market, but they do so in terms that (consciously or not) bolster the economic value of their occupational productivity. Even if they attempt to expose their concealed labour, writers still reproduce the market logics to which they are subject. In *The Gift*, for instance, Browning's direct, stylistic intimacy smooths over the technical specificity of the academic labour that she ostensibly brings into view. While defining Occupy organizer David Graeber's concept of "baseline communism", Browning's fictional double notes that it is "what happens when you grab the check at a restaurant because you know you make more money than the person you're dining with. You may think that's bourgeois politesse, but, like Graeber, I'd prefer to call that communism."[7] Style here papers over the complexity of scholarly work via anecdotal illustration, a conversational second-person voice, and the implication that analytical claims are formed around preferences rather than rigour. In this fictocriticism, structural transparency gives way to feigned simplicity according to the logic of professional occupation. Browning may laudably attempt to democratize scholarship but she does so in terms that smooth the rough edges of academic activity into a saleable commodity. Such a tack is anything but anathema to the marketized university where scholars are told to adopt styles and modes of delivery that make research accessible and impactful, "relatable", and commercially friendly. The problem with which Browning and Lerner wrestle is the financialization of the writer's occupation. Through a public reading of the short story, occupiers in Zuccotti Park may have made Herman Melville's Bartleby into their mascot for his understated refusal of professional occupations—"I'd prefer not to"—but he was also driven to madness and death by finance, by Wall Street's "dead letters". How can writers navigate this struggle between capital and labour? What does a professional occupation like writing matter if the markets care more about our spending than our working?

Eugene Lim's novel *Dear Cyborgs* (2019) is distinct among occupation fictions in its unwavering focus on these specifically corporate-financial conditions and their relation to aesthetic theory. The novel comprises recounted vignettes from various middle-class discontents as they mill from karaoke bar to café, from book store to restaurant, and discuss the predicaments of their financialized lives. One such episode recounts the occupation of a skyscraper that served as "the headquarters of a global energy company".[8] Lim pessimistically undermines the tension between the occupiers and the forces of capital— the "legions of riot cops and rows of armored vehicles, noise cannons and prison vans"[9]—by showing the extent to which their opposition can be integrated into financial circuits. The occupation becomes a welcome means of containing the protestors who were roaming the streets so that, once contained, this political occupation can be converted into a professional one with bleak offers of work in "a standard corporate labor camp" which consists of "low-level data analysis in exchange for their consumer spending units and daily gruel".[10] Those who refuse are eventually forgotten: after years, their occupation dissolves once "ruthless corporate-government actuaries" determine that "granting [the occupiers] geographic mobility was heavily and decisively outweighed by the debt incurred in the continuing wages paid and resource spent to hold [them] captive".[11] Aaron Sorkin's HBO show *The Newsroom* (2012–14) attempted to skewer Occupy for this apparent lack of pragmatism. By constructing a scene in which an #OWS interviewee flounders under basic scrutiny, Sorkin's straw-man drama implied that there is no "virtue of a leaderless movement" that "protests against lots of things" endlessly. Ironically, Sorkin's criticism evokes what recent occupation writers suggest is the movement's chief virtue, namely that its anarchical methods are precisely how it resists enclosure.

The radical indeterminacy of this uncontained movement was prefigured by the Occupy ballerina's question "What is our one demand?", which emphasizes the occupation as not only a political but also an artistic activity, one not bound by instrumentalist logics. *Dear Cyborgs* offers a theory of the aestheticization of protest through the suggestion that "a protest, like a work of dance or a work of music, is something done, in part, by the protestor *for* the protestor".[12] On first glance, the abstract individualism inherent in such an approach might be disconcerting: the protestor has only an imagined interlocutor and participates in no actual dialogue of either confrontation or solidarity. But by formulating the activity of protest as an aesthetic action that serves its creator, Lim yanks it from the jaws of the professional occupation: an artistic performance such as this does not require either its purchase or sale. Moreover, as Graeber was keen to stress, politics constitutes a category of activity rather than a category of identity: politics is not something we are but something we do continually. It is by token of the same logic that artistic occupations are not determined by the condition of *having made* art, and certainly not by *having sold* art, but by *making* art. Occupations are an end in themselves, an ongoing process of making new: new art, new spaces, new politics. The aesthetics of the occupation centralize this sense of persistent incompleteness.

Perhaps the clearest example of the openness of occupation aesthetics is the Human Microphone. Also known as People's Microphone, it became synonymous with #OWS demonstrations as a means for protestors to achieve amplification through sheer numbers: a crowd repeats phrases like a rolling, living echo that spreads a message across distances that are otherwise inaccessible to any single human voice. This form of collective and creative statement is key to many Occupy fictions—Browning, Lerner, and Crain all depict it. As a live human expression, it is the dialectical sister of the internet, which also features in most Occupy texts as a reified social relation that retains the possibility for collectivity.

Lim's novel depicts the historical occasion when #OWS protestors used the People's Mic to convey a message from a solitary protestor in South Korea, Kim Jin-suk, who was staging a solitary nine-month occupation of a crane in a Busan shipping yard. This is not a utopian moment of connection across a global underclass: speaking for the collective, Lim's narrator states: "our attention drifted, and we soon found ourselves leaving the park".[13] Yet, the encampment's dissonant voice comprises an imperfect collection of common bodies, words, phrases, thoughts, feelings, rhythms, sounds that Lerner has termed "essentially [the Occupy movement's] own greatest poem".[14] If capital breaks social relations through alienation, occupation aesthetics uses forms like the people's mic to evoke an assemblage of people who are linked by their inability to connect meaningfully with each other. It is a negative capability: its failure shows that a collective remains possible.

Notes

1 Christian Lorentzen, "Fictitious Values. Boom and Bust in Twenty-First-Century Lit", *Bookforum*, August 2012, www.bookforum.com/print/1902/boom-and-bust-in-twenty-first-century-lit-9453.
2 Magdaléna Platzová, *The Attempt*, trans. Alex Zucker (New York: Bellevue Literary Press, 2016), 140.

3   Mark McGurl, *The Program Era* (Cambridge, MA: Harvard University Press, 2011).

4   Barbara Browning, *The Gift* (Minneapolis, MN: Coffee House Press, 2017), 31.

5   Ben Lerner, *10:04* (London: Granta Books, 2014), 4.

6   Paul Crosthwaite, *The Market Logics of Contemporary Fiction* (Cambridge: Cambridge University Press, 2019), 4.

7   Browning, *The Gift*, 139.

8   Eugene Lim, *Dear Cyborgs* (New York: Farrar, Straus and Giroux, 2017), 61.

9   Ibid.

10   Ibid., 62.

11   Ibid., 64.

12   Ibid., 24.

13   Ibid., 20.

14   Ben Lerner, "A Note on the Human Microphone", *Critical Quarterly* 54, no. 2 (2012), 66–68, 66.

Organization | Joshua Clover and Annie McClanahan

(Bondage), (Circulation), **Counterfeit**, (Crisis), (Logistics), (Platform), (Stagnation), (Struggle), (Supply), **Work**

We can tell the story of the recent economy with two images of stopped vehicles. We might begin in late 2020 with Ali Badir, a recent immigrant to the US from Egypt barely making ends meet while driving for three different gig work apps. Unable to afford car payments on the vehicle that was his only source of income, Badir took out loans with two subprime lending-and-leasing companies targeting gig economy workers. When Badir couldn't make the ballooning payments on his leased vehicle, the lender called in the car as stolen property, and Badir was stopped on his way to work by six cop cars, who set a police dog on him. We might end one year later, in late 2021, with the semis stalled outside the port of Los Angeles, evidence of a supply chain crisis caused by pandemic- and climate-change-related shutdowns in global production. Truck drivers—who, like Badir, had financed their own vehicles with debt—waited in hours-long lines with no guarantee of being paid for time spent without moving any goods around.

These stories have much to say about a series of entangled transformations of national and global economies that demand a reconsideration of the category of organization itself. This knotted shift travels under a variety of names, as is inevitable given the contradiction between the variety of underlying changes and the desire to give them a unifying concept. It may be "neoliberalism" or "post-Fordism" or "financialization"; it may feature the "shift to circulation" or the "gig economy" or "platform capitalism"; its paradigmatic subject may be the "precariat" or "knowledge workers" or a "new lumpenproletariat".

Of some things we can be certain. In the US (our nation of residence and the most overdeveloped capitalist power), workforce participation remains far below its peak years; union density, especially in the private sector, remains at similarly historic lows. Underlying both of these data, a dramatic fact: while about a century ago the three standard labour sectors approached parity, at present we find manufacture around 10%, agriculture tilting towards zero, and services thereby accounting for more than 80% of employment. Industrial profits never recovered their postwar jouissance; so-called "capital formation" (bourgeois economics' best proxy for reinvestment of profit into production) remains unmoved by astounding pours of liquidity into the markets; the bond yields said to predict future growth predict something else entirely. There is no indication these tendencies will reverse. In turn, there is no reason to believe that the basic modes of political organization that arose from those lost conditions will be the forms that suffice in the future, whether "suffice" means to secure adequate lives for some significant portion of the population or to challenge the present social ordering. Redistribution, reproduction, retribution, revolution—none of these things seems likely to arrive on the shoulders of organization in its once conventional senses.

The insurrectionary struggles that orient contemporary social contest in the capitalist core have diverged decisively from the organized workplace antagonisms of the past. In their content they persistently concern access to basic subsistence, with fuel costs playing a central role once monopolized by food prices. They concern just as dramatically the mediation of access to those reproductive goods by finance and debt. They address a wide spectrum of "political" issues ranging from policing and the carceral state to climate crisis. The forms they take, in turn, range from wildcat strikes and work stoppages in response to cost-of-living struggles or protests against police brutality (often denounced by traditional unionists as mere "bad organizing"), to riots, blockades, and prison uprisings, to mutual aid efforts on the part of sex and gig workers alike.

We have elsewhere gathered these forms under the rubric of "circulation struggles".[1] A circulation struggle designates a social contest that launches not from the halls of production but from within the political-economic sphere of circulation, where goods are exchanged and eventually consumed, where the movement of goods and peoples rather than their production becomes a privileged site of conflict, and where participants may be labourers but are not structurally required to be so. These struggles therefore move the centre of balance among subjects of social contestation from the historical working class to an expanded proletariat characterized by the broad presence of the dispossessed and excluded as well as the exploited.

In this we see not simply a transformation in flight within what Charles Tilly calls the "repertoire of collective action", but a contemporary political economy in a state of crisis, riven by increasingly intractable structural contradictions.[2] Peering through our stalled motion allegories for the broader phenomenon of economic stagnation,[3] we find a growing indistinction between what Marx termed the "big storms" of crisis, in which "the antagonism of all elements in the bourgeois process of production explode", and the impasses of tendential slow-down.[4] The intractably low productivity of the service sector which now makes up the vast bulk of US employment (a trend visible as well not just in Western Europe but also China and other centres imagined to be sources of manufacturing growth) means that its wages will inevitably fail to provide for workers' subsistence. This obtains especially in the gig economy, which depends on the availability of workers compelled to accept below subsistence wages, dependent on tips or piece-rate wages excluded from regulation, and detached from traditional principal-agent contractual obligations. For them there will never be a shop floor, a workplace, nor even a paymaster. The gig economy, like sex work or criminalized hustles, offers only derivative and inadequate access to the wage; it simply formalizes this informalization for a growing number. It can scarcely be surprising that counterforms—that is to say, modes of "organization"—are changing.

In this formal informalization, finance provides a peculiarly thick and powerful mediation. Access to subsistence is often mediated less by employment than by financialized debt; collecting on that debt, in turn, becomes not a workplace issue but a criminal matter. It is neither Uber nor the bank that sets loose the dogs on Badir, but the police. Notably, this is today no less true of the truckers stuck in their big rigs in LA than it is of drivers like Badir: forced to finance their own trucks, many truckers are trapped by debt and forced into virtually wage-less piece-rate work. Stuck in the "indentured servitude" of this arrangement, they are further idled by the radical instability of the circulation economy in which they operate. When the COVID pandemic demolished the leisure, travel, and hospitality portion of the service sector in a single blow, the abrupt shift in spending to physical goods revealed supply chains far less flexible than promised by the breathless rhetoric of a "logistics revolution". This simply added to the concatenation of crises in the global circulation of goods increasingly caused not simply by "economic" circumstances but also by the disruptions consequent on global climate collapse.

The drivers idling at the port without wages or work were not consciously engaged in what we typically mean by "workplace action". And yet they had in some sense downed their tools, marking an increasingly common sort of work stoppage, one driven by conditions rather than intention, by the wild disorganization of the conjuncture rather than the organization of a union. It is here that we would like to focus our attentions: on the action that does not seem conventionally planned or even intended, which arises from concrete and often dramatic conditions but remains illegible to those with an orthodox sense of organization. Such actions have a long history and are increasingly prevalent in our present. An account of them might begin with what W.E.B. Du Bois called the "black general strike", comprising withdrawals of black labour from the South in the various forms of refusal of work on the plantation as well as escape from captivity to the North, into the Union Army, or into *marronage*. It is on the basis of this that Du Bois famously concluded that the slaves freed themselves.[5] We might note three features. First, the character of a widely shared and effective action; second, the absence of conventional organizing forms like the union, the party, or the charismatic leader; and third, the illegibility of this action *as an action* until disclosed by later accounts. That this force, form, and lack of legibility are racialized should not escape our notice.

We do not wish to be over-casual in comparing a hollowing labour market or deindustrializing exurbs to the conditions of chattel slavery. To seek a historical trajectory for organization means tracking the features set forth above more than the contents of classed, raced, and gendered domination. Five contemporary episodes seem to us instructive, none of which can be set forth in the detail they deserve.

The *Gilets Jaunes* uprising in France across 2018–19 seems paradigmatic: a provincial *jacquerie* happening everywhere and nowhere (until descending inevitably upon Paris), focused entirely on the circulation of goods and people, and the prices thereof, organized beyond union halls and party offices. This last feature was so decisive that it cast a perplexing ambiguity over the entire sequence, leaving observers—absent the movement's explicit or implicit alignment with political institutions—uncertain as to its political valence. Moreover, the uprising stood predictably accused of lacking organization, though it is quite hard to suppose how small groups of people kept arriving at roundabouts in a timely fashion, devising shelters, and standing watch so as to bring commercial traffic across the nation to a standstill, absent some sort of collective planning.

Arguably even more instructive was the 2019 action taken by coal miners left without jobs when their employer, Blackjewel, dissolved without warning. Playing out in Kentucky's Harlan county, a historical centre of heroic union struggles, this last act by the labourers and their associates was in the first instance a wage conflict and a labour action. The company had reneged on considerable final wages. Their demand—give us our pay—was without argument in the tradition of workplace struggles. Except: no workplace. The only threat available to them was not the strike but the blockade, something like the obverse of the downing of tools: gathering on the tracks, with a small encampment to the side, by way of preventing Blackjewel's final coal trains from launching the coal into the marketplace. This leap of antagonism from production to circulation was not freely chosen; it was proffered by material conditions beyond the participants' control. It would be hard to imagine a more schematic demonstration of the shift in forms of organization.

If miners sitting on the Harlan tracks represent the blockade of the circulation-extraction economy, the San Francisco gig workers who block the private commuter buses used to transport tech workers from the city to their jobs in Silicon Valley echo a similar strategy in the circulation-service economy. These actions expressed rage not just at the low wages and brutal precarity of gig work but also at the astronomical increases in rental prices in the Bay Area, driven up by the twinned afflictions of financialization and a booming tech sector. Rioters blocked traffic with their collective mass of bodies and raised a hasty memorial to a bike-delivery gig worker struck and killed by a car months before—managed by algorithm, he had been promised "bonus pay" to deliver in torrential rains. Two years later, as the pandemic ravaged the in-person service sector, many of those same gig-worker activists would join with sex workers to create mutual aid funds towards providing one another basic subsistence. Such projects exposed gaping holes in a social welfare infrastructure built by the compromise between organized labour and the capitalist state during the mid-century industrial boom. They also registered the specific forms of precarity suffered by a modern lumpenproletariat of informal workers, tip workers, and those performing criminalized labour, and they captured the unwaged nature of most socially reproductive labour. Here too, then, we find both a set of conditions and a set of responses that cannot be organized under the signs of wage struggle, point of production unionization, or work stoppage.

About the George Floyd Uprising in the summer of 2020 there is too much to say. Most salient is certainly the condensation of counter-struggle against durable, unendurable racialized domination organized and enforced by the deep unity of political and economic violence. While a racialized class domination has never lacked for these features, they take on developing contours in the present: the more that wage discipline seems to dematerialize into debt and algorithms, the more it must be materialized in the form of the police. And if uprisings against deadly police enforcement, and the ceaseless production of hierarchies of survival, form a time-worn story, the intensity of 2020's condensation gave it the character of the new. Again, it seemed to happen everywhere almost at once, its forms recurring across distances, a racialized proletarian movement we might call the Black General Riot. For present purposes we might note only a few small, significant details that emerged from within this complex. Consider the passing of the counterfeit bill that served as the purportedly triggering event: a striking synecdoche for the contemporary economy wherein cash is at once king and entirely derealized, where both the lord and the pauper have at their disposal only funny money and fictitious capital towards fatally different results. But we might also note the innovative use of coordinated, automobile-based looting as a recurrent feature of the uprising across the nation. As we have argued elsewhere, looting is an entirely non-exceptional historical feature of circulation struggles, providing immediate or derivative access to subsistence goods. The circulatory verve and automobility of this tactic, an innovation in flight, links it to numerous other global antagonisms, while demonstrating considerable and careful coordination.

All of these new and renewed tactics return us to the port of Los Angeles and environs. Among the underlying conditions, we might linger over the workforce participation rate, which reached its high point at the cusp of the millennium, began falling during the financial crisis of 2008, and never restored its upward trajectory. Having plummeted to a previously unthinkable nadir of 60% during the first phase of the global pandemic beginning in 2020, it has scarcely improved since, despite modest wage gains. Readers will recognize the suggestive phrase "the Great Resignation". Here, we might posit, is another kind of "general strike" unfurling behind the back of consciousness, concealed by its concatenated nature, gathering seemingly disparate reactions and rationales into a unitary effect, albeit one unrecognizable from the limited vantage point of traditional organization.

It may at first seem possible to claim that the change in forms of political organization follows the change in forms of capital, with the immanence and dispersion characteristic of finance and platforms reappearing as decentralized and leaderless protests. This offers homology in its weaker sense. Given the spatialization of circulation struggles, it is perhaps no surprise that we might be drawn into the spatial models that bedevil homology. However, if we are to spatialize, it is better to say that the contemporary, informal modes of organization arise in response to underlying changes, rising where long-standing features of expanded reproduction fall—something no less true regarding the powers of finance and the algorithm. Each of these phenomena meets the withdrawal of industrial capital with its own orienting counterforms. Such an understanding allows us in turn to recognize that revolutionary movements spread *neither by contamination nor resonance*, as they do not expand across a two-dimensional surface. They burst through the surface in a thousand places, akin because they share the same soil.

Notes

1   See Joshua Clover, *Riot. Strike. Riot: The New Era of Uprisings* (London: Verso Books, 2016).
2   Charles Tilly, "Speaking Your Mind without Elections, Surveys, or Social Movements", *Public Opinion Quarterly* 47, no. 4 (1983), 461–478, 463.

3   See Sarah Brouillette, Joshua Clover, and Annie McClanahan, "Late, Autumnal, Immiserating, Terminal", *Theory & Event* 22, no. 2 (2019), 325–336.

4   Karl Marx, *Capital: A Critique of Political Economy*, trans. Ben Fowkes (New York: Penguin, 1991), 681.

5   W.E.B. Du Bois, *Black Reconstruction in America 1860-1880* (New York: Free Press, 1998), 55–127.

Orthodoxy | Annie McClanahan

Black–Scholes, Mont Pèlerin, Resilience, Sacrifice, The University

In 2017 and 2018, I received funding from the Mellon Foundation to take a year and a half of undergraduate economics courses. I was interested in writing an intellectual history of methodological individualism (MI): the presumption that social phenomena (the macro) can be explained by attending to the intentional states that motivate individual actors (the micro).[1] MI is increasingly the dominant orthodoxy of a range of social science fields, but as the *Stanford Encyclopedia of Philosophy* notes, "the discipline that most clearly satisfies the strictures of methodological individualism is microeconomics".[2]

At the beginning of nearly every Introduction to Microeconomics textbook, you'll find one of these two claims: although you might assume rent control is good for renters, actually it's bad; although you might assume minimum wage laws are good for workers, actually they're bad. These two arguments are not just the orthodoxy of mainstream US economics; they are also widely accepted as gospel within much US political discourse. They are, in other words, the orthodoxy of a discipline that is itself an orthodoxy. But in class, because these ideas are examples of "how an economist thinks", they are recounted as brave apostasy. The presumed audience for this rhetoric, then, is the student who has been introduced to certain liberal shibboleths but has always congratulated himself that he can think outside the box. The tone is like being buttonholed at a party by a dude who is sure you'll appreciate the "not-PC" candor of his racist jokes.

Doing interdisciplinary work from the humanities into microeconomics is challenging because microeconomics begins by asserting its distance from the social sciences and humanistic disciplines. From Aristotle to Adam Smith, "political economy" treated economic questions as both political and historical. However, after the so-called "Marginalist Revolution" of the 1870s—later seen as the advent of modern microeconomics—the discipline thenceforth called simply "economics" aligned itself with physics and mathematical formalism. For late-nineteenth-century marginalist William Stanley Jevons, for instance, economics "must be a mathematical science ... because it deals with quantities".[3] By the turn of the twentieth century, economics increasingly saw itself not as a form of historical, political, or social theory but as an empirical science.[4] By the last third of the century, doing even an introductory course in microeconomics would require about a year of college calculus.

Despite having multiple tutors, I still struggle with the maths in these classes. By the end of the year, I despair of this ever becoming a feasible project in part because I realize that I will never be able to understand the discipline from the inside. But the problem of disciplinarity is deeper, too, as I come to realize the intensity of the field's resistance to self-reflection. When I present my work to econ faculty at the end of the year (a disaster I am led into by a well-meaning liberal macroeconomist), I ask how many of them have read early predecessors in classical political economy like Adam Smith and Jeremy Bentham, or marginalists like Carl Menger or Vilfredo Pareto, or major neoclassical social thinkers like Friedrich Hayek or Ludwig von Mises. Fewer than a third say yes. It becomes clear to me that they think their own intellectual history is irrelevant precisely because they think of their field as strictly a science: from this view, the wrong or even simply superseded ideas of the past are irrelevant. I come to suspect that economists have to insist that they are scientists precisely because the field's claim to scientificity is dubious. If my snarky colleague in the maths department is right, the math is pretty bad too.

MI tends to claim that its individualism is "merely" a methodological imperative—not only value-neutral but also epistemologically modest. By the time Joseph Schumpeter coined the term "methodological individualism" in 1909, however, the stakes of the debate were clearly political.[5] Since the 1870s Carl Menger and the Austrian marginalists had been engaged in a pitched war of method against the German Historical School—and, more important, against its socialist politics. In the Austrians' view, economic historicism was yoked to a rationalist belief in social engineering. That claim would take on even more urgency during the "socialist calculation debate" of the 1920s and 1930s, a debate between second-generation marginalists like Ludwig von Mises and Marxist economists Oskar Lange and Maurice Dobb. In 1944, Karl Popper would connect socialist politics to all "holistic" social theory committed to understanding "the development, not of aspects of social life, but of 'society as a whole'".[6] Indeed, the primary aim of MI was to refute the politics of collectivism, socialism, and social engineering by asserting that a well-ordered market society would arise automatically or naturally without interventions on the part of states or institutions—what Friedrich Hayek would describe as a "spontaneous collaboration".[7]

I learn to be very sceptical anytime a microeconomics professor mentions history. Historical "facts", the students are told, include the following: the primary reason homelessness increased in the 1970s in California was the overregulation of SRO apartments. The "tragedy of the commons" thesis refers to a real historical event where common land was overused. Modern insurance began with Lloyds of London underwriting the exchange of gold (in this last instance I have to press my lips together to keep myself from shouting "SLAVERY! It was to insure the slave trade!").

Strangely, though, the psychological individual deep at the heart of microeconomics ultimately was neither deep nor psychological—indeed, the second-generation marginalists became increasingly wary of their previous association with psychology. To retain individualism while eschewing psychology, they insisted that they were not interested in the *origin* of preferences but only in the ways preferences were revealed through decisions. Following the insights of Vilfredo Pareto, microeconomic theory turned from models of cardinal utility, which sought to measure utility absolutely, to models of ordinal utility, which measured utility relatively.

Ordinalism came with conceptual entailments: the "action-theoretic" account of choice insists that individuals themselves "usually do not know why they do what they do".[8] It also reflects a form of radical individualism: because my preference for apples can only be compared to my preference for oranges and not to *your* preference for apples, it is both impossible and, indeed, selfish to attempt to maximize utility for the community as a whole. "Social reformers believe they are solving an objective problem: what is the *best* form for a society?" Pareto writes. "But in fact they are dealing with solutions to a subjective problem: what form of society is best fitted to *my* sentiments?"[9] Embracing Lionel Robbins's famous definition of economics as no more than "the forms assumed by human behavior in disposing of scarce means", the field refused to offer a criterion of judgement for creating a social state that would most justly distribute those ostensibly scarce resources.[10] For microeconomic MI, there is no such thing as a social good transcending individual preferences—no "to each according to their needs".[11]

The first day of class in game theory is the same "econ as red-pill" vibe again, with a hard emphasis on let's-all-admit-we're-rationally-self-interested-individualists. As I'm listening, I think about the student next to me who let another student he'd never met use his phone; the student who gave another student her pen; the student who held the door open for me; the two students I hear agreeing to collaborate on note taking: all examples of what David Graeber calls "everyday communism" and a strong indication that most of the time we actually don't *act like pure self-interested rationalists.*[12] *Also, possibly relatedly, this class is hella sexist. One of the most famous game theory problems is "Battle of the Sexes": she wants to attend the ballet; he wants to attend a boxing match; which will they choose? The textbook for the class rewrites it as "Bach versus Stravinsky". But the prof doesn't think much of this "politically correct" choice and so doubles down, jokingly pretending to have to correct himself every time. To introduce Nash Equilibrium, he plays the clips from* A Beautiful Mind *in which Nash theorizes the solution at a bar after playing a game theory scenario called "Blondes versus Brunettes". Wisecracks about the preference for blondes will structure the professor's lectures for the remainder of the quarter. I'm not convinced we're* all *selfish assholes, but I'm definitely convinced that* this *guy is one.*

After the Paretian turn to ordinalism, orthodox economists like Paul Samuelson began to seek out a microeconomic theory entirely "independent of any psychological, introspective implications".[13] In an influential 1938 essay, Samuelson noted that we have no way of measuring or studying individual *preferences* but only individual *decisions*. Rejecting self-conscious deliberation, Samuelson was deeply influenced by concomitant work in behavioural psychology.[14] Yet in 1948 Samuelson abandoned this attempt to rid microeconomic theory of utility entirely, and instead introduced the idea of "revealed preference".[15] Whereas psychological behaviourism had embraced a radically mechanistic view of human behaviour, reducing preferences almost entirely to conditioning and stimuli, Samuelson's revealed preference theory would reassert the claim he had formerly disavowed—that choices reflect underlying preferences—while also excluding the internal states that created those preferences from the domain of consumer choice theory.

So why did Samuelson—and most of the consumer choice theory that came after him—turn so abruptly away from behaviourism? The reasons, I think, are historical and political. A strong behaviourism is entirely committed to an idea of control—including social control. It is this emphasis that links early behaviourism to the institutionalist economics of thinkers like Veblen, and to the very social engineering that the microeconomic individualists abjured. In the early twentieth century, the rise of both scientific management and centralized economic planning had created an atmosphere friendly to Samuelson's behaviourist theory of consumer choice; quickly thereafter, however, the terrain started to shift rather decisively. That is, by the late 1940s, as Samuelson published his far less mechanical theory of revealed preference and as his more explicitly neoliberal colleagues were meeting in Mt Pelerin to discuss the rising tide of socialism, consumer choice theory had to *appear*, if not to actually *be*, a theory of individual *freedom*. Dispensing explicitly with volition, as the behaviourists had, would be anathema to this aim: the idea of freedom as both a political and a moral imperative was increasingly central to the perceived difference between free markets and other ways of organizing economic activity.

In a class on the microeconomics of corporate decision making, we do a lot of problems around compensation, problems which always lead to a critique not just of minimum wage laws but of all *forms of hourly compensation. Microeconomics* *disdains hourly compensation because it guarantees compensation regardless of output whereas piece-rate ensures that the worker has to bust her ass all the time. The professor of this class is a full professor in his seventies who has been at UCI for decades, so it's pretty galling when—over and over again—he uses the tenure system as his example of a "highly inefficient employment model". Later, I happen across the news that he's received $1.5 million in grant funding from the Koch Foundation.*

The individual of microeconomic MI—and of revealed preference—thus had to be individual in order to be free. But he *also* may have had to be volitionally free precisely because he was not actually very individual. Turning away from cardinal utility, microeconomics had surrendered Jevons's fantasy that it might someday "measure the feelings of the human heart" and asserted instead that individual desires are too particular and subjective to be quantified.[16] Embracing the homogeneity principle and the theory of the representative agent in order to reduce macroeconomic theory to its supposed microfoundations, it had also asserted that all individuals were the same. The result was that microeconomics' methodological individual began to look like a rather strange figure indeed: so particular that he could not possibly be known by anyone else, and yet also, in his subjection to abstract formal logic, generically universal. None of this lent itself very well to a *positive* ideology of individual freedom in a free market society. Nor did economics' post-Cold War turn towards what Philip Mirowski describes as a "cyborg" theory of the human, with its purely computational theory of mind.[17] Offering this mindless machine apparent freedom to choose was, in a sense, the least the microeconomic individualists could give him.

In a discussion of the "choices" workers make on the labour market, the professor says that people accept risky jobs like long-haul trucking "because they are not risk-averse". In a discussion of homelessness in another class, the professor urges us to eschew the language of "inequality" and think instead of homelessness as "rational choice": the homeless person simply chooses to allocate their resources towards non-housing consumption. In these examples we can see the intellectual poverty of revealed preference, the way it depends on vacuous tautology: it isn't interested in whether the worker really is *non-risk-averse but simply takes the fact that she will do a risky job as proof that she must be. Because of its resistance to any form of social determination, the theory cannot accept stark, awful necessity—cannot see the way we are made by circumstances as much as we make them. Never does such a theory acknowledge that a risk-averse person might have to take such a job simply in order to survive, since acknowledging that would contravene the fantasy that free markets are the best means for human flourishing and freedom. For microeconomists, if you've made the choice to work a dangerous job or to eat rather than pay rent, you must have had a choice, as if when asked the question "Your money or your life?" we can be said to "choose" life. Recasting brute necessity as market freedom, microeconomic orthodoxy becomes the helpmate of late-stage capitalism.*

Within a year of finishing my courses, I abandon the intellectual history project entirely, deciding instead to think a lot more about risky jobs and unfree choices, and about the lived experience of post-industrial workers who are, as Marx put it, "free in a double sense": free to work or free to starve.

Notes

1   For an intellectual history of MI, see Lars Udehn, *Methodological Individualism: Background, History and Meaning* (London: Routledge, 2014).
2   "Methodological Individualism", *Stanford Encyclopedia of Philosophy*, https://plato.stanford.edu/entries/methodological-individualism/.

3   William Stanley Jevons, *The Theory of Political Economy* (New York: Palgrave, 2014 [1871]), xxix.

4   See Philip Mirowksi, *More Heat than Light: Economics as Social Science, Physics as Nature's Economics* (Cambridge: Cambridge University Press, 2014); Ben Fine and Dimitri Milonakis, *From Political Economy to Economics: Method, the Social and the Historical in the Evolution of Economic Theory* (New York: Routledge, 2014).

5   Joseph Schumpeter, "On the Concept of Social Value", *Quarterly Journal of Economics* 23, no. 2 (February 1909), 213–232. For an example of the claim to apolitical method, see Ludwig von Mises, *The Ultimate Foundation of Economic Science: An Essay on Method* (Princeton, NJ: D Van Nostrand Company, 1984 [1962]).

6   Karl Popper, "The Poverty of Historicism II: A Criticism of Historicist Methods", *Economica* 11, no. 43 (August 1944), 119–137, 123.

7   Freidrich Hayek, *Individualism and Economic Order* (Chicago, IL: University of Chicago Press, 1948.

8   Ibid., 87.

9   Vilfredo Pareto, *Mind and Society*, Vol. 4, trans. Andrew Bongiorno and Arthur Livingston (New York: Harcourt Brace, 1935), 1477.

10 Lionel Robbins, *An Essay on the Nature and Significance of Economic Science* (New York: New York University Press, 1937), 15.

11 See S.M. Amadae, *Rationalizing Capitalist Democracy: The Cold War Origins of Rational Choice Liberalism* (Chicago, IL: University of Chicago Press, 2003).

12 David Graeber, *Debt: The First 5000 Years* (Brooklyn, NY: Melville House, 2011), 326.

13 Paul Samuelson, "A Note on the Pure Theory of Consumer's Behaviour", *Economica* 51, no. 17 (1938), 61–71, 62.

14 See D. Wade Hands, "Paul Samuelson and Revealed Preference Theory", *History of Political Economy* 46 (2014), 85–116.

15 Paul Samuelson, "Consumption Theory in Terms of Revealed Preference", *Economica* 15, no. 60 (November 1948), 243–253.

16 William Stanley Jevons, *Theory of Political Economy*, second edn (Middlesex: Penguin, 1970 [1871]), 83.

17 Philip Mirowski, *Machine Dreams: Economics Becomes a Cyborg Science* (Cambridge: Cambridge University Press, 2002).

P

Period | Torsten Andreasen

Decadence, (Deindustrialization), (Dystopia),
The Invisible Hand, Mont Pèlerin, (Stagnation),
(Struggle), **Utopia**

The point of the period is the end of it—the fact that it ends. Therein lies its analytical usefulness and its political purpose. The period is where the syntax of words, images, sounds, deeds, and events can be reconstructed as meaning and opened for not only interpretation and diagnosis, but also new use, new creation, new communal praxes, a new beginning. Positing the period as the necessity of an end inspires hope that what is does not exhaust possibility: *Ça suffit la connerie.*

The period is, then, a tool for taking a stand against time, for creating a distance to the past and a release from the present in order to bring about a time to come. What counts is that we are *at the end of* something, and not just the end of the day to begin yet another but the end of a certain measurement of time altogether: shots fired at the clocks measuring out the working day, the microseconds of HFT, the maturity of debt, the persistence of property, the steady, beating rhythm of the upward mobility of wealth. Periodization is a means for ending the end of history, all the more urgent as the end of history turns increasingly genocidal in its own catastrophic demise. That things "just go on" *is*, literally, the catastrophe.

From the perspective of the period, the vagaries of syntax can be reconstructed as the grammatical possibility of meaning. The struggle for possibility therefore begins with the syntactic constituents, the identifiable traces left by the machinations of obscure logics: names, deeds, and occurrences are inscribed in our bodies and our minds, as, for example, in Édouard Louis's short narrative *Who Killed My Father*:

Macron, Hollande, Valls, El Khomri, Hirsch, Sarkozy, Bertrand, Chirac. The history of your suffering bears these names. Your life story is the history of one person after another beating you down. The history of your body is the history of these names, one after another, destroying you. The history of your body stands as an *accusation* against political history.[1]

The syntax of a life's occurrences is reconstituted as a grammar of violence and accusation: the subjects and their names, the verbs and their deeds, the object and occurrences of their violence, the political history that must be brought to an end.

Sean Bonney similarly screams at "those who sit on the various committees. The names of those responsible for the massacres": "The names of power. The forbidden syllables. The names of those whose names it is impossible to pronounce in certain combinations and continue to simply live. ... I start to scream. I arrange the pieces on the ground. With each scream I name one of them. The bones of Boris Johnson. The face of Theresa May."[2] But arranging the syntactic constituents of the massacres in their proper grammar of violence requires a period.

Mourning the victims, seeking out and screaming at the names, the deeds, the faces, and the bones of the perpetrators—those responsible for the misery—are necessary for the struggle; it *is* struggle. However, it does not tell the time: are we there yet? The period, on the other hand, is a stake in the ground, a tentative historico-philosophical sundial, trying to determine the end and a new beginning.

Periodization unveils the names, the deeds, the bones as character masks of a period piece, as forms of appearance of the machinations, relations, and processes of the obscure logics and moving contradictions that constitute the period. Only in the period does the character of the names and deeds appear as clearly determined by the particular historical and social structures, the mute compulsions, the increasing subordination of the networks of power to the networks of accumulation. Only the period demonstrates the absurdity of the moral showdown between the good industrialist and the evil greed of financial capital—Edward Lewis and Gordon Gecko, the character masks.

The period situates the naming of names and deeds in the context of the "inexpressible things" that made them possible, seemingly necessary. In *Margin Call*, Jeremy Irons's character, John Tuld—a less than subtle reference to Lehman CEO Dick Fuld—lists the financial crises of "1637, 1797, 1819, '37, '57, '84, 1901, '07, '29, 1937, 1974, 1987 '92, '97, 2000", "and whatever we want to call this", i.e. 2008. He then concludes: "It's all just the same thing over and over; we can't help ourselves." They can't help themselves, abandon all hope, ye who enter …

The period revolts against this list, the insignificant "whatever" of every new incident, its abandonment of hope. The period articulates its historical grammar, its historical units of meaning: the age of the Genoese, the Dutch, the British, the US; the end of *les trentes glorieuses* producing the financialization of the long downturn, the end that must end. Periodization insists on the discontinuous regimes of accumulation and oppression—their names, their deeds, their occurrences, and events—but also on new modes of struggle and community that continuously scan the position of the sun: are we there yet? The hope that those momentous seventy-two days of 1871 could, once again, become the present, but anew.

The point of the period, then, is to force the moment to its inherent crisis, its vortex of destruction and creation, bringing the end and willing the new, while stressing that in order to will the new, we must not just will the bones of the perpetrators but also will our own destruction, rooted as we are in the past we set out to destroy.[3]

The point of the period is the end of it—the fact that it ends. Therein lies its analytical usefulness and its political purpose, to create a distance from the present and release us from the past in order to bring about a time to come. And

when everything is at an end, give me your hand, so that we may begin again from the beginning. ... [W]e must expose the old world to the full light of day and shape the new one in a positive way. The longer the time that events allow to thinking humanity for taking stock of its position, and to suffering mankind for mobilizing its forces, the more perfect on entering the world will be the product that the present time bears in its womb.[4]

Notes

1   Édouard Louis, *Who Killed My Father*, trans. Lorin Stein (New York: New Directions, 2019).
2   Sean Bonney, *Our Death* (Oakland, CA: Commune Editions, 2019), 18, 75.
3   Diane Di Prima, *Revolutionary Letters* (San Francisco: City Lights Books, 2021, 12.
4   Karl Marx, *Letter to Ruge – Cologne, May* 1843, www.marxists.org/archive/marx/works/1843/letters/43_05.htm.

The Pit | Christian Borch

(Algorithm), (Chicago), HFT, Men, Speculation, (Trader)

Can financial panic be smelled? In contemporary, through-and-through digital financial markets, the answer seems to be no. A possible exception is if data transmission cables were to catch fire, since in today's digital market space, almost all orders to buy or sell securities are entered manually on computers or, increasingly so, automatically by algorithmic systems, and arrive at securities exchanges and trading venues through complex digital infrastructures. This was not always the case. From the inauguration of the first stock exchange in Amsterdam in 1611 and almost four centuries on, trading was above all an analogue affair where traders would meet physically on exchange trading floors to buy or sell commodities and securities. When traders were physically co-present, there was a sense in which imminent financial panic could be immediately perceived, perhaps even smelled.

Being physically co-present does not in itself say much about how trading was carried out more specifically, and through history different exchanges have implemented different ways of organizing the ways in which face-to-face trading was conducted. One of the most iconic designs remains the architectural structure known as "the pit" and adopted most famously by the Chicago Board of Trade (CBOT) and later closely associated with the Chicago markets. Briefly, the history behind the introduction of trading pits runs like this. Established in 1848, the CBOT soon became a central location for the trading of agricultural products such as grain.

However, a victim of its success, by the end of the 1860s more than 2,000 CBOT members were flocking the exchange floors, generating a widespread sense of turmoil. The exchange therefore decided to introduce a new architectural design to facilitate more orderly trading. As a result, in 1870 the flat trading floors that previously hosted the CBOT's trading activities were replaced by sets of octagonally shaped structures, with each of these trading pits having steps descending from the periphery to its centre.

The trading activities emerging in and from this new architectural design had several formal and informal characteristics which were largely shared across the different exchanges that adopted pit trading. For example, the trading of a particular commodity or security would have its designated pit, and trading it outside of that pit would be prohibited. Moreover, all bids to buy and offers to sell had to be explicitly communicated in the pit. This is known as "open-outcry trading", that is, literally shouting one's buy or sell interest to the other market participants in the pit. As some pits may attract hundreds of market participants, they could evolve into frenetic, noisy spectacles (an image often reproduced in popular representations of financial markets, including the movie *Trading Places*). To further facilitate communication in the pits, traders therefore supplemented verbal outcries with hand signals, and over time, traders at different exchanges developed locally refined ways of signalling by hand the amounts they wanted to buy or sell as well as other pieces of information relevant to their orders. (Speaking only of traders here is a matter of convenience. In reality the Chicago pits were populated by two groups of people: traders or market makers—also called "locals" in Chicago—who would trade on their own account, and brokers who would trade on behalf of clients.)

Given that seeing and hearing the others in the pit was critical to the ability of making the best possible deals, traders with a strong physical stature would have a natural competitive advantage. In her wonderful ethnography of Chicago pit trading, Caitlin Zaloom[1] observed that some traders would compensate for being physically smaller than others by adding inches of black foam to the soles of their shoes. Similarly, the analogue nature of pit trading rendered physical impression management important. Zaloom reported that pit traders would carefully train not only their voice (to be heard properly in the pit) but also their facial and other expressions. If other pit traders could sense from a trader's facial expressions or stressful voice that he (most traders were indeed men) was trying desperately to get out of a bad position, they could exploit this. Accordingly, traders would spend considerable efforts on learning to not give off unintended signals.

From a sociological perspective, one of the interesting aspects of the pits is that their ongoing interactions among the same groups of people over extended periods of time in effect meant that the pits' formal rules were overlaid with informal ones, based in part on trust and some form of gentlemanship. For example, a key formal rule in the Chicago pits was the "first" rule, according to which the first person a trader perceived to have responded to his buy or sell interest was also the person with whom the trade must be consummated. However, as several accounts of trading pits have detailed, including Zaloom's, traders would often circumvent this rule if the person who responded first had a poor reputation. As the first rule left plenty of room to the initiating trader's discretion, the rule could easily be evaded. While such examples testify to the social norms characterizing the pits—demonstrating that these norms existed alongside the cold capitalism of which financial markets are often seen to be emblematic—they also point to a problem often associated with this form of analogue trading: that it lent itself to collusion and manipulation. In fact, the quest for replacing pit trading with more electronic forms of trading was based in part on a critique of the kinds of manipulation that some pit traders were accused of.

The rise of electronic trading and the accompanying demise of the pits began in the 1990s, and with few exceptions this form of analogue trading has vanished and no longer forms a central part of modern capitalism—which is why using the past tense to describe pit trading is appropriate. However, as market manipulation has not disappeared with the rise of anonymous automation, one might be forgiven for looking back on the pits with a bit of nostalgia. For all their drawbacks, they demonstrated that high finance can be embedded in social relationships that might at times curb financial panic.

Note

1   Caitlin Zaloom, *Out of the Pits: Traders and Technology from Chicago to London* (Chicago: University of Chicago Press, 2006).

Property | Emma Sofie Brogaard

(Body), (Bondage), (Colonialism), **Debt, Extraction, Flesh,** (Land), **Mapping, Repossession,** (Resilience), **r>g,** (Sabotage), (Struggle), (Violence), (Whiteness)

Holes have been punched in the map of Denmark. It worries me deeply. Because of the fact that the ghettos are also ejecting tentacles out on the streets, where criminal gangs create unsafety. Into the schools, where neglected children are hanging on by a thread. Down into the municipal coffer, where income is scarcer, and expenses are greater than they need to be. And out into society where Danish values such as egalitarianism, liberality and tolerance are losing ground.[1]

Those were the words of the former prime minister of Denmark Lars Løkke Rasmussen a few months before he and the rest of the Danish government on 1 March 2018 announced the legislative strategy "One Denmark without parallel societies. No ghettos in 2030", or what has become known as the so-called "Ghetto package". With this package of laws and amendments, that was passed by a wide majority of the Danish parliament the same year, certain non-profit social housing neighbourhoods with more than 10,000 residents could be designated either "exposed housing area", "ghetto", or "tough ghetto", if they met two out of four criteria on education, employment, income, and crime. The defining metric, however, of whether a neighbourhood would be categorized as a "ghetto" was ethnicity: if more than 50% of the residents in an area were what are (still) termed "immigrants or descendants of non-Western countries", the area was labelled as a "ghetto". After four years, it changed to "tough ghetto".

With this designation, an area is subject to various provisions in order to change the assumed "homogeneous residential constitution",[2] including economic sanctions, special local laws such as obligatory daycare for children from the age of one, the doubling of criminal sentencing, and the requirement to reduce the family housing units to 40% by 2030, by way of a strategy of either "development" or "demolition". The latter entails forced eviction and relocation of residents, sale to private investors, and tearing down buildings to make room for new private construction. In effect, in 2020 this meant the demolition of 3,745 residential units, privatization of 730 residential units, affecting around 11,000 people.[3]

The highly discriminatory and stigmatizing implications and effects of these laws have faced criticism in Denmark as well as internationally. Perhaps most noticeably, the network of residents Almen Modstand has organized resistance on a variety of levels,[4] but also other organizations, lawyers, and researchers have expressed their critical concerns, and Danish media has often quoted the Danish sociologist Aydin Soei for calling the law the "biggest social experiment ever launched by the Danish welfare state".[5] In 2020, a group of residents from the neighbourhood Mjølnerparken in central Copenhagen sued the Ministry of Social Affairs and Housing for ethnic discrimination. The same year UN human rights experts urged "Denmark to halt the continuous sales of 'ghetto' buildings" and levelled a strong critique of the ill-defined term "non-Western" as it "disproportionately means Denmark's non-white, non-European ethnic populations", which raises "serious concerns of discrimination based on race, ethnicity, national origin, and other protected grounds".[6]

Yet, the critique of the so-called "Ghetto package's" clear violation of right of equality before the law seems to have largely peeled off the changing Danish governments. Although, in 2021, there was a legislative altering of the "Ghetto package" in which the terminology was changed from explicitly using the controversial term "ghetto"—Denmark was the *only* country in the world to use it in an official definition[7]—to now targeting "parallel societies", "prevention areas", and "transformation areas".[8] However, the defining criterion "non-Western" remains unchanged, and the measures to "enhance cohesion in Denmark"[9] by developing or demolishing low-income, largely Muslim minority neighbourhoods in non-profit social housing were increased.

"All property is loss because all property is the loss of sharing,"[10] write Stefano Harney and Fred Moten in *All Incomplete*. In the instance of the laws on "parallel societies", this claim seems on point: to sell off non-profit family housing units—in Danish termed *almennyttige boliger*, which also translates as "common housing" or "housing of public utility"—to private investors is a concrete loss of large parts of the non-profit social housing sector. A sector previously excepted from financial speculation, exactly with the purpose of securing good, affordable housing to the growing Danish working class after the end of World War II.[11] This propertization of housing that used to be common, public, social, non-profit, is undeniably a loss of something shared, a loss for/of a state of welfare, a state of law, not to mention the obvious loss of shared life, living, home, and community for the residents.

But the loss of sharing is not only a consequence of property. It is a loss foundational to the concept of property that has come to constitute Western modernity and its individuals, according to Harney and Moten. Following their argument, the "Package on parallel societies" does, thus, not only pose a problem of a breach of a fundamental juridical principle of equality before the law, although it certainly also does that. It also poses a crucial question of whether the law has ever concerned everyone.

Beginning with the English jurist John Locke and his concept of the mind as *tabula rasa*, Moten and Harney unfold how Enlightenment interiority emerges in the conquest of owning, thus filling this supposed emptiness. "For this emptiness to become private property," they write, "it must be filled with and located in the coordinates of space and time. Space emerges as the delimitation of what is mine, and time begins with the theft and imposition of when it became mine."[12] What enables the mind to take possession of itself is its capacity to take possession of something beyond itself, its ability to "grasp property". Possession and self-possession thus constitute a reciprocal circuit of the enlightened individual, a feedback logic, wherein the more someone owns, the more they own themselves, which, again, makes them capable of owning even more.

This individuation, however, is only for those who from the outset are granted the ability to self-possess. As the principles of Enlightenment dualism prescribes, the contours of the rational (transcendental, universal, singular, etc.) individual appears when contrasted against a background of those (immanent, particular, plural, etc.) others, who are presumed to lack that ability. Possession and individuation run in tandem with dispossession and subjugation, and the genres of Man, as Sylvia Wynter would have it,[13] are defined against those racialized, gendered others who are consistently excluded from entering the category of the Human.

"This is to say that from the outset, the ability to own—and that ability's first derivative, self-possession—is entwined with the ability to make more productive,"[14] Harney and Moten

continue, emphasizing Locke's labour theory of property in
this line of reasoning. This theory appears in the context of
land tenure, is derived from the principle of usufruct in Roman
law, and it posits that someone can be granted the ownership
over a piece of land if they, by way of their labour, can improve
the productivity of that land. In order to do so, earth must
be reduced to its measurable and manageable productivity,
a violent reduction that requires a double-edged process of
speciation: speciation of earthly generativity that submits it
to "techniques of domination that isolate and enforce particular increases in and accelerations of productivity" and
speciation of (necessarily European) man, "who imposes
speciation upon himself, in an operation that extracts and
excepts himself from the earth in order to conform his supposed dominion over it".[15] In other words that "racialization
is present in the very idea of dominion over earth; in the very
idea and enactment of this exception; in the nuts and bolts of
possession-by-improvement".[16]

Speciation, differentiation, racialization, segregation constitute the (literal) ground from which Western modernity is
growing, and is foundational to the very ideas of possession,
ownership, property. Not only is property of earth, land, and
all the capacities within it deeply entangled with the properties of the self, but this circuit is regulated by a capitalist idea
of improvement (or, say, productivity, growth, progress, uplift,
etc.). Meaning that *proper* individuality, with the juridical
and moral attributes of political status and rights it entails,
is shaped through the extractive mechanisms of what Cedric
Robinson in 1983 termed *racial capitalism*.[17]

Within this onto-epistemological configuration of the
world, the principle of possession-by-improvement legiti-
mizes the ability for someone to own what belongs to someone else, or what didn't belong to anyone, and furthermore

allows for the consideration of someone else *as* property. In other words a principle that has underpinned the violence of colonialism, of the destructive extraction of natural resources, what(or whom)ever that concept might include, that has caused Moten and Harney to quote Hortense Spillers for saying that "the transatlantic slave trade was the supply chain of the Enlightenment", and that has led Cheryl Harris to identify whiteness as a form of property in itself.[18]

To be regarded improper, on the other hand, is thus to be presumed to lack the ability of, or to refuse, improvement within and beyond oneself, as Harney and Moten elaborate:

Continuous improvement is the metric and metronomic meter of uplift. Those who won't improve, those who won't collectivize and individuate with the correct neurotic correctness, those who do the same thing again, those who revise, those who tell the joke you've heard and cook the food you've had and take the walk you've walked, those who plan to stay and keep on moving, those who keep on moving wrong—those are the ones who hold everybody back, fucking up the production line that's supposed to improve us all. They like being incomplete. They like being incomplete and incompleting one another. Their incompleteness is said to be a dependency, a bad habit. They're said to be partial, patchy, sketchy. They lack coordinates. They're collectively uncoordinated in total rhythm. They're in(self)sufficient.[19]

When Lars Løkke Rasmussen presented a plan to enhance the social cohesion in Denmark, with the object being supposed "parallel societies" and the aim of having "no ghettos in 2030", based on the often repeated argument, that also disturbingly opens this entry, that there are "holes in the map of Denmark" and that "Danish values ... lose ground", the resonances of this Enlightenment legacy are almost palpable.

The cohesion of the social, of a certain (yet unspecified) idea of Danishness, a shared set of values that binds together the nation, is in this argument delineated as proper ground, emplotted space and time, coordinates on a map—that *someone* has punched holes in. And that someone, who is without coordinates, who resides in the holes on the map, on the lost ground, who "huddles together in ghetto areas",[20] is, according to this reasoning, necessarily *improper*. This uncoordinated impropriety is exactly perceived to be the result of the lack of ability or willingness to *improve*, or "actively participate",[21] as it is put on the first page of the draft bill. Such insufficient improvement, incomplete individuation, is, as Harney and Moten show, not only an obstacle to progress. It is seen as sabotage, terrorism, a planned subversion of the order of things, or as no one said better/worse than the former prime minister himself, as a tentacular entity, that causes criminality, exploits public funds, and corrupts values as equality, freedom, and tolerance: "A threat to *our* modern society",[22] as bluntly stated in the initiative.

The obvious question is what cohesion, tolerance, what equality and freedom, and for whom, is actually lost in this undertaking of property. But behind that lies a question of whether this loss is just an unfortunate casualty in the doing of the proper, as has become a widespread rhetoric in Denmark ("we discriminate you to help you"[23]), or, if this discriminating and racializing designation of impropriety in fact is constitutive of the proper, of capitalized Property, of the very capacity of claiming something like "modern society" as *ours*. And if so, at last, how does one collectively edit, endure, and end it in coalitional self-(in)sufficiency?

Notes

1 Lars Løkke Rasmussen, "Lars Løkke Rasmussens nytårstale 1. januar 2018", transcript of speech delivered at the Prime Minister's Office, Copenhagen, Denmark, 1 January 2018,

www.regeringen.dk/aktuelt/statsministerens-nytaarstale/lars-loekke-rasmussens-nytaarstale-1-januar-2018/ (my translation).

2   Government of Lars Løkke Rasmussen III (2016–2019), Prime Minister's Office, "Ét Danmark uden parallelsamfund. Ingen ghettoer i 2030", 1 March 2018, 12, www.regeringen.dk/media/4937/publikation_%C3%A9t-danmark-uden-parallelsamfund.pdf.

3   Farhiya Khalid, "4. Hvor skal vi så bo?", 30 March 2020, in *Mere end Mursten*, produced by Respons, podcast, MP3 audio, 12:10, www.responsmedie.dk/mere-end-mursten-afsnit-4/.

4   See more about Almen Modstand at www.almenmodstand.dk/.

5   Farhiya Khalid, "4. Hvor skal vi så bo?", 1:50 (my translation).

6   United Nations, "UN Human Rights Experts Urge Denmark to Halt Contentious Sale of "Ghetto" Buildings", UN press release, 23 October 2020, www.ohchr.org/en/press-releases/2020/10/un-human-rights-experts-urge-denmark-halt-contentious-sale-ghetto-buildings.

7   Anna Mikaela v. Freiesleben, "Et Danmark af parallelsamfund: Segregering, ghettoisering og social sammenhængskraft", (PhD dissertation, University of Copenhagen, 2016), 127.

8   Ministry for the Interior and Housing, Kaare Dybvad Bek, "L 23 Forslag til lov om ændring af lov om almene boliger m.v.", enacted 23 November 2021, www.ft.dk/samling/20211/lovforslag/L23/som_vedtaget.htm.

9   Government of Lars Løkke Rasmussen III, "Ét Danmark", 4.

10   Stefano Harney and Fred Moten, *All Incomplete* (Colchester, New York, Port Watson: Minor Compositions, 2021), 14.

11   Farhiya Khalid, "2. Drømmen om bedre boliger", interview with associate professor Troels Schultz Larsen, *Mere end Mursten*, 08:29.

12   Harney and Moten, *All Incomplete*, 16.

13   Sylvia Wynter, "Unsettling the Coloniality of Being/Power/Truth/Freedom: Towards the Human, after Man, Its Overrepresentation—An Argument", *CR: The New Centennial Review 3*, no. 3 (2003), 257–337.

14   Harney and Moten, *All Incomplete*, 29.

15   Ibid.

16   Ibid., 21.

17   Cedric J. Robinson, *Black Marxsism: The Making of the Black Radical Tradition*, third edn (Chapel Hill, NC: University of North Carolina Press, 2000).

18   Cheryl I. Harris, "Whiteness as Property", *Harvard Law Review* 106, no. 8 (1993), 1707–1791.

19   Harney and Moten, *All Incomplete*, 41.

20   Government of Lars Løkke Rasmussen III, "Ét Danmark", 5.

21   Ibid., 4.

22   Ibid., 5.

23   Farhiya Khalid, "2. Drømmen om bedre boliger", 2:53 (my translation).

R

r>g

Repossession

Resilience

Risk

Rollover

r>g | Goldin+Senneby

(Art), Interest, Money, Property

There are some people who own so much that they don't need to work. But there are many more people who do need to work. They work hard just to survive. Sometimes they think that if they work even harder, they can also own enough to not work. They can just own. You know the owners—they lunch, they shop, they take vacations from their cycles of lunching and shopping. Often, they are just like poor people who sleep, eat, and roam the earth searching for meaning in their lives, except they are not poor.

In 2013 the French economist Thomas Piketty revealed a startling statistic in his *Capital in the Twenty-First Century*: since antiquity, the rate of return on capital has always been higher than the rate of economic growth, which is to say that it has always been more rewarding to own rather than to work. The value of investing what you own always exceeds that of working for what you might eventually own. The only identifiable exception was in the late twentieth century, when, for a short time following World War II, the value of labour peaked slightly above that of capital in a tendency towards relative income equality. Which is to say that, for a short time in documented history—in 1970s Sweden, for example—work paid better than money. According to Piketty's projections, that time is now over, and we are sliding back to inequalities not known since antiquity—what Marx called primitive accumulation. Yet, what is perhaps most surprising in Piketty's study is how exceptional—how special, and how fragile—that small moment was when one would be better off working than owning.

In 2017 the artists Goldin+Senneby entered an international competition set up by Public Art Agency Sweden to develop a public artwork for an underground rail station to be built as part of one of the largest construction projects in Gothenburg's history. The colossal production budget of 7 million kr (approximately €700,000) must have appealed to the two artists who have developed numerous works on financial mechanisms. For their public art project, they proposed to invest the entirety of this budget in a foundation, which would generate sufficient capital gains to pay a full-time salary for a single person. This single person would be employed at Korsvägen station, yet the position would hold no specified duties or responsibilities beyond checking in at the beginning of each working day at Korsvägen Station and then checking

Figure 45.1   Goldin+Senneby, "Eternal Employment". (detail from proposal: "working light", visualized by Anna Heymowska, 2017; commissioner: Public Art Agency Sweden/the Swedish Transport Administration)

out at the end of the day. A "working light" installed throughout the station would notify the public when the employee
would be at work.

One can only imagine the uproar in Sweden when their
project was appointed as one of the winners of the competition. Old Social Democrats accused them of using financial
realism to mock the transcendental accomplishments of the
welfare state. Neoliberal "progressives" accused them of wasting taxpayers' money to stage a nostalgic return to that same
welfare state. But many others in Sweden were probably deeply
moved, and perhaps even shocked, to consider that a functioning socialism could emerge from financial calculation.
After all, well-distributed resources under socialism did not
come from God, just as unequally distributed resources under
neoliberalism did not come from an interest in the common-
wealth. How uncanny Eternal Employment is: a functional
monument to the bygone aspirations of social democracy that
implants a fully functioning welfare model within capital itself.

Brian Kuan Wood

Repossession | Johanna Isaacson

(Bondage), (Chicago), (Deindustrialization), **Property**, (Social Reproduction), (Violence)

"Myth is constituted by the loss of the geographical quality of things … the more events are wrenched from their constitutive geographies, the more powerful the mythology." Neil Smith

"What hauntings result when an entire community becomes a ghost?" Tananarive Due

Repossession is repetition, cycling, recurrence—capitalist violence as eternal return. Eviction, occupation, predatory profit loop endlessly forming punctual centrifugal horrors, pushing "surplus" people *out* into crushing debt, homelessness, bare life. Yet this movement creates waves of centripetal reaction, proving that people cannot simply be cleansed and expunged—repossession as resistance, as riot, as payback, as swarm.

Repossession is *horror*—"the struggle for recognition of all that our civilization represses or oppresses"[1]—and manifests as such.

Repossession *looms*, constantly threatening racialized expropriation, "a structural component of the ongoing reproduction of the capital relation through dispossessive processes conditioned by exploitation but not reducible to it".[2]

Repossession *zombifies*, as "part of a larger ideological frame that normalizes state violence and conceals the fundamental inequalities of late capitalism".[3]

Repossession *snatches bodies*, "*confiscating* capacities and resources and *conscripting* them into capital's circuits of self-expansion".[4]

Repossession *crushes cities*, creating and manipulating crisis, then launching "urban pioneers" who seek to "scrub the city clean of its working-class geography and history".[5]

Repossession *preys on pain*, draining living labour, then morphing into "accumulation by repossession", feeding on rent debt, asset stripping, and punitive enforcement while clearing the way for intensified capital investment and development.[6]

Repossession *massacres*, creating racialized, surplus populations who "will never be fully integrated into capitalist accumulation processes except as bodies to be policed, warehoused, or exterminated".[7]

Repossession *haunts houses*, depending on unwaged reproductive labour while withholding necessary resources and support, becoming a "free rider" on "activities of provisioning, care-giving and interaction that produce and maintain social bonds".[8]

And yet when all seems lost, repossession *resurrects the dead*, sparking insurrection. The riot, a "counterproposal of unmanageability", swells to confront the state's violent carceral solutions to crisis and surplus.[9]

In Nia Da Costa's 2021 version of *Candyman*, a folk hero arises to *repossess* the bodies and land treated as valueless nature by a rapacious gentrifying elite.

In the infamous Cabrini-Green towers, Chicago, 1977, a Black child goes about his daily reproductive labour, venturing into one of the massive building's basement laundry rooms. Outside, a swarm of cops menace, brandishing signs depicting their prey, the "Candyman", a monster that serves as pretence for their hostile occupation. It's no wonder that innocent Sherman Fields hides in the walls. When he emerges, startling the boy, the cops descend on him, killing him on the spot.

This is the film's only depiction of violence in the Cabrini-Green towers, once labelled a dangerous slum but rarely acknowledged as home to a wealth of collective social reproduction. When, in 1999, the decision was made to tear down the buildings and replace them with mixed-income housing, Mayor Daley claimed his "Plan for Transformation" was a gift to the poor, Black, tower residents: "I want to rebuild their souls." But the real story is one in which the soul-killing failures of the towers were foreordained.

As the Cabrini-Green towers filled with poor Black people, all funding for maintenance and social services evaporated, leaving the buildings decrepit and open to gang violence. Despite this craven abandonment, many who lived in the towers reported a feeling of belonging and collectivity. The towers were infamously associated with violence and blight, but rarely acknowledged as home to a wealth of collective social reproduction, "like a little village: everybody knew everybody," says a former inhabitant.[10]

After the towers fell, this social reproduction lost its collective dimension. The task of reproducing one's life became an act of drudgery and isolation, as residents were torn from their communities and pushed into even more segregated, under-resourced neighbourhoods or into abject homelessness. Even if a former Cabrini-Green tower resident managed to gain one of the few vouchers that allowed them to occupy the mixed-income housing that Daley claimed would "rebuild their souls", they faced horrific class hatred from "market rate" tenants who were bent on driving their new neighbours away by harassing them, calling in the police, and finding ways to mask their racist violence with gentrified language of concern about crime, traffic, and education.

As tenants were evicted, the Cabrini-Green towers were *repossessed*, razed, and transformed into lucrative privatized assets. The monster of finance capital went about its business of commodifying pain, speculating on loss, pushing its residents further into the grasp of market capitalism, the poverty industry and the debtfare state, under the capitalist logic of "accumulation by repossession".[11]

In *Candyman,* a kaleidoscopic shot takes us from these disappeared towers to the present day, where they have been replaced by sleek, high-rise apartments. Brianna Cartwright and Anthony McCoy, a beautiful, ambitious Black couple who have carved a precarious place for themselves in the Chicago art world, newly occupy one of these gentrified residences. But they don't make it past their house-warming party before Brianna's brother peels back the neighbourhood's shiny surface to reveal the ghosts beneath. Dimming the lights and igniting candles, he tells the campfire story of Cabrini-Green, once called "smokey hollow", "little hell", and then "combat alley". Here, by looking in the mirror and saying his name five times, one can conjure the murderous spirit of the Candyman.

Brianna and Anthony seem to have it all, but no amount of talent and beauty can save them from this haunting. They are not so much part of the art world as useful to it as sources of slickly packaged Black trauma. Anthony, once "the great Black hope of Chicago", is now considered yesterday's news and faces his own imminent obsolescence.

An agent threatens to cut Anthony off unless he searches out, subsumes, and excretes some new terrain of Black experience in a form suitable to entertain and profit the Chicago elite. It is with a mixture of craven ambition, desperation, and enthralled fascination that Anthony dives into the history of Cabrini-Green, searching for artistic inspiration. Drawn to the neighbourhood's remaining row houses, he is stung by a bee, the agent of death for the original Candyman (1992). Pierced by history, he will lose his place as a tokenized artist in Chicago's public-facing legends of meritocracy and class mobility. However, as the new incarnation of the vengeful

Candyman, he will gain his footing in the city's subterranean legacy of racial retribution, the swarm. In the end he will *repossess* the grounds of Cabrini-Green, if not for the living then for the dead.

Meanwhile, voices of the dead are channelled by William Burke, the now-grown boy who inadvertently led the cops to the innocent Candyman lurking in the tower walls. One of the few remaining poor residents of the former Cabrini-Green neighbourhood, Burke is stuck in Sisyphean cycles of isolated and low-waged reproductive labour, working alone in a laundromat. While Anthony is caught in his own uncanny spin cycle—returning obsessively to the remains of the original Cabrini-Green housing, ravenous to learn more about the Candyman—William becomes the willing Virgil in Anthony's Dante-esque descent.

Punctured by William's stories, sharp as the infected bee sting, Anthony is now repossessed with the avenging spirit of history. Necrosis oozes and spreads over his body as he moults from upwardly mobile artist into the nascent form of the Candyman. He still creates art that depicts the suffering of the Black community, but it no longer fortifies the walls of the gentrified buildings on which it hangs. Instead, his art is passage work, through which the Candyman can emerge and take his revenge. In a swank uptown gallery, Anthony's new work penetrates boundaries, appearing as a mirror, but opening into its own microcosmic gallery of pain. Any bored art world denizen may gaze into the reflective surface and summon their own doom, individually re-enacting the fatalistic cycles of denial and retribution brought on by racist expropriation.

The ever-innovating city must be kept alive by an ever-innovating commoditization of Black trauma, and, as the ice-cold critic judging Anthony's work puts it, the "knee-jerk cliches" of everyday suffering are of no use to this project. But

Anthony is no longer making art for the critic's gaze. When the Candyman tears through the bodies of his art world overlords, they are baffled by their vulnerability. Bleeding out, one young hipster can't believe she has left the simulacra of gentrification. Jerrica's last words are: "is this real?"

Seeking this "real", Anthony haunts the remnants of Cabrini-Green. He learns that Candyman isn't a single being; he's "the whole damned hive" of racial capitalism's victims. William schools Anthony in the Candyman's series of repossessions, all bearing common scars of violence through ongoing accumulation by dispossession. One was killed during white housing riots in the 1950s, another lynched after he refused to be financially cheated by a white man, and several were executed in the name of defending pure, white womanhood. Each murder Anthony learns about served to justify the ongoing accumulation of land and resources, once thought to initiate capitalism as "primitive accumulation" but now understood as an unending form of dispossession.[12] The transformation of these victims into the Candyman turns the tables. From the ashes of racialized violence, a figure of retribution arises to expropriate the expropriators. The Candyman is both monster and victim, depriving whites of their once exclusive entitlement to fear, a paradoxical "sign of empowerment" in typical horror films.[13]

The scarred witness of Candyman's most recent lynching by the police, William remains in the neighbourhood as the griot who recites and preserves this historical litany of pain. He recounts the original Candyman, Daniel Robitaille, whose arm was sawn off and replaced with a hook before his assailants smeared him with honey, inciting a hive of bees to sting him into an unrecognizable mass of agony, which they then set on fire. The myth of Candyman is neither "real" nor "unreal": it's "how we deal with the fact that these things happened".

William can only repossess his territory and his story by continuing the cycle of death. He kidnaps Brianna, bringing her to the dilapidated husk of the Northside Stranger's Home Missionary Baptist Church, a former thriving social centre of the Cabrini-Green towers community. There, he forces her to witness Anthony's final transformation. As he saws off the Candyman's now completely atrophied hand, he meditates on the cycling etiolation of social reproduction in his community: "When something leaves a stain, even if you wash it out, it's still there. You can feel it. A thinning deep in the fabric. This neighbourhood got caught in a loop. This shit got stained in the exact same spot, over and over until finally it rotted from the inside out."

William's connection to laundry throughout the film is no accident. The companion to repossession, reproduction is twofold: it is repetitive and draining, but also, when done collectively, the essence of community. If Mayor Daley really wanted to "rebuild the souls" of the poor, he would have supported liveable, self-managed social reproduction, rather than cementing a whole community's dispossession.

The logical antithesis to collective social reproduction is the "accumulation by repossession" staged by the police, who have made the city of Chicago the "code word for racist fear".[14] And so William sets up the Candyman to wreak revenge on this most potent symbol of capitalist violence. Staging Anthony as the boogeyman responsible for the spate of recent murders, William knows intimately that the cops will shoot first and ask questions later. But William also knows that the artist's death will mark Anthony-as-Candyman's ultimate transformation into a force of retribution by and for the disappeared community of the Cabrini-Green towers.

After the inevitable police murder and attempted cover-up, Brianna too leaves her aspirational persona behind and enters the Candyman's realm of weaponized abjection. Now a perverse incarnation of the "final girl", she summons the Candyman to attack the police who have just killed off the last remnants of Anthony's humanity. In the final face-off, the cops and the Candyman (now lost in a throng of bees) are two swarms that represent the dual nature of repossession. There is the swarm that seeks to take everything from us and the swarm ("the writing on the walls, the sweet smell of blood on the street, the buzz that echoes in the alleyways") that will arise to take everything back.

Notes

1   Robin Wood, "An Introduction to the American Horror Film", in *On the Horror Film: Collected Essays and Reviews*, ed. Barry Keith Grant (Detroit, MI: Wayne State University Press 2018), 79.
2   Christopher Chen and Sarika Chandra, "Remapping the Race/Class Problematic", in *Totality Inside Out: Rethinking Crisis and Conflict under Capital*, eds. Kevin Floyd, Jen Hedler Phillis, and Sarika Chandra (New York: Fordham University Press, 2022), 154.
3   Travis Linnemann, Tyler Wall, and Edward Green, "The Walking Dead and Killing: Zombification and the Normalization of Police Violence", *Theoretical Criminology*, 18, no. 4 (2014), 507.
4   Nancy Fraser, "Expropriation and Exploitation in Racialized Capitalism: A Reply to Michael Dawson", *Critical Historical Studies* 3, no. 1 (2016), 163–178.
5   Neil Smith, *The New Urban Frontier: Gentrification and the Revanchist City* (New York: Routledge, 1996), 26–27.
6   Vickie Cooper and Kirsteen Paton, "Accumulation by Repossession: The Political Evictions under Austerity", *Urban Geography* 42, no. 5 (2021), 598.
7   Christopher Chen, "The Limit Point of Capitalist Equality: Notes Toward an Abolitionist Antiracism", *Endnotes 3* (September 2013).
8   Nancy Fraser, "Contradictions of Capital and Care", *New Left Review* 100 (July/August 2016), 101.

9   Joshua Clover, *Riot. Strike. Riot.* (Brooklyn, NY: Verso, 2016), 163.

10   Andrew R. Chow, "How Candyman Reclaims the History of Cabrini-Green", *Time*, 27 August 2021, https://time.com/6092375/candyman-cabrini-green-true-story/.

11   Vicky Cooper and Kirsteen Patton, "Accumulation by Repossession", *Urban Geography* 42, no. 5 (2021), 598.

12   David Harvey, "Accumulation by Dispossession", *The New Imperialism* (Oxford: Oxford University Press, 2003), 137–182.

13   Aviva Briefel and Sianne Ngai, "'How Much Did You Pay for This Place?' Fear, Entitlement, and Urban Space in Bernard Rose's *Candyman*", *Camera Obscura* (1996), 7.

14   Geo Maher, *A World without Police* (New York: Verso, 2021), 30.

Resilience | Tina Turnheim

Orthodoxy, Property

Figure 47.1 Still shot from the performance *Anastrophe Now*, theatre collective EGfKA, *Ringlokschuppen Ruhr*, 2017. (*source*: photograph courtesy of Stephan Glagla)

A: Dear audience, sustainability no longer has a main role to play: Resilience is the new imperative.

The key message is: crises cannot be prevented; we can only adjust to them.

Often unnoticed, resilience has replaced the discourse of sustainability as a strategy of system preservation. What kind of system that is ...

B: ... and why it should be worth saving is not even up for debate!

C: "Too Big to Fail!"—WELCOME TO RESILIENCE CAPITALISM!

A: Resilience originates from the Latin verb resilire: "to bounce back", "to rebound".

The word refers to the ability to cope with crises and to use them as an opportunity for growth. Make the most out of every crisis!

B: Since the end of the 1990s, the concept of resilience has been applied in the field of economics, especially in global financial and economic policy. After 9/11, and at the latest with the onset of the financial crisis in 2007, the term became ubiquitous in the public discourse ...

A: The pandemic then took the whole thing to the top!
Resilience is not only the ability to coping with a crisis but to return to the pre-crisis status quickly.

E: BACK TO NORMALITY!

D: Resilience is not only about overcoming a deeply stressful situation but also the said situation "proper functioning"—or even with "improvement in functioning".
So it's not just true for the US Army:
"Strong Minds, Strong Bodies: Building Resilience, Enhancing Performance!"

E: "Invincible like a Navy SEAL: resilience and mental toughness for success at the highest levels."

A and B: STRONGER THAN EVER.

C: Everything has to be resilient nowadays:
Urban planning no longer has to be sustainable. It has to be resilient.
Mitigating risk is the mark of resilient companies. Business has to be kept resilient globally.
Development policymakers must always consider the rising in sea levels.
Health experts the increase in pandemics ... well, theoretically speaking ...

B: Today, hardly anyone believes that capitalism can regulate or prevent its own crises ... If we assume that crises cannot be prevented, that the invisible hand of the market does not regulate everything, the solution is simple: everyone must become resilient.

A: Because politics barely goes beyond reactive crisis management, resilience appears to be the most appropriate way to deal with the prevailing crisis or disaster dynamics ... Theoretically speaking ...

D: Of course, it is vital to help people to protect themselves better against crises or even catastrophes. But it becomes absurd when the effort for "disaster preparedness" is used as a justification for not taking action against the causes of crises, e.g. against climate change or growing social inequality.

C: Everything has been privatized. Even responsibility. Even stress!

A: Resilience is OWNERSHIP.

E: Already school children are trained in resilience: they are expected to endure what is happening, ideally to let it bounce off them.

A: (shows a book cover) *The Resilience Book: How Parents Strengthen Their Children for Life*

B: *Resilience. The Strategy of the People Who Stand with Their Feet on the Ground: Mastering Crises with Inner Resilience*

D: *Resilience: The Undiscovered Skill of the True Achiever*

B: *Resilience – The Secret of Inner Strength: Developing Resilience and Living Authentically. With 12-Point Self-Test*

C: *Resilience: Inner Strength for Executives*

A: *The Resilience Training: For More Meaning, Satisfaction, and Motivation at Work*

E: *Resilience – Competence of the Future: Balancing Performance and Health*

C: *Resilience in Times of Extreme Change: Actively Shaping Personal and Social Change*

B: *Successful Leadership with Resilience: How to Steer Yourself and Your Team Serenely through Pressures and Crises*

C: *Get Resilient! Resilience Training through Hypnosis*

D: (to the audience) Don't laugh! These titles reveal a great deal of truth: they show what makes the resilience concept so attractive. Resilience primarily responds to unpleasant experiences: fears of failure, the feeling of not being able to meet the expectations of others and of oneself, the need to protect oneself in a world that is becoming increasingly insecure—in other words a growing lack of confidence in the state of affairs.

And therein lies the double-edged nature of the resilience concept: it responds to this unease and at the same time nourishes the conditions that allow this very unease to grow!

E: WELCOME TO THE SOCIETY OF FEAR! Insecurity is no longer the exception, but the norm.

I hope you enjoy catastrophes ... I recommend you do. There is no escape anyway. Hahaha.

A: SHOW YOU'RE NOT AFRAID! GO TO THE RESTAURANTS! GO SHOPPING!

B: Consider the great promises of freedom and happiness of modernity: they remain unfulfillable for more and more people.

C: *The Pursuit of Happiness* is History. Resilience is all about remaining functional.

A: Always. Remain. Functional. Always. Produce. Surplus Value.

B: Consider the economization of human existence:

Homo sapiens has already been transformed into *homo economicus*, who aligns his interests, her social relations, and their behaviour with business considerations.

D: *The entrepreneurial self* has no emotional anchor.

C: Failure keeps knocking on the door.

D: And that's what triggers fear: fear of failure. Fear of depression. Fear of fear. Failure from exhaustion. Failure from fear. I can't take it anymore! I'm so tired of all this shit!

A: The entrepreneurial self becomes the exhausted self.

C: Depression keeps knocking and knocking AND KNOCKING!!!

A, C, D, and E: (mutually) MEDITATE. EXERCISE. SOCIALIZE. EAT. PRAY. LOVE.

BECAUSE YOU'RE WORTH IT!

B: (begging) Please! Make me resilient. Make me a stand-up guy. I wish I could be an achiever.

Relieve me of my scruples. I am no longer resisting. I give up resistance.

I want to be brimming with resilience, even if I have to become a manager or a soldier to do it. Train me! Please! Help me to get rid of my emotions. I would like to embrace even the most traumatic experiences as an opportunity for self-discovery. I strive to become a fully resilient human being who can shake off even the most extreme circumstances.

E: There is no safety for more than one day.

A: When the future resembles an endless chain of threats, many weaponize themselves.

They transform into tanks.

D: (shouting in German) KÖRPERPANZER CHARAKTERPANZER GEFÜHLSPANZER!

B: Forget the *Anti-Oedipus*, forget Wilhelm Reich, forget Theweleit! Today, the therapeutic goal consists no longer in breaking down such armour.

Resilience programmes transform thin-skinned characters that are frightened and full of self-doubt into thick-skinned characters that are ready to conquer the world.

C: Whether at school or university, the battlefield is everywhere:

universities offer workshops on how to become a resilient researcher in a world marked by career stress, competition, and rejection.

D: Obviously, the goal of such programmes is no longer to create decent living conditions but to help people adapt individually to an increasingly hostile world.

A: Always. Remain. Functional. Always. Produce. Surplus Value.

C: The idea that has crept into the resilience discourse is simple: Resilience as a technique that can be taught and learned.

If you are willing to learn, you can become resilient.

E: (cheering) JUST DO IT!

B: (cheering in American English) YES, WE CAN!

C: If they fail to adopt, it's at the expense of the individuals themselves. It's all yours. The whole failure is yours.

No one else is responsible. It's not the economy, stupid!

B: (in British English) They are casting their problems at society. And, you know, THERE'S NO SUCH THING AS SOCIETY. There are individual men and women and there are families. And no government can do anything except through people, and people must look after themselves first. It is our duty to look after ourselves and then, also, to look after our neighbours.

E: Everyone is the architect of their own happiness. Or unhappiness. Or failure.

D: But paranoia was socialized. Resilience is an ideology of the permanent state of emergency.

A: Resilience stands for a new (old) conception of the state. One that ultimately cancels the social contract on which modern states were founded. It's the TIME OF THE WOLVES again ...

C: Social cohesion should no longer arise from the promise of progress and a better future but only from the common defence against an invisible enemy that has as many names as capitalism has crises.

D: (speaking through a megaphone) Caution, caution: the following is a warning from the OECD in times of high debt!

Risks have migrated from the banking system to other financial institutions and credit intermediaries.

These vulnerabilities require an integrated response to enhance the resilience of economies in the advent of adverse shocks. Be aware of Zombie firms!

A: AN EYE FOR AN EYE! Big Dada ... Data Brother is watching us.

B: (making a presentation) Come on guys, BUSINESS RESILIENCE IS A CHOICE AND IT CAN BE MANAGED! Most losses can be prevented.

Let me show you how to KEEP YOUR BUSINESS RESILIENT WORLDWIDE!

The 2021 FM Global Resilience Index ranks the overall resilience of 130 countries and territories based on their economy, risk quality, and supply chain.

Use it to make informed decisions about where you do business! Creating Resilience Means Creating Success! LET'S MOVE TOGETHER TOWARD GREATER RESILIENCE!

A strong resilience strategy must aim to:

strengthen existing crisis-management capabilities

take the various crisis phases (preparation, mitigation, and adaptation) into account

address the various levels (politics, economy, society), including their interplay.

May I introduce you to the magic formula?

GROWTH— CONSERVATION— COLLAPSE— REORGANIZATION.

E: Isn't it beautiful? SAY HELLO TO THE ETERNAL RETURN OF THE SAME!

C: (developing a choreography and inviting the others to join in) GROWTH— CONSERVATION— COLLAPSE— REORGANIZATION— GROWTH— CONSERVATION— COLLAPSE— REORGANIZATION— GROWTH— CONSERVATION— COLLAPSE— REORGANIZATION— GROWTH—CONSERVATION—COLLAPSE …

Rollover | Mikkel Krause Frantzen

(Crisis), **Debt,** (Oil), (Risk), (Struggle)

Anything can roll over if left standing on its own too long—or if faced with a force too strong to oppose. A cat can roll over on its back for any number of reasons. A musician can roll over to make room for a new musician and an emergent style of music—none other than Beethoven was asked to do so by Chuck Berry in 1956. This is *roll over*, as a verb: something you can do, or an action you are asked, ordered, or forced to do, roll over. It can thus be a neutral description and imperative both.

Etymologically, the word comes from roll (noun) plus over (preposition), the former dating back to the fourteenth century, and the Old French word *roeller*, the Medieval Latin *rotulare*, and the Latin *rotula*. The wheel is thus inscribed in the word, the roulette in the rollover.

In the parlance of our times, rollover as a noun is first and foremost a financial term with multiple meanings (more on that below). It is also the name of a movie from 1981: *Rollover*, directed by Alan J. Pakula, starring Jane Fonda and Kris Kristofferson. *Rollover* is a thriller about high finance, a melodramatic financial thriller as it were.[1] Here is a good, if rather hilarious, summary:

In Rollover, Hubbel Smith (Kris Kristofferson) is a no-nonsense financier put in charge of the recently bailed out Borough National Bank by First New York Bank chairman, Maxwell Emery (Hume Cronyn). Looking for a way to meet the failing bank's next dividend, Smith devises a plan to facilitate a loan for a company in even worse shape, Winterchem Enterprises. When Winterchem's chairman is murdered, his widow, Lee Winters, (Jane Fonda), an actress turned socialite, takes control of the company. Hubbel and Lee become financially and romantically involved, unearthing the circumstances behind her husband's murder, and a plot with dire implications for the world economy.

The tagline of the movie? "The most erotic thing in their world was money."

Rollover as a financial operation doesn't seem particularly *erotic*, though. It denotes the transfer of funds, of debt, of risk, from one period in time to the next. As such, rollover is integral to the metabolism of finance capital. Instead of liquidating a deposit on maturity, you can roll it over into a new deposit. Instead of repaying the principal, when a debt becomes due, you can enter into a new agreement. The former is what is about to happen in *Rollover*. The latter is what finance really is about: borrowing time, in the words of Wolfgang Streeck.[2] You buy yourself some extra time to pay off your debt, you postpone the payment—and in fact there is a certain eroticism to this temporal deferral, a sort of never-ending tantric jouissance, endless edging.

Any finance and/or tantra expert will tell you that there is a certain risk involved in this operation. Hence the term *rollover risk*. When a debt matures, you may *not* be able to find anyone who will lend you money to roll over the old debt into new debt. Maybe it is because the interest rates have risen in the meantime, or because your personal financial situation has changed, or because, at a more general level, liquidity has dried up and a credit crunch is on its way. In fact, the rollover risk pertains much more to objective than to subjective conditions; prevailing economic conditions have more to say than the financial condition of the individual borrower. In any case, for some reason or other, you—a person, a private company, a government—cannot refinance your due liabilities. Or you cannot do it without taking a severe hit. This is rollover risk. And the thing is, the more short-term debt you hold, the greater the risk. The financial crisis of 2007–08 was a perfect illustration of this. As scholars Zhiguo He and Wei Xiong write: "failure to roll over maturing debt is the direct cause of the collapses of both Bear Stearns and Lehman Brothers".[3]

But back to the film. Its first images are all about the aesthetics of finance, showing screens with currency rates (currency speculation was all the rage in the post-Bretton Woods world of the 1970s due to fluctuating exchange rates) and numbers everywhere. Then comes a tracking shot scanning a trading floor at night-time, empty except for a woman literally rolling (*roeller, rotulare, rotula*) a little cleaning trolley in the shadows—articulating, either unwittingly or in an act of deliberate subtlety, an axiom of the world of finance (and the representations thereof): work must remain unnamable, invisible, and in the margins. The camera pans again, and now it's morning and it's busy. Phones are ringing. There is a cacophonic chatter and a certain office buzz, as acoustic as it is visual. The movie wants to let its viewers know that we are in a hypermodern, technological setting with computers and phones everywhere and that finance is international: the traders on the phones are speaking—or trying to speak—German, French, Japanese, *jawohl, merci*.

The critics were not happy when the movie came out. "Is the Arab Euro-dollar really a good subject for movie banter?" *The New York Times* asked rhetorically. "Somehow, somebody thought so," the review continues. "In 'Rollover,' Kris Kristofferson and Jane Fonda play a banker and a board chairman who confer incessantly about financial matters at the multi-multi-megabuck level."[4] And in his influential *Movie Guide*, Leonard Maltin delighted in delivering this verdict: "Laughably pretentious, barely comprehensible drama about petrochemical heiress (and former film star) Fonda, banker-trouble-shooter Kristofferson, and their high-financial dealings. Cronyn excels as a cunning banker. A rare example of financial science fiction."[5]

It's rather striking to note the extent to which critics dismissed the movie on grounds of realism. The universe depicted by Pakula is outlandish, otherworldly, unrealistic, pure science fiction—or, in the words of *Variety*'s review: "there's a certain lack of reality".[6] Nonsense, gibberish, mumbo jumbo. But in reality, *Rollover* is, simultaneously, a grotesquely complex movie and a very simple movie. It is a movie about money, gold, and oil, indexing the financial reality of the aftermath of the oil crisis and embargo of 1973, when a number of oil-producing countries in the Arab world accumulated so many petrodollars that they did not know what to do with them. Suddenly, some oil sheiks simply had too much money.[7] This not only led to a recycling of a considerable amount of these petrodollars into the global financial system and American banks (as deposits, as loans) but also to a conversion of some of this money into gold. This, in turn, threatened to collapse the world—read: American—economy and the whole banking system, as it caused the value of the dollar to drop like a stone. This is a familiar plot to any reader of 1970s financial thrillers, whether written by Paul Erdman or Arthur Hailey or someone else.

The title of the movie refers to the specific moment when the aforementioned Arabs—portrayed, as expected, in an overly stereotypical and racist manner, with tents in the desert, Muslim calls to prayer sounding from an offscreen mosque, etc.—threaten to *not* roll over $95 million that they deposited in an account in the Borough National Bank in New York. This could and would create a great deal of panic in the bank, on Wall Street, and around the world, but the rollover *does* roll over, and everyone can breathe a sigh of relief. The Arabs kept their money deposits in the American bank. That's it, as far as the rollover of *Rollover* is concerned.

It could have been a lot more complicated. Clearly, Alan Pakula is not that interested in rollover as a technical term or strictly financial operation. He may have been aware that Western bankers were, at the time, scared witless that Arab deposits continued to be largely short term. In his 1979 book *How to Prosper during the Coming Bad Years*, prepper Howard Ruff writes: "The threat of withdrawal of Arab money from the New York bank is only one of several major potential banking problems as this book is written."[8] In a 1980 article, David Rockefeller, son of John D. Rockefeller, prophesied that "[w]hat we see ahead are treacherous economic seas and gale-force financial winds, strong enough to capsize even large, well-manned ships", before asking: "Is the wobbly world of international finance and banking about to be buried under a mountain of endlessly multiplying petrodollars?"[9] A similar question was asked in 1981 by George Goodman, writing under the pseudonym Adam Smith, in *Paper Money*: "What if the Arabs yanked the money the first of the month?"[10] Pakula may have been aware of this archetypical anxiety among New York bankers at the time, but his real interest and, by extension, the real drama of *Rollover* lie elsewhere.

The true risk in *Rollover* has nothing to do with rollover. At least not in the sense just indicated and described. The real drama is about the wheeler-dealer world of international finance. "I am not taking that rollercoaster again," says the villain Maxwell Emery, the lion of American banking and First New York Bank chairman who is out to set up Hub. The drama is about the game of finance, the roulette implicit in the rollover. "This is not some sort of game," someone says to Hub at a party at the beginning of the movie, to which Hub replies: "Yes, it is. That's exactly what it is", adding: "You can't beat the system, but you can win a game." Some win and some lose, and some do it quicker than others. And at the end of the movie, we get, like it was some Adam Curtis-documentary, full-blown panic, we get a "world economic crisis"; we get protests and riots; we get news images from Seoul, London, New York, Cairo. We are, the movie tells us, "at the edge of anarchy". But *whose* anarchy? Chaos and crisis for *whom* exactly? Can these riots be rolled over? Can the panic be postponed—and is this panic an effect of the system crashing or the cause of its collapse?

So many questions because of so many contradictory stories, told both by the film's director and its characters. At one point Maxwell Emery explains capital to Hub: "It's a force of nature, like gravity. Like the oceans. It flows where it wants to flow. This whole thing with the Arabs and gold is inevitable. We're just going with the tide." Watching after 2008, we recognize this statement as pure ideology. We know the people who, like Emery, say: in the face of finance, in the face of this force of nature, there is nothing to do but roll over.

More questions, proper ones: don't play with the end of the world, a banker from the West says to one from the Middle East at another point during *Rollover*—but what if that is all that's left to play with? What if, as the Arab banker and negotiator also points out to his Western interlocutor, it is only the end of the world as *you* know it? And what if even the hero, Kris Kristofferson's Hub, is wrong: what if the system *can* be beaten? What if the emergency break could be pulled on the rollercoaster ride of finance capital? What if the most erotic thing is not money but its negation?

Notes

1   See my forthcoming book on the subject: Mikkel Krause
     Frantzen, *The Birth of the Financial Thriller: Making a Killing in
     the 1970s* (Edinburgh: Edinburgh University Press, 2025).

2   Wolfgang Streeck, *Buying Time: The Delayed Crisis of Democratic
     Capitalism* (London: Verso, 2017).

3   Zhigou He and Wei Xiong, "Rollover Risk and Credit Risk",
     Journal of Finance, LXVII, no. 2 (2012), 391–430.

4   Janet Maslin, "KRIS KRISTOFFERSON AND JANE FONDA IN
     'ROLLOVER' ", *The New York Times*, 11 December 1981.

5   Leonard Maltin, *Leonard Maltin's Movie Guide – 2010 Edition*
     (New York: Plume Books, 2010), 1174.

6   https://variety.com/1980/film/reviews/rollover-1200424889/.
     Not everyone was critical though: "This seriously underrated
     movie sees Alan Pakula now locating the corridors of paranoia
     in the world of high finance, where money not only talks but
     shouts", https://ifi.ie/film/rollover/.

7   For more on oil—the embargo, the crisis—and the world of
     finance, see, for example: David M. Wright, *Oil Money: Middle
     East Petrodollars and the Transformation of US Empire,
     1967–1988* (Ithaka, NY: Cornell University Press, 2021); Helen
     Thompson, *Disorder: Hard Times in the 21st Century* (Oxford:
     Oxford University Press, 2022); Daniel Yergin, *The Prize: The Epic
     Quest for Oil, Money & Power* (Florence, MA: Free Press, 2008).

8   Howard Ruff, *How to Prosper during the Coming Bad Years* (New
     York: Times Books, 1979), 81.

9   David Rockefeller, "Business: World Bankers Juggle the Huge Oil
     Debts", *Time Magazine*, 3 March 1980.

10   Adam Smith, *Paper Money* (New York: Summit Books, 1981),
     251. In *Oil Money* David M. Wright tells the story of the head of
     the foreign department of a major New York bank who, to the
     question of how much one-year money the bank had received
     from Arab investors, exclaimed: "One-year money! ... I wish I
     could get it for more than 24 hours!" (Wright, *Oil Money*, 75–76).

S

Sacrifice

Speculation

Sacrifice | Max Haiven

Counterfeit, Gaming, Orthodoxy

In a sense the conspiracy theorists are right: we do live in a world of hideous human sacrifices, superintended by a financially enriched elite. But whereas the conspiracists hallucinate a coordinated cabal of evildoers, the more complex and the more disturbing truth is that the forms of human sacrifice that characterize financialization do not require (and would, in fact, be imperilled by) any such intentional orchestration of efforts. Rather, financialized capitalism must be reckoned as a *system*, one that reproduces a set of imperatives, enticements, rewards, and punishments for competitive economic behaviour that only in sum creates an overall movement of capitalism towards a sacrificial world order. No individual needs to utter the prayers or wield the dagger for this system to enact human sacrifice. And whereas the conspiracist imagination fixates on the purity of the innocent victim, notably children, today's sacrifices are not only individuals in all their complexity but messy and entangled entities: the climate, the biosphere, the cultural fabric, the very possibility of the future.

The urge to misimagine systemic violence as the work of wicked individuals is not new; it is both symptomatic and constitutive of capitalism's development. Marx and later Marxist analyses of anti-Semitism indicate how residual racist myths can furnish an explanation for socio-economic pain and uncertainty among both elites and the exploited.[1] The recent QAnon "conspiracy fantasy", which has gained terrifying worldwide popularity, rehashes many of these tropes with its seductive participatory narrative about a secret war being waged by the righteous against a cabal of blood-drinking child abusers.[2]

Michael Taussig has studied the reappearance of the devil in rural Latin America during periods of seismic economic change and social dislocation.[3] Silvia Federici's account of the role of the witch trials in the development of capitalism's phase of "primitive accumulation" likewise details how accusations that specific people (mostly but not exclusively women) were engaged in ritual and conspiratorial human sacrifice were key to the destruction of the commons and the uniquely capitalist renovation of patriarchy.[4] In these cases, a charismatic narrative of human sacrifice, focusing on the evil intentions of individuals or groups, distracts political attention from the broader sacrificial social order.

The rise of conspiracism is typically the result of a combination of, on the one hand, a genuine effort by suffering people to understand a world that seems to be collapsing all around them and, on the other hand, the efforts of predatory manipulators, grifters, and entrepreneurs. The line between the two is rarely sharp. This line is even more blurred in an era of financialization, where each subject is exhorted to recast themselves as a speculator and manipulator. The QAnon phenomenon, for example, sees a fluid movement between true believer and online huckster, thanks in no small part to the opportunities provided to monetize attention by corporate social media platforms.[5] But to focus on the cynicism and opportunism is to lose sight of the reality that such theories in fact take root not in obedience to dogma but in a misaimed critical thinking, in a scepticism towards dominant narratives, in a desire to discover and interrogate the workings of power, and in a more or less genuine humanitarian wish, all gone terribly wrong.

At stake is the poverty of a conspiratorial theory of power, which, in line with dominant neoliberal narratives, sees the world as defined by the intentional actions of powerful individual actors, rather than a more capacious critical theory that can analyze systemic and institutional power and, crucially, their contradictory nature.

Yet on a discursive level, a narrative of sacrifice has important systemic functions within such a system.[6] As Wendy Brown notes, under both the economic and cultural shifts of financialization, the notion of sacrifice has been crucial.[7] Individuals are expected to sacrifice time, energy, pleasure, and health on the altar of *homo oeconomicus* in the hope that that idealized figure of competitive risk taking might offer his dark blessing in the form of a return on investment. On a broader political level, the forms of neoliberal policy and austerity, which might have once been cloaked in a rhetoric that suggested that a sacrifice today might bring better tomorrows, now admit that sacrifice is here to stay. In reaction, resurgent far-right and fascist political formations today thrive in the environment of endless sacrifice. They gain traction by claiming only they can clearly see and manage the sacrifices that must be made for security: the restoration of the patriarchal family, murder on the border, expulsion, war.[8] It's sacrifice or be sacrificed.

And yet behind and beyond these more ideological mobilizations of sacrifice is a deeper truth: the term financialization indicates what can be framed as a vast global order of human sacrifice. Here, thanks to the abstract movements of gamed markets, millions of people are condemned to death from completely preventable diseases or privation, or by the effects of anthropogenic climate chaos derived almost entirely from the past centuries of capitalist accumulation. Encoded in the interlaced digital ledgers of this financial empire is an authorless, decentralized sacrificial order with a metahuman bloodlust, hidden in plain sight. It's a truth both obvious to everyone and also somehow unspeakable that the poor will die and suffer to protect the privileges of the rich and the competitive vitality of corporations.

Perhaps, however, while sacrifice offers an evocative and provocative metaphor for financialization's forms of lethal indifference and unintended humanitarian and ecological catastrophes, it is a poor analytic tool. After all, can it be said to be human sacrifice if it is not intentional and not accompanied by religious ritual? Does the spectre of human sacrifice simply rehearse a long-standing vulgar critique of capitalism that, by calling up the spectre of an allegedly premodern barbarism, seeks to cast down a hyper-modern political-economic system?

But maybe we have learned to think of human sacrifice the wrong way. Most of what we know about the practice of human sacrifice is irredeemably clouded by modern colonial prejudices that have sensationalized the violent practices of non-Western human sacrifice while ignoring or rationalizing Western, modern forms of human sacrifice. A vast diversity of civilizations practised some form of human sacrifice at some time in their history, and for very different reasons.[9] While the practice perhaps seemed normal or at least justified in the eyes of those who practised it, it has perennially been used by outside observers as evidence of barbarism. More often than not, it has been pointed to by outsiders and rivals as a justification for war or in some sense as a distraction from the accusers' own sacrificial practices. As Tzvetan Todorov noted, the sensational scenes painted by the conquistadors of the Aztec "society of sacrifice" helped justify that empire's liquidation while at the same time mystifying the Spanish "society of massacre".[10] I have written elsewhere about how the human sacrifices practised by the Edo Kingdom (located in what is today Nigeria) were used by the British Empire as a justification to, in 1898, invade and destroy that Kingdom, part of a broader tendency towards a kind of capitalist imperialism that sacrificed millions of lives around the world on the altar of white supremacy Christianization and "free trade", though of course it never understood itself as such.[11]

It is often assumed that the heinous practice of human sacrifice originated in the dark crypt of prehistoric mysticism. But recent evidence seems to suggest that, more often than not, orders of human sacrifice took form as societies became more stratified and imperialistic.[12] Though it may have been disguised in the trappings of religious necessity to appease fickle gods and ensure the continued vitality of the nation, typically elites used human sacrifice as a dramatic means to intimidate the lower classes, vassals, and enemies. It was a convenient method for eliminating potential rivals and usurpers and for disguising state terror as cosmological necessity.

If such arguments are to be believed, human sacrifice was always already about what we, today, might call "risk management" on at least two levels. On the one hand, the elites who practised it used it as a means to eliminate risks to their continued dominance and enrichment; on the other, they presented it to the world as an act undertaken for the public good, a regrettable necessity to control the uncertainty of supernatural providence. Were the sacrifice not made, the gods might be angered, or might starve, portending doom for a whole society. It helps that, often, those sacrificed are not even considered fully human at all.

How unfamiliar and exotic to us are these metaphysical justifications, really? Today, defenders of global financialized capitalism legitimate its profound sacrificial violence with recourse to the idea that, somehow, to interrupt or intervene in it would be to jeopardize the spirit of economic growth: progress that is said to be universally beneficial. Few today would earnestly parrot the maxims of turn-of-the-millennium capitalist optimism (e.g. "a rising tide lifts all boats"). Yet in the dominant neoliberal ideological framework, the progress of the market (its "creative destruction" and "disruptive innovation") is said to lead to greater overall economic growth, technological innovation, and a higher standard of living. It is even rumoured to lead to a "capitalist peace" and the "end of history", where humanity's inherent competitive and acquisitive urges are safely sublimated into market activity which, in aggregate, are universally beneficial.[13]

At stake for me in this comparison is the possibility that the cosmological dimensions of financialized capitalism might come into better view. Of course, financial markets are, in an extreme way, made up of a multitude of competing hyper-rational decisions.[14] Yet, while market philosophers like Hayek predicted that, left to their own devices, such markets would usher in a rational political-economic order, the reality is a largely irrational order where growing gaps in wealth are accompanied by profound ecological sacrifices as well as humanitarian catastrophes.[15] According to those thinkers, the market represented the apotheosis of reason, the emergence, for the first time in human history, of a kind of metahuman intelligence free of prejudice, superstition, and bias.

At some level a global market-dominated society justifies the human sacrifices it demands in terms of a kind of regrettable but ultimately providential cosmological necessity: it is indeed terrible that those children died of malnutrition or preventable disease, but to prevent it would be to disrupt the transit of the holy market (by, say, raising taxes or by regulating free trade). Such profane actions would, ultimately, have *more* catastrophic consequences. Such consequences, we are told, might not only include the stagnation of economic growth but the appearance of the demonic forces of unfreedom.

If we look at the global financialized capitalist system from the right angle, squint, and defamiliarize ourselves with the normalized justifications, it appears as an empire built on human sacrifice not unlike any other. But what is perhaps different in the reigning cosmology of the market is how it shapes our actions and dispositions, whether we believe in the finer points of its theology or not. Financialization encourages each of us to adopt the dispositions of the imagined financier, the risk manager. I have suggested that this contributes to the conditions within which certain far-right and post-fasicst ideologies can find footing.[16] The daily experience of uncertainty, insecurity, individualism, and competitiveness reinforces a cosmological view of a universe made up of similarly uncertain, competitive, speculative beings.[17]

Within such an imagined world, ever greater human sacrifice can be envisioned and justified. The losers of a competitive system are now recast not as momentarily unlucky but fundamentally flawed, poor imitations of the idealized figure of financialization. Worse still, the dependency of the losers of financialization on the winners is, in a world of increasingly scarce resources and relentless competition, a threat to the continued success (and survival) of the winners. Financialization is in some sense a global order of human sacrifice in which we are all both participants and potential victims. Like the sacrificial empires of old, ours justifies its bloodletting in the name of cosmological necessity: the market demands it, and to fail to heed or feed the market would be to invite both personal and collective doom. In other sacrificial empires elites use mystical theology and gory spectacle to consolidate their rule, and claim that their sacrificial acts are in the public interest. Today, the sacrificial blade and altar are dematerialized and diffused. We are all, to greater or lesser extents, compelled to participate, even those who are destined to be sacrificed. Their sacrifice will typically take the form of invisibilized abandonment, rather than hyper-visible ritual. Yet like other orders of sacrifice, it stems from a largely unquestioned cosmology, a cosmology no one might actually fully believe in and yet which still structures our imaginations.

For Sylvia Wynter, the cosmology of *homo oeconomicus* is one whose origins stem from the Euroepan colonial project and transatlantic slave trade at the birth of the capitalist-imperialist system.[18] This cosmology, which I am here associating with sacrificial financialization, is both fundamentally built on racist notions of what it means to be human but also, in a global neoliberal age, suggests that *homo oeconomicus* is a model that all people can and should strive to emulate and embody. But its success in capturing the imagination and shaping the material world is bound up with the way it vanquishes or delegitimates many other "genres" of being human practised by other civilizations, which it takes to simply be poor, unreflexive emulations of the truth of *homo oeconomicus*. If we are to have a chance of surviving the cosmology of financialization, we must do nothing less than reimagine what it means to be human. Such a reimagining would be a material practice of rebellion and experimentation and would necessarily imply not the end of sacrifice but a different mode of sacrifice, perhaps more in line with George Bataille's theories that understand sacrifice as among the highest purposes for any society.[19]

Notes

1   Moishe Postone, "Anti-Semitism and National Socialism", in *Germans and Jews since the Holocaust*, ed. Anson Rabinbach and Jack Zipes (New York: Holmes & Meier, 1986), 356–361.

2   Wu Ming 1, La Q Di Qomplotto: *Come Le Fantasie Di Complotto Difendono Il Sistema* (Rome: Alegre, 2021).

3   Michael Taussig, *The Devil and Commodity Fetishism in South America*, thirtieth anniversary edn (Chapel Hill, NC: University of North Carolina Press, 2010).

4   Silvia Federici, *Caliban and the Witch: Women, Capitalism and Primitive Accumulation* (New York: Autonomedia, 2005).

5   Wu Ming 1, *La Q Di Qomplotto*.

6   Keren Wang, *Legal and Rhetorical Foundations of Economic Globalization: An Atlas of Ritual Sacrifice in Late-Capitalism* (London and New York: Routledge, 2019).

7   Wendy Brown, "Sacrificial Citizenship: Neoliberalism, Human Capital, and Austerity Politics: Neoliberalism, Human Capital, and Austerity Politics: Wendy Brown", *Constellations* 23, no. 1 (March 2016), 3–14, https://doi.org/10.1111/1467-8675.12166.

8   Max Haiven, "From Financialization to Derivative Fascisms: Some Cultural Politics of Far-Right Authoritarianism in an Era of Unmanageable Risk", *Social Text* 41, no. 2 (2023), 45–73, https://doi.org/10.1215/01642472-1038320S7.

9   Jan Nicolaas Bremmer (ed.), *The Strange World of Human Sacrifice* (Leuven: Peeters, 2007).

10   Tzvetan Todorov, *The Conquest of America: The Question of the Other*, trans. Richard Howard (New York: Harper & Row, 1984).

11   Max Haiven, *Palm Oil: The Grease of Empire* (London and New York: Pluto, 2022).

12   Joseph Watts, Oliver Sheehan, Quentin D. Atkinson, Joseph Bulbulia, and Russell D. Gray, "Ritual Human Sacrifice Promoted and Sustained the Evolution of Stratified Societies", *Nature* 532, no. 7598 (April 2016), 228–231, https://doi.org/10.1038/nature17159.

13   Gerald Schneider and Nils Petter Gleditsch (eds.), *Assessing the Capitalist Peace* (London: Routledge, 2013); Francis Fukuyama, *The End of History and the Last Man* (New York: Perennial, 1993).

14   Edward LiPuma and Benjamin Lee, *Financial Derivatives and the Globalization of Risk* (Durham, NC, and London: Duke University Press, 2004).

15   Randy Martin, *Knowledge LTD: Towards a Social Logic of the Derivative* (Philadelphia: Temple University Press, 2015).

16   Haiven, "From Financialization to Derivative Fascisms".

17   Aris Komprozos-Athanasiou, *Speculative Communities* (Chicago, IL, and London: University of Chicago Press, 2022).

18 Sylvia Wynter and Katherine McKittrick, "Unparalleled Catastrophe for Our Species? Or, to Give Humanness a Different Future: Conversations", in *Sylvia Wynter: On Being Human as Praxis*, ed. Katherine McKittrick (Durham, NC, and London: Duke University Press, 2015), 9–89.

19 Georges Bataille, *The Accursed Share: An Essay on the General Economy*, Vol. 1, trans. Rob Hurley (New York: Zone, 1988).

Speculation | Aris Komporozos-Athanasiou

(Chicago), Debt, (Future), HFT, Mapping, The Pit, (Trader)

Uncertainty has always been a two-sided coin. An endemic feature of life, it represents the limit of what we can possibly know and what we can confidently predict about the future. On the one hand, doubt about what lies ahead during periods of crisis and heightened volatility—such as financial crashes, global pandemics, or military conflict—can be a cause of devastating insecurity and paralyzing anxiety. On the other, as Ursula Le Guin puts it: "the only thing that makes life possible is permanent, intolerable uncertainty: not knowing what comes next".[1] If the only certainty about our future is its inherent indeterminacy, *another* future will always be possible, and fighting for it will never be futile. But how do economies and societies take up this challenge?

Speculation has been one of the most enduring and complex answers to unpredictable uncertainty. Whether in markets and gambling, or in philosophy and religion, speculation tosses the coin of uncertainty in the hope of seeing through a haze-draped future. A mirror (*speculum*) and a watchtower (*specula*), it animates a certain *vision*: from the leaps of scientific revolutions and technological futurity to the pursuit of dreams and mystical theologies. Searching the world for signs and portents, speculators have always sought to capture what lies ahead. Driven by such visions, they breed prophecies that tie people together into shared fates, taming the future's obscurity. Or they place high-risk wagers, whose volatile yields exacerbate uncertainty further still. Speculation, in that sense, stands for both *closure* and *openness* to the unknown.

Closer to this critical glossary's subject matter, speculation encompasses a duality perching at the core of all financial activity. When pushed to its outermost limit, it can unleash formidable destructive forces, the stuff of frenzies and fads, leading to the burst of market bubbles like seventeenth-century Amsterdam's notorious Tulip craze and the Victorian era's railway manias (so poignantly lamented by John Francis), or last century's Great Depression and the more recent 2008 global financial crisis. During these periods, market "passions" (memorably described by the Fed's totemic chairman Alan Greenspan as "irrational exuberance") take hold; traders venerate ethereal values with no material referents or links to "fundamentals"—they take leave of reality itself. Yet, speculation is also the market's indispensable lubricant. All speculative trades, in essence, calibrate risks in order to generate yields, and in doing so they prevent markets from "overheating".

Somewhat counterintuitively, then, speculation's greatest gift to markets is stability, not crisis: absorbing volatility by "smoothening out price fluctuations" and generating much-needed liquidity. For those in the business of trading, speculation means betting on possible future movements of asset prices, but it also involves dealing in risky assets (like derivatives and futures) with the goal of providing insurance *against* price movements in the "wrong" direction. Speculators, in other words, both short *and* hedge uncertainty. Throughout capitalism's history, defenders and opponents of speculation have foregrounded one function over the other to mark it, respectively, as a virtue or as a vice.

Iconic anarchist thinker Pierre-Joseph Proudhon, in his 1857 *Manuel du spéculateur à la Bourse*, famously distinguished between the greedy financiers of the Paris stock market—whom he lamented as "pure, corrupt, and unproductive gamblers"—and what he saw as more productive forms of speculation. When sought for its own sake, speculation is circular, autotelic, and parasitic on the real economy. But when put to "productive use" it can be not only insulating but also generative, exciting, and imaginative, in Proudhon's words: "a source of progress [that] provides orientation for labour, capital and trade" and "the genius of discovery ... that invents, innovates ... and ... creates something from nothing".[2]

As markets in the global centres of capitalism sought to expand their insatiable financial activities over the course of the nineteenth century, they vied fervently for control over the power of speculation. Just as Proudhon was writing his *Manuel*, a new kind of speculative market was being established some 4,000 miles west of the Paris Bourse. In 1848, the Chicago Board of Trade (CBOT) became the world's first organized exchange for *futures contracts*: standardized agreements to buy or sell an "underlying asset" (predominantly grains such as wheat from the city's hinterland), at a guaranteed price for delivery at a specified future time. Ostensibly, the trading of futures served the hedging side of speculation's coin, functioning as insurance against volatility for farmers whose harvest was exposed to radical and incalculable weather uncertainties. Speculators stepped in to take on the unwanted risk at a discount (performing thus a social function), while farmers got security and the market remained liquid. Yet, no bushels of grain were being moved because of these trades, and even actual contracts never exchanged hands in the CBOT. Soon after the launch of the future contract, the circulation of "phantom wheat" in the pit vastly overtook that of the real grain produced in farms; futures traders were engaging in "fictitious dealings" that were entirely unmoored from the corporeal economy. Was this kind of speculation ethical? Was it different to ordinary gambling?[3]

Advocates of futures contracts and the CBOT's influential allies answered these questions unequivocally in the positive.[4] State courts enshrined the legal right of futures traders to short sell for their alleged positive effect on setting off prices in the real economy, and successive governments sanctioned the promise of even the most fictitious of trades to stabilize an inherently unstable capitalism.[5] Importantly, speculative bets made in the pit were painstakingly distinguished from the wagers placed outside of incorporated commodities, which were systematically slated. In the mushrooming *bucket shops* (informal establishments allowing access to anyone who wanted to wager small sums on the price movements of stocks in formal exchanges) strewing American cities of the *fin de siècle*, speculation was becoming a game for the many.

This was the disorganized speculation associated typically with farmers and people of colour, with migrant urban workers and women—groups that were not only excluded from the futures markets (even though, for some, these markets defined the prices of their products and hence their livelihoods) but were also derided as morally repugnant. The imagined netherworld of dingy gambling houses served as a convenient scapegoat to the celestial halls of futures trading. By transposing the evils of speculation to outcast lay betters, the pits' denizens and their powerful institutional allies buttressed the legitimacy of *homo economicus*. They cast it as a noble figure and stood it at the helm of American capitalism.[6]

Yet, speculative activities across organized exchanges and informal bucket shops had deeper affinities in the Victorian era. Speculators from all walks of life wielded a vivid imagination to navigate the inherent opacity of staking the future. Numinous ambulation and flights from reality were not the exclusive purview of irrational and exuberant "crowds"; professional financiers regularly turned to occult technologies of market prognostication, their speculations too meandering through the worlds of magic, superstition, and tarot card reading. Stock markets' close encounter with astrology is perhaps the most telling of this enmeshment of the rational/scientific and the irrational/spiritual: Wall Street traders lined up to heed the predictions of financial astrologers like the notorious Evangeline Adams, while mainstream financial technologies were adopting horoscopic methods that sought to map the movements of markets on to those of stars.[7]

In the dawn of finance capitalism's modern era, speculation created a world that was at once obscure and spectacular, full of stardust and bitter conflicts—a world, importantly, that was far from insulated from broader social reality. Speculators were a mirror image of society rather than a deviation from it, reflecting its assiduous drive to lay wagers on the unknown in the face of radical uncertainty.

This world is one that we still recognize as ours. Following a period of unbridled financialization during the later part of the twentieth century (turbocharged by the repeal of the Glass–Steagall legislation in 1999 allowing commercial banks to act as financial traders), contemporary economies and societies are once again steeped into the whirlpool of speculation. In today's turbocharged financial markets, speculation is even more opaque because of the highly complex technologies on which it relies: machine learning, algorithmically powered, superfast trading systems whose inner workings are often indiscernible even to traders themselves. High-frequency and automated trading takes place in virtual pits, with data scientists and coders sat quietly in front of rows of screens monitoring a ceaseless search for patterns through stacks of data, including predictive analysis of social media content that informs trading decisions (not all that different to the practices of yesteryear's financial astrologists).[8]

On the most obscure end of these markets, speculators submerge themselves in "dark pools": exclusive forums of block trading of securities that evade transparency requirements of formal exchanges, where dealings appear even more detached from reality. The complexity of this kind of trading means that it is often impossible to tell whether a product like the derivative will be used to hedge an uncertain event or derive profit out of it. At the same time, speculative wagers are now placed not merely on the uncertainty of the future but also *on the volatility of uncertainty itself.* At Chicago's CBOE, the successor of the CBOT and America's largest modern options exchange, volatility has its own index commonly called the VIX or the Fear Index—a measure of expected price swings in the S&P options market. CBOE's virtual pit even trades volatility as an "asset class" with its own "index futures".

The denizens of these new temples of finance continue to fire up the public imagination. On first brush, we may intuitively recall the greedy-yet-charming hedge funders—immortalized by Leonardo DiCaprio's gregarious Wolf of Wall Street—as the exemplary speculators of our time. But on closer inspection, a new, more tragic figure is emerging to usurp the suave megatrader of financialized capitalism from its throne. The modern-day speculator resembles a "high-tech Frankenstein" like Dr Alexander Hoffmann, the tragic protagonist of Robert Harris's 2012 bestseller *The Fear Index*: a tormented physicist-cum-financier confronted with VIXAL-4, an omniscient AI algorithm with the power of predicting fear—including Dr Hoffman's own fear of losing himself entirely in a battle with the mercurial forces of finance. It was adapted to a successful TV series with actor Josh Hartnett rummaging the streets of Geneva injured, haunted, limping, and sweating, while searching for clues on his own past and future, plunged into a nightmare reality where it's impossible to tell fact from fiction.

Yet, beyond this dreamlike world of hyper-technologized finance, the markets' thirst for volatility is now reminiscent of contemporary societies' own immersion in the gamified reality of financialized digital media, where speculation breaks out of the organized digital pits to become a mass spectacle. With retail trading of highly volatile assets exploding in the post-2008 crisis era, meme and crypto trading platforms, decentralized finance ("defi"), and "dApps" provide the online bucket shops for our time's virtual punters. Mass "shorting" events like the GameStop saga—a grassroots short squeeze on the price of the iconic video game retailer organized via social media and making headlines in January 2021—betray a world where volatility is treated as an opportunity in society writ large, with ordinary people sowing (rather than averting) uncertainty in order to reap profit. Following a long trail of speculators for whom the worlds of wizardry and reason were never too far apart, today's short-sellers care little about untangling reality and fiction in their "augmented" everyday lives, from the Metaverse and Web 3.0 to the halls of in-game trading of non-fungible tokens. They are drawn to strange narratives, increasingly untethered from material reality and weaved into the mainstream. Perhaps most alarmingly, the confusion sown by this radical fragmentation of everyday experiences fans the rise of right-wing conspiracy fantasies and regressive movements like QAnon, which are moving rapidly from the fringes of political discourse to centre stage.

Under such conditions, speculation once again emerges as an apt and imaginative response to the chaotic volatility wrought by financialized life—importantly, as a collective rather than merely individual act. The kind of speculation involved in these gamified worlds evokes a yearning for community and imagined connectivity, a joint "hedging" of uncertainty. Wagers across economy and politics—from "crypto-bros" coordinating their short sells around meme stocks to profit from destabilized prices to voters in Middle England sowing Brexit chaos in the hope of disrupting the liberal-technocratic status quo—are oriented towards new solidarities and often confusing political alliances. Such speculations place demands on the future in ways that encompass (rather than redress) doubt, ambivalence, and cynicism.

Speculation, in that sense, is not merely a *symptom* (as mainstream critiques in both economic and political theory often suggest) but a *structure*, something more foundational and generative, and therefore it may also contain valuable answers to the financialization of modern life. This proposition has implications for our ways of rethinking the political use of speculation as a weapon that can be mobilized not only against neoliberal democracy (like in the case of nativist conspiracists and right-wing populists) but *against* finance itself: as an instrument for orienting a radical collective imagination towards more inclusive myths and future narratives that help those in the margins of capitalist society to resist the logic of capital. As such, speculation should also be understood as a *field of action* that may also enable movements that challenge the paradigm from which they emerge, by driving us towards figuring out who we are and who we can be in the face of radical uncertainty. It provides an invisible thread holding speculators together even though it is constitutive of our collective experiences of adrift-ness. We may call these types of radical and progressive speculation *counter-speculation*.

Notes

1　Ursula Le Guin, *The Left Hand of Darkness* (London: Orbit, 1997), 66.

2   Pierre-Joseph Proudhon, *Manuel du spéculateur à la Bourse* (Paris: Garnier Frères, 1857).

3   For a detailed, fascinating, historical account of these events in Chicago and other US financial centres during the nineteenth century, see: Jonathan Ira Levy, "Contemplating Delivery: Futures Trading and the Problem of Commodity Exchange in the United States, 1875–1905", *American Historical Review* 111, no. 2 (2006), 307–335.

4   Economic historians (Ann Fabian, *Card Sharps and Bucket Shops: Gambling in Nineteenth-Century America* (London: Psychology Press, 1999), and Jamie Pietruska, *Looking Forward: Prediction and Uncertainty in Modern America* (Chicago, IL: University of Chicago Press, 2017)) have richly documented this process.

5   See Levy, "Contemplating Delivery".

6   This is also a story, however, of disparaging the mass psychology of "the mob", which served to systematically delegitimate lay speculators and return us to a noble figure of formal elite speculator. Ever since Charles McKay's *Extraordinary Popular Delusions and the Madness of Crowds* from 1841, the vice of speculation is seen as a disease spreading among the "plundered people": Charles McKay, *Extraordinary Popular Delusions and the Madness of Crowds* (New York: Crown Trade Paperbacks, 1980), 74. Historian Richard Hofstadter, *The Age of Reform: Form Bryan to FDR* (New York: Alfred A. Knopf, 1956), famously posited that early American populism was a form of "paranoid" politics.

7   W. D. Gann, R. N. Elliott, and Charles Dow (of the Dow Jones index) pioneered a practice called "chartist investment analysis", drawing directly on gnostic and astrological fields to hedge future uncertainties.

8   For a brilliant discussion of the affinities between big data science and astrology, see: Alexander Boxer, *A Scheme of Heaven: Astrology and the Birth of Science* (London: Profile Books, 2021).

T

Trader

Trust

Trust | Rob Hawkes

Credit, (Faith), Fictions, (Insurance), Liquidity, Money, Utopia

Let me begin with three quotations. The first, from Disney's computer-animated fantasy *Raya and the Last Dragon* (2021), is a conversation between the warrior princess Raya and the dragon Sisu:

Raya: The world's broken. We can't trust anyone.
Sisu: Maybe it's broken because you don't trust anyone.[1]

Next, the plot of *Avengers: Endgame* (2019)—the culmination of Marvel's twenty-three-film "Infinity Saga"—arguably pivots on this moment, when a billionaire tech genius and a super soldier, whose rivalry has energized the entire *Avengers* series, finally shake hands:

Tony Stark/Iron Man: You trust me?
Steve Rogers/Captain America: I do.[2]

Finally, the following exchange, between lawyer Chuck, his arch-rival and hedge fund manager "Axe", and Wendy (Chuck's wife and the in-house psychiatrist/performance coach for Axe's fund), is from the third season of Showtime's financial drama *Billions*:

Chuck Rhoades, Jr: How do I know I can trust him?
Bobby "Axe" Axelrod: How do I know I can trust him?
Wendy Rhoades: Trust me.[3]

On the face of it, this is a disparate group of fictional characters, drawn from an equally incongruous selection of late-2010s/early-2020s popular cultural texts. Nevertheless, these texts share a common preoccupation with the topic of trust. In each case, characters must overcome their antagonism towards one another in order to achieve mutually beneficial goals (either saving the world/universe from the evil Druun/Thanos or simply staying out of jail). Of these examples, only *Billions* explicitly addresses the world of contemporary finance, and yet each one projects an imaginary microcosm of the fundamental role that trust plays in facilitating and indeed enabling social and economic life. As the economist Benjamin Ho highlights in his recent book *Why Trust Matters* (2021), trust "is deeply important to economics" and "is essential to structuring our workplace relationships, our relationships with brands, our investment relationships—right down to our relationship with national currencies and the institutions that guarantee their value".[4] Indeed, social scientists have been arguing for several decades that trust is an invaluable (and hitherto under-acknowledged) driver of economic prosperity. Francis Fukuyama's *Trust* (1995), for example, sets out to demonstrate that there is a strong correlation between economically successful and "high-trust" societies, and, drawing on this perspective in *Bowling Alone* (2000), Robert Putnam suggests that:

When each of us can relax her guard little, what economists term "transaction costs"—the costs of the everyday business of life, as well as the costs of commercial transactions—are reduced. ... A society that relies on generalized reciprocity is more efficient than a distrustful society, for the same reason that money is more efficient than barter. Honesty and trust lubricate the inevitable frictions of social life.[5]

Thus, according to a wide range of commentators, including sociologists, political scientists, historians, and philosophers, trust plays an indispensable role in the functioning of complex, modern societies by "lubricating" social relations, facilitating cooperation, and supporting individuals to maintain a sense of confidence or "faith" in other people and institutions in the midst of uncertain and unpredictable circumstances. Indeed, Anthony Giddens defines trust as both "a form of 'faith'" and an expression of "confidence in the reliability of a person or system", while Barbara Misztal describes it as "a device for coping with the contingency and arbitrariness of social reality".[6] Importantly, as Onora O'Neill observes, the need for trust only arises under conditions of uncertainty: "Where we have guarantees or proofs, placing trust is redundant."[7] The question "how do I know I can trust him?"—which both Chuck and Axe pose in *Billions*—is therefore something of a paradox. If it *were* possible for Chuck to *know* (or to be guaranteed) that he could trust Axe, he would no longer need to trust him.

The references to money and barter in the quotation above emphasize an even more specific connection between trust and finance which points, in turn, towards the social underpinnings of money itself. Etymologically and conceptually, there is a close connection between the words trust and credit, which derives from the Latin *crēdere*: to trust, to believe.[8] For Georg Simmel, in *The Philosophy of Money* (1900), the relationships between money, credit, and trust emerge via a consideration of the difference between "metallic money" and "credit money".[9] While the value of a coin made from a quantity of precious metal that's equal to its nominal worth might appear fixed in a way that negates any need for trust, Simmel demonstrates that "material money", too, relies on credit in that it requires trust both in the government that issues it and in the idea that it will retain its value in order to be spent again.[10] As Simmel goes on to underline: "Without the general trust that people have in each other, society itself would disintegrate, for very few relationships are based entirely upon what is known with certainty about another person. ... In the same way, money transactions would collapse without trust."[11]

Again, uncertainty plays an important role here. No user of money can know for certain that the issuing authority will not collapse or that the money they receive today (whether metallic, paper, or digital) will be accepted tomorrow. Similarly, Steve Rogers/Captain America cannot know that the "time heist" he and his companions have embarked upon in *Avengers: Endgame* will be a success or, more specifically, that Tony Stark/Iron Man has accurately calculated the crucial date to which the pair must travel back in time.

These issues resonate, perhaps with even greater profundity, in literature as well as in film and television. In the 2013 essay collection *Incredible Modernism: Literature, Trust and Deception*, Max Saunders highlights the fundamental questions of trust raised by the figure of the unreliable narrator in Ford Madox Ford's *The Good Soldier* (1915).[12] More recently, Hernan Diaz's fascinating 2022 novel *Trust* repeatedly calls the reliability of its multiple narrators into question while exploring the connections between trust and finance. Each section of Diaz's multi-layered work adopts a different narrative form—novel, autobiography, memoir, diary—and each casts doubt upon the previous section's account of the story of the Bevels: the reclusive financier Andrew and enigmatic philanthropist Mildred. At one stage the novel's third narrator Ida Partenza recalls her father's assertions that "money is a fiction" and, furthermore, that "finance capital is the fiction of a fiction. That's what all these criminals trade in."[13] Thus, a fictional work that directly addresses the topics of honesty, storytelling, deception, manipulation, and the fictionality of finance continually foregrounds the trust demanded of the reader—at both formal and thematic levels—by the text itself, and indeed by the very act of reading. Beyond Ida's father's anti-finance stance in *Trust*, proclamations of money's fictionality abound in contemporary scholarly discourse; for example, Nigel Dodd describes money as "essentially a fiction: a socially powerful—and socially *necessary*—illusion".[14] However, we might claim with equal force that *trust is a fiction* and that to rely upon and cooperate with others is to partake in a mass delusion (albeit one that is "socially *necessary*"). As Laura Finch observes: "The fictionality of finance is, of course, a fiction itself."[15] Indeed, if we accept the view that money is a social relation founded upon credit—as opposed to an imaginary or merely symbolic representation of a piece of metal (or of a "real" transaction within the "real" economy)—the very contention that "money is a fiction" appears increasingly untrustworthy, if not untenable.

Putnam's assertion that "money is more efficient than barter", in the same way that a trusting society is more efficient than a "distrustful" one is, therefore, revealing in other important ways, since it points to the widespread understanding of money as having developed from and eventually replaced barter as a system for exchanging goods. From Simmel's perspective, for example: "The exchange of the products of labour, or of any other possessions, is *obviously* one of the purest and most primitive forms of human socialization; ... in the sense ... that exchange is one of the functions that creates ... a society, in place of a mere collection of individuals."[16] Simmel goes on to affirm that the "frequently emphasized inconveniences and deficiencies of barter" led to the invention of money, which is "the reification of exchange among people".[17] However, in recent years major challenges to this view of money (and, by extension, to this understanding of the role of trust) have been presented by the (re)emergence of chartalist theory within the field of heterodox economics. Coined by Georg Friedrich Knapp in *The State Theory of Money* (1924), the term *chartalism* is based on the Latin word *charta* and refers to the understanding of money as a state-authorized "ticket or token" and as "a creature of law".[18] In *A Treatise on Money* (1930), John Maynard Keynes refers to "Knapp's chartalism" as "the doctrine that money is peculiarly a creation of the State" and asserts that: "the age of chartalist or State money was reached when the state claimed the right to declare what thing should answer as money. ... To-day all civilised money is, beyond the possibility of dispute, chartalist."[19]

More recently, neochartalist economists have returned to Knapp's ideas in order to argue in favour of radical alternatives to the orthodox view of money as "a veil, a simple medium of exchange, which lubricates markets and derives its value from its metallic content".[20] As Pavlina Tcherneva explains, one of the first propositions of (neo)chartalism is that: "The atomistic view of money emerging as a medium of exchange to minimize transaction costs of barter among utility-maximizing individuals finds no support in the historical record."[21] Perhaps surprisingly, this has far-reaching implications for culture and aesthetics as well as for economics.

We began with the observation that a children's animated fantasy, a superhero movie saga, and a television drama set in the world of high finance share a vision of trust in which antagonists must (more often than not reluctantly) enter into interdependent relationships, making themselves vulnerable in the process, in order to achieve shared goals. These are just three examples of a ubiquitous tendency in the cultural representation of social and especially monetary relations and the forms of trust underpinning them: in each case, as in the barter myth, competition and friction precedes cooperation and trust. However, the neochartalist perspective on money opens up on to an entirely different understanding of trust and its role in social and economic life. In place of the "mere collection of individuals" that Simmel imagines as *obviously* pre-existing social interaction in the form of exchange (and, thus, the need to trust others), we can posit a relationship between self and other that is always already interdependent, always already vulnerable, and always already founded upon trust.

Notes

1   *Raya and the Last Dragon*, dir. Don Hall and Carlos López Estrada (Walt Disney Animation Studios, 2021).

2   *Avengers: Endgame*, dir. Anthony Russo and Joe Russo (Marvel Studios, 2019).

3   "The Third Ortolan", *Billions*, Season 3, Episode 6, Showtime, 29 April 2018.

4   Benjamin Ho, *Why Trust Matters: An Economist's Guide to the Ties That Bind Us* (New York: Columbia University Press, 2021), 3. As Ho also points out: "Even the word 'trust' is deeply entwined with how we think about the economy. A bank is sometimes called a trust; many corporations are managed by trustees; money saved for our children can be placed in a trust".

5   Francis Fukuyama, *Trust: The Social Virtues and the Creation of Prosperity* (New York: The Free Press, 1995); Robert D. Putnam, *Bowling Alone: The Collapse and Revival of American Community* (New York: Simon & Schuster, 2000), 135.

6   Anthony Giddens, *The Consequences of Modernity* (Cambridge: Polity Press, 1990), 27, 34; Barbara A. Misztal, *Trust in Modern Societies: The Search for the Bases of Social Order* (Cambridge: Polity Press, 1996), 96–97.

7   Onora O'Neill, *A Question of Trust* (Cambridge: Cambridge University Press, 2002), 6.

8   See "credit, n.", *OED Online*, March 2022, www.oed.com/view/Entry/44113.

9   Georg Simmel, *The Philosophy of Money* (Abingdon: Routledge, 2011), 190.

10 Ibid., 190–192.

11 Ibid., 191.

12 Max Saunders, "Ford Madox Ford, Impressionism and Trust in *The Good Soldier*", in *Incredible Modernism: Literature, Trust and Deception*, ed. John Attridge and Rod Rosenquist (Farnham: Ashgate, 2013), 117–133.

13 Hernan Diaz, *Trust* (London: Picador, 2022), 216.

14 Nigel Dodd, *The Social Life of Money*, with a new preface (Princeton, NJ: Princeton University Press, 2016), 6.

15 Laura Finch, "The Un-Real Deal: Financial Fiction, Fictional Finance, and the Financial Crisis", *Journal of American Studies* 49, no. 4 (2015), 732.

16 Simmel, *The Philosophy of Money*, 187. Emphasis added.

17 Ibid., 187–188.

18 Georg Friedrich Knapp, *The State Theory of Money* (London: Macmillan, 1924), 32, 1. Knapp's monograph was first published in German in 1905.

19 John Maynard Keynes, *The Collected Writings of John Maynard Keynes, Volume V: A Treatise on Money, 1: The Pure Theory of Money* (London: Macmillan, 1971), 4.

20 Pavlina R. Tcherneva, "Chartalism and the Tax-Driven Approach to Money", in *A Handbook of Alternative Monetary Economics*, ed. Philip Arestis and Malcolm Sawyer (Cheltenham: Edward Elgar, 2006), 69.

21 Tcherneva, "Chartalism and the Tax-Driven Approach to Money", 70.

U

The University

Utopia

The University | Shannan Hayes

Debt, Disruption, Occupation, Orthodoxy, (Risk)

Naturalizing

Although colleges have existed in the US since 1636, the now common notion that one proceeds to college after high school to develop life prospects didn't emerge until the second half of the twentieth century.[1] The belief that higher education is how one builds "a good life", gains upward mobility, and/or achieves some notion of "the American Dream" simply did not exist until the Servicemen's Readjustment Act of 1944. This so-called G.I. Bill marked the first time in US history that higher education was opened to a population beyond elites.[2] The initiative established a governmental grant—not a loan—paid directly to colleges. Its goal was to incentivize military service, leverage FDR's popularity, promote consumer spending, and keep immiserated World War II veterans from challenging the social order.[3] Under the G.I. Bill, the number of people earning college degrees more than doubled between 1940 and 1950.[4] As part of the Keynesian postwar context, the grant made going to college a possibility for many (primarily white men) who otherwise would not have been able to afford it.[5] With union power still strong and a Fordist model of rising wages popular, a college degree was likely to increase one's life standings, and college as a path towards upward mobility became part of a popular imaginary.

Support for higher education as a publicly subsidized good did not last long. The National Defense Student Loan programme (NDSL) of 1958 initiated a hegemonic transition from government grants to private loans. Whether higher education should take the form of a grant or a loan was actively debated. While President Truman promoted the idea that higher education should be a general right, tuition costs—on the rise as colleges took advantage of the guaranteed $500 government voucher—impeded universal access to college.[6] In the Cold War context of anti-communism, state-sponsored higher education also proved controversial. Investing in education was nonetheless seen as critical to strengthening the nation's image and STEM capacities, in competition with the Soviet Union. By the time the USSR successfully launched Sputnik in 1957, two US political mandates had crystallized: more citizens needed to enrol in college, and the individualized responsibility emblematic of capitalism was the way to do it. President Eisenhower passed the National Defense Education Act complete with a paired ideology of scientific progressivism and US nationalism.[7] Hailing good, individualized, economically obliged, and nationally obedient subjects, the NDSL even required one to pledge allegiance against communism upon signing their future to a loan.[8]

That individual families and/or students would be made to pay for their privatized good-life aspirations through wagers on individual future earnings was thus not inevitable but instead an emergent ideology of a particular historical moment. The late 1950s marked this pivot from grants to loans, and with it the subsequent naturalization of individualized debt burdens. Even as the NDSL made college more accessible to non-veterans and non-elites,[9] the cultural embrace of this programme normalized the now presumed private cost of job training. It is during this first half of the so-called golden age of higher education that the burdens produced by, and promises invested in, college became thoroughly individualized and individualizing.[10] The view that college was a personal investment became sedimented in the cultural imaginary, and the first step in this critical story thus involves denaturalizing the notion that higher education must be, or always has been, a privately borne cost.

Financializing

It is helpful to place the subsequent developments within the context of the credit system and global economy more broadly. Personal credit was growing as an industry through advancements in digital technology, the spread of neoliberal ideology, the exporting of US domestic manufacturing abroad, and an excess of capital needing new investments. Private lines of personal credit became an important means of supplementing stagnant wages for those impacted by deindustrialization in the US, while also producing profit for "FIRE" (finance, insurance, and real estate) shareholders.[11] Adrienne Roberts succinctly characterizes this process when she observes that private credit "ultimately serves to redistribute wealth upward, from the poor to the rich, from single women to men and from certain racial minorities to white men and their families".[12] Put differently, the so-called democratization of credit over the past several decades has cornered already disadvantaged populations into relationships of debt and dependency on financial systems that benefit from their disenfranchisement.

The financialized student loan industry developed squarely within this story of neoliberalism. Financialization started with the Guaranteed Student Loan programme (GSL) of 1965, wherein the government institutionalized a mode of lending that was detoured through banks. President Johnson pushed the programme with an agenda of equal opportunity in the context of increasing social demands for racial justice amid the Civil Rights movement.[13] The US's involvement in the Vietnam War produced a deficit deemed too high to add student lending.

To expand the loan programme without expanding the deficit, Johnson incentivized banks to keep loans on their books. Banks became the lenders to colleges (who distributed loans to families), and the government offered insurance to banks if families couldn't pay (covered through taxpayer dollars). In this way, the government has subsidized banks by transferring risk to private borrowers and taxpayers, since the beginning.[14]

Congress created Sallie Mae in 1972 in response to lingering shareholder concerns. As loan demands increased, bank funds became scarce.[15] Investors were not convinced that student loans were a smart investment due to government caps on interest. Moreover, student loans lacked collateral and remained illiquid for long terms. Sallie Mae addressed these issues by buying commoditized student debt from banks and thus producing liquid capital. As a "government sponsored enterprise" (or GSE), Sallie Mae functioned as a "servicer", moving debt commodities around to create liquid capital for banks and shareholders, while the government stood by to bail shareholders out if students couldn't pay.

A fully financialized structure of student lending arrived in the 1990s and 2000s, when Sallie Mae incorporated Student Loan Asset-Backed Securities, or SLABS, into its operations.[16] SLABS name a process of bundling debt commodities. Bundling offsets risk by pooling loans, ranking their risk-to-yield levels, and commodifying the likelihood of both repayment and default.[17] Without an asset like a house or car to collect, student loans are backed by the "asset" of the government bail-out promise, the creation of laws that prevent student loans from being dismissed through bankruptcy, and the distribution of risk across bundles. With these security measures, SLABS have become an appealing way for investors to make "at-scale" profit by gaining access to large sums of investment capital in the form of packaged debt. Debt becomes liquid capital in this way, able to be traded or used as a source of income.[18] In turn, liens on students' futures become a lucrative, tradable resource for profit extraction. The profit extracted gets accumulated by banks, private investors, and colleges. This is the student loan industry.

Colleges directly benefit from this system. Most immediately, loans enable schools to coordinate a culture of inflated tuition. In the decade following the creation of Sallie Mae, the cost of college exploded.[19] The first formal ranking of colleges by the *US News & World Report* in 1983 allowed colleges and universities to organize tiered tuition mark-ups. The advent of loan consolidation in the late 1980s enabled colleges to raise tuition further. Monthly payments would now remain relatively low in appearance (once the loan extended from ten to thirty years), while interest collected greatly increased. Once Congress let Sallie Mae sell some of the company's shares on Wall Street in 1978, colleges became some of the company's largest shareholders. Colleges have thus benefited from student indebtedness through tuition hikes, cuts as a lending middleman, and, starting in the 1980s, stock in Sallie Mae.

With all this it becomes clear that student lending has always operated more as a profit-generating enterprise than a structure of public support. As Sallie Mae CEO Edward Fox stated in 1982, two decades before Sallie Mae went private: "We are a private corporation, and as such, with stockholders and bondholders, we have a fiduciary responsibility to those individuals ... We are not charged with subsidizing the Guaranteed Student Loan Program or subsidizing the students."[20] Student loan regulations promote effective debt trading rather than conditions to help students avoid delinquency or default.[21] When, already by 1975, people were not able to get the jobs needed to pay loans back, default too became a commodity. Securitizing incentivized the lending of unpayable loans.

High-risk loans could deliver high yields through the circulation of risk, charged default fees, bankruptcy prohibitions, wage garnishing, and higher interest returns through longer repayment periods. Between 1976 and 1978, and again in 1990 and 2005, Congress passed several policies making student loans increasingly non-dischargeable through bankruptcy.[22] The industry was deregulated to let lenders set their own fees and penalties on borrowers. The state has ultimately facilitated a system that makes delinquent debt profitable while minimizing shareholder risk. As a result, Sallie Mae's profit grew from 0.3 billion in 1975 to 47.5 billion in 1995.[23] By the mid-1980s, the banking industry's lobbying efforts centred issues pertaining to student lending, and by the mid-2000s, SLABS became one of the hottest asset categories.[24]

Student lending is naturalized and depoliticized by a lack of public awareness about the systematic steps the state has taken to ensure that government, banks, schools, and investors—i.e. shareholders—profit at the expense of already disadvantaged students trying to get ahead. This has forced people to treat themselves as both investments and investors in themselves, making high-stakes wagers on their inherently unknowable futures. The future thereby becomes a source of great anxiety, rather than the joyful horizon it could be. Social problems are internalized as personal inadequacies, further obscuring the fact that students are afforded no protections for dealing with circumstances outside of their control, while shareholders are protected to the end. Student debtors are channelled towards more debt via credit cards to access basic needs and/or maintain the normative lifestyle their education hails them into. All the while, higher education is promoted as a great equalizer.

Expanding access to higher education through personal loans has in fact increased structural inequality.[25] BIPOC and working-class families tend to lack the inherited family wealth that affords debt-free college. They also tend to lack the nepotistic social connections that give entry into both top-tier universities and high-paying jobs. Even when students find post-college employment aligned with their professional goals—which many do not—women generally, women of colour particularly, and people of colour broadly continue to be paid less for the same work as their male and white counterparts. These factors set minoritized borrowers up for taking longer to pay off their loans, "hence spen[ding] more money over time for the same degrees [as] their wealthier peers".[26] For many first-generation students, finishing school is also often interrupted by life demands and/or a sense of alienation within the white professional disciplinary climates of higher education.[27] On top of this, for-profit institutions with low employment statistics target black, Hispanic, low-income, and non-conventional students most aggressively.[28] Despite the carrot of individual success, and the stick that not going to college makes precarity, criminalization, social stigma, and despair-oriented death far too likely,[29] access to college through the current loan system has never been an adequate solution. Even when "successful", it extracts wealth and life from the hopeful and the extorted while reintensifying state, capital, and disciplinary power over people.

Detaching

It should be clear that the institution of higher education is set up to accumulate capital and power for those who already have it at the expense of those who don't. Accumulation happens at scale by letting more people into college, specifically those who cannot afford the culturally inflated costs of learning and "earning a living". The problem at hand is therefore not to get more people into the classrooms of higher learning but rather to start dreaming more freely and aggressively outside of the classroom. To become disobedient in the face of "the future", to withdraw the force of our social and intellectual yearning by getting together to do some discerning, some non-reactive thinking, and some other unnamed things somewhere else. I say all this as someone with over 100K in student debt, who never intends to stop learning.

Notes

1   Craig Steven Wilder, *Ebony & Ivy* (New York: Bloomsbury Press, 2013).

2   Josh Mitchell, *The Debt Trap* (New York: Simon & Schuster, 2021), 15. See also US Department of Veterans Affairs, "Born of Controversy: The GI Bill of Rights", Celebrating America's Freedoms, www.va.gov/opa/publications/celebrate/gi-bill.pdf.

3   Franklin D. Roosevelt, "Statement on Signing the G.I. Bill", quoted in "The GI Bill", Khan Academy, www.khanacademy. org/humanities/us-history/postwarera/postwar-era/a/the-gi-bill. See also US Department of Veterans Affairs, "Born of Controversy".

4   James T. Patterson, *Grand Expectations: The United States, 1945–1971* (New York: Oxford University Press, 1996), 68.

5   While this grant was promised to all veterans, functionally it was distributed to a majority of white men. Women at the time were rarely recognized as vets, and colleges and housing lenders rarely included black people in their services. See Mitchell, *The Debt Trap*, 16. See also Robert H. Scott III, Kenneth Mitchell, and Joseph Patten, "Intergroup Disparity among Student Loan Borrowers", *Review of Evolutionary Political Economy* 3 (2022), 515–538.

6   David Witman, "Truman, Eisenhower, and the First GI Bill Scandal", The Century Foundation, https://tcf.org/content/report/truman-eisenhower-first-gi-bill-scandal/. See also Matthew Fuller, "A History of Financial Aid to Students", *Journal of Student Financial Aid* 44, no. 1 (July 2014), 51.

7   Fuller, "A History of Financial Aid to Students", 42–68; Elizabeth Tandy Shermer, "What's Really New about the Neoliberal University?", *Labor: Studies in Working-Class History* 18, no. 4 (2021), 75.

8   Mitchell, *The Debt Trap*, 20.

9   By 1960 the percentage of young adults attending college had increased to 30%, from 15% in 1940. Financial aid offices were also created at this time: Fuller, "A History of Financial Aid to Students", 52.

10   Astra Taylor, *Can't Pay, Won't Pay: The Case for Economic Disobedience and Debt Abolition* (Chicago, IL: Haymarket Books, 2020). See also Maurizio Lazzarato, *The Making of the Indebted Man* (Los Angeles, CA: Semiotext, 2012).

11   Julie Froud, Sukhdev Johal, Johanna Montgomeire, and Karel Williams, "Escaping the Tyranny of Earned Income?", *New Political Economy* 15, no. 1 (2010), 147–164. See also Susanne Soederberg, "Student Loans, Debtfare, and the Commodification of Debt", *Critical Sociology* 40, no. 5 (2014), 689–709.

12   Adrienne Roberts, "Financing Social Reproduction", *New Political Economy* 18, no. 1 (2013), 21–42.

13   Scott III et al., "Intergroup Disparity among Student Loan Borrowers".

14   This is also the time that credit scores became digitally archived and credit records became widely monitorable, further displacing risk from banks and investors to individuals' futures.

15   See also Soederberg, "Student Loans, Debtfare"; Annie McClanahan, "Investing in the Future", *Journal of Cultural Economy* 6, no. 1 (2013), 78–93.

16   The precedent for financializing debt was established in the 1970s with Fannie Mae. Unlike Fannie Mae, Sallie Mae garnered special confidence through the government's unique promise to cover defaulted loans. See Soederberg, "Student Loans, Debtfare", 696–698. See also See Eli J. Campbell, "Wall Street Has Been Gambling with Student Loan Debt for Decades", *open-Democracy*, 24 October 2019.

17   Jack Du, "Student Loan Asset-Backed Securities: Safe or Subprime?", *Investopedia*, www.investopedia.com/articles/investing/081815/student-loan-assetbacked-securities-safe-or-subprime.asp.

18 Elizabeth Popp Berman and Abby Stivers, "Student Loans as a Pressure on U.S. Higher Education", *Research in the Sociology of Organizations* 46 (2016), 135.

19 For comparison: between 1980 and 1990, consumer prices rose 62%, annual earnings rose 68%, and college tuition rose 145% for private schools or 113% for public schools: Mitchell, *The Debt Trap*, 76.

20 Thomas H. Stanton, "Reducing Government Involvement in a Market", *Public Budgeting & Finance* 28, no. 1 (2008), 101–123.

21 Ibid. See also Soederberg, "Student Loans, Debtfare".

22 Soederberg, "Student Loans, Debtfare", 696. See also Scott et al., "Intergroup Disparity among Student Loan Borrowers".

23 Stanton, "Reducing Government Involvement in a Market".

24 Berman and Stivers, "Student Loans as a Pressure", 137, 140. See also Stanton, "Reducing Government Involvement in a Market".

25 See, for instance, Shermer, "What's Really New"; Scott et al, "Intergroup Disparity among Student Loan Borrowers"; Justin Ortagus and Rodney Hughes, "Paying More for Less?", *Third Way*, 3 March 2021, www.thirdway.org/report/paying-more-for-less-a-new-classification-system-to-prioritize-outcomes-in-higher-education.

26 Shermer, "What's Really New", 81.

27 Scott et al, "Intergroup Disparity among Student Loan Borrowers".

28 Tressie Cottom McMillam, *Lower Ed* (New York: New Press, 2018).

29 Anne Case and Angus Deaton, *Deaths of Despair and the Future of Capitalism* (Princeton, NJ: Princeton University Press, 2020).

Utopia | Paul Crosthwaite

Care, Comedy, Counterfeit, Mont Pèlerin, Period, Trust, Value

The aesthetics of finance have a profoundly utopian dimension. For many of those who work with or theorize about financial markets and instruments, such phenomena possess a beauty and perfectibility lacking from the world at large, but with the potential to make over that world in their own image. To this way of thinking, finance is—or at least tends towards being—an idealized domain in which absolute equilibrium, precision, and synchronization preside; and all that is required for social and economic life in general to assume these same qualities is the thoroughgoing expansion of financial logics. Like all utopias, financial utopias are simultaneously technical—a matter of optimally constructed policies, practices, and procedures—and deeply aesthetic: visionary projections whose sublimity is to be contemplated with reverence, awe, and wonder.

Finance's utopian aesthetic finds its purest expression in claims for capital markets' maximal "efficiency". The "efficient market hypothesis" (EMH) is a central plank of the now canonical body of finance theory that began to transform American universities' economics and business departments in the 1960s and 1970s, and became integral to financial professionals' models, practices, and assumptions over succeeding decades. Most closely associated with the leading financial economists Eugene Fama and Paul Samuelson, the EMH refines a vision of the market as a perfect aggregator of dispersed knowledge and action that stretches back through pioneering neoliberal thinkers such as Friedrich Hayek to the foundations of modern political economy in Adam Smith and the notion of the "invisible hand". In Fama's canonical formulation, mature securities markets in advanced capitalist economies can be defined as "efficient" in that their "prices always 'fully reflect' all available information".[1] Because—so the theory runs—numerous investors and traders devote their attention to identifying divergences between the prices of stocks and other financial assets and their "true" values, such divergences will vanish almost before they appear, as market participants immediately act en masse to exploit the arbitrage opportunity. On this account the market's collective wisdom has always already "priced in" everything that can be known about the past and present, as well as everything that can be anticipated about the future. Since the efficient market consistently incorporates an aggregated "best guess" about what the future holds, impending price movements are, in effect, random—no more predictable than the successive coin tosses that, recorded on a chart, form the meandering "random walk" paths invoked by Burton Malkiel in his celebrated popularization of the EMH, *A Random Walk down Wall Street* (1973).[2]

Underlying efficient market theorists' technical disquisitions is thus a conception of financial markets as functionally omniscient phenomena in whose price records every event (even every merely prospective event) is weighed, registered, and preserved. What makes this conception properly utopian (in several senses of the word) is the way in which it answers to a profoundly human, and ultimately theological, yearning for a transcendent realm in which the ephemera of the everyday would be redeemed and immortalized. Slavoj Žižek refers to such a space as the "Other Scene in which the accounts are properly kept, [the] fictional Other Place in which, from the perspective of the Last Judgement, our acts will be properly located and accounted for" (Thomas More's original Utopia, we might recall, is literally a "no place").[3] Žižek is here echoing

the kabbalistic and messianic utopianism of Walter
Benjamin's "Theses on the Philosophy of History", which
imagines a divine chronicler for whom "nothing that has
ever happened should be regarded as lost for history", and
whose "recit[al]" of events both "major and minor" permits
a "redeemed mankind" to receive "the fullness of its past",
now "citable in all its moments".[4] The EMH vision of financial
markets would thus lend weight to Benjamin's intuition, in
the fragment "Capitalism as Religion" (written in 1921), that
a "religion may be discerned in capitalism", since "capitalism serves essentially to allay the same anxieties, torments,
and disturbances to which the so-called religions offered
answers".[5] The EMH suggests the possibility of something like
the ascension of temporal life into the realm of the eternal
that religious faith once uniquely extended.

The utopian vision that glimmers within efficient market
theory—of the market as a radiant, redemptive space, with
the power to elevate even the most quotidian occurrences of
our fallen world on to a transcendent plane—helps to explain
why the EMH retains such a hold across the discipline of economics and the financial profession, even in the face of events
(most obviously, the global financial crisis of 2007–08) that
would seem conclusively to have disproved it. At stake is not
simply a theoretical explanation of the functioning of the securities markets, but the very possibility of some secular proxy
for the kind of omniscient state—traditionally attributed only
to the divine—that might bestow meaning, significance, and
permanence on events and experiences otherwise destined to
lapse into historical oblivion.

This vision likewise helps to explain why the EMH has
provided the underlying rationale for the neoliberal extension of market logics to virtually every domain of contemporary life, from health and education to criminal justice and

even the environment. If markets "know best", the argument runs, then all social and economic fields will function efficiently to the extent to which they are organized on a market basis. Via this process of expansion, the utopia that is the market need not merely be an idealized "reflection" of the ordinary, everyday world (with financial markets, on the one hand, "reflecting" wider socio-economic reality, on the other) but immanent to that world, a fully achieved utopia at the level of daily life, whose every interaction would be miraculously coordinated and optimized. If, in the efficient market imagination, the social world is perfectly mirrored by the stock market, then the ultimate expansion and fulfilment of this vision would see the world in effect become coterminous with and indistinguishable from the market. Such a condition is glimpsed by the narrator of a recent story by Jonas Eika, who, shortly before describing his experiences as an obsessive derivatives trader, reflects that "my entire working life felt like one big coincidence, or like the inevitability of a network of connections that belonged not to me but to the market".[6] What looks to some like a utopia may—viewed from a different perspective, as in Eika's hallucinatory narrative— take on a starkly dystopian aspect. Sometimes, in a certain light, and after nearly half a century of market ideology's political dominance, it may seem as though a condition of this kind is already with us.

Notes

1   Eugene Fama, "Efficient Capital Markets: A Review of Theory and Empirical Work", *Journal of Finance* 25, no. 2 (1970), 383.

2   Burton G. Malkiel, *A Random Walk down Wall Street* (New York: W.W. Norton, 1973). On the significance of Malkiel's work, see Paul Crosthwaite, Peter Knight, Nicky Marsh, Helen Paul, and James Taylor, *Invested: How Three Centuries of Stock Market*

Advice Reshaped Our Money, Markets, and Minds (Chicago, IL: University of Chicago Press, 2022), 237–243, 245–246.

3   Slavoj Žižek, *The Ticklish Subject: The Absent Centre of Political Ontology* (London: Verso, 2000), 340.

4   Walter Benjamin, "Theses on the Philosophy of History", in *Illuminations: Essays and Reflections*, ed. Hannah Arendt, trans. Harry Zohn (New York: Schocken, 2007), 254. For more on the Benjaminian resonances of efficient market theory, see my *The Market Logics of Contemporary Fiction* (Cambridge: Cambridge University Press, 2019), 170–179.

5   Walter Benjamin, "Capitalism as Religion", trans. Rodney Livingstone, in *Selected Writings, Vol. 1: 1913-1926*, ed. Marcus Bullock and Michael W. Jennings (Cambridge, MA: Belknap Press of Harvard University Press, 1996), 288.

6   Jonas Eika, "Alvin", in *After the Sun*, trans. Sherilyn Nicolette Hellberg (London: Lolli Editions, 2021), 9.

V

Value

Violence

Void

Value | Beverley Best and Richard Dienst

(Circulation), Commodity, Credit, Extraction, Gaming, Work

By the time it is over, this essay should provide a critical gloss on the concept of "value" in the context of a collective elaboration of "finance aesthetics". That's a promise. In order to keep that promise, it will be necessary to think not just about value but also about finance, about aesthetics, and what each concept has to do with the others. The possibility that this essay might not be able to keep this promise is an essential part of the theoretical problem it is trying to examine. Promises are like debts but they are also like hopes: grasping that simple but massively important distinction is roughly where we will try to end up a few pages from now.

First of all, it is necessary to take the measure of the words we will need. On one hand, the concept of value is too vast. You can see it everywhere if you look for it, which is precisely the problem: it is an imperial concept, capable of rewriting everything according to its logic. On the other hand, finance aesthetics is a newfangled, rather specialized term, conjoining two ambitious words that might not go together so easily. It doesn't help that value operates on either side of the divide: there is a lot to say about financial value and just as much to say about aesthetic value, but the language of fiscal policy and derivatives cannot be meshed with the language of beauty and wonderment without surrendering all chances of critique.

Everybody thinks they know what value is when they see it: it is an old metaphysical slippage turned into a global economic machine. Evidently, nobody has been able to correct the logical error far enough to upset the system. That is because every appearance of value must conjure an aura of ignorance (recoded as risk or mystery) in order to set it aglow. And that is why it is time to set aside inquiries into the nature of value itself as remnants of an earlier age and concentrate instead on "actually existing" value, value as capitalist formation, value that is constitutively perverted and topsy-turvy. When there is no such thing as value apart from its capitalist manifestations, no value apart from the dream factory of markets, the critique of value must learn how to track the trickery of representation through all of its twists and turns. Most of the time it's not that complicated, because everyday economic exchanges must seem natural enough to function. But some of the time the arrangements look very complicated indeed, as if a sublime degree of complexity could open a wormhole through the current architecture of wealth. That is a signal of what is usually called "financialization", which is both relentlessly inventive and perpetually vulnerable to failure. Value may be the tortured soul of capital, but its monstrous appetite for further expansion—the production of surplus value—remains capital's all-too-embodied raison d'être, and Achilles heel.

We need to think about value as the machinery of staggering irrationality and misery, and, at the same time, as that machinery's dissimulator. Right now, as we speak, value names the movement of socialization; it is, as Marx says, "pure sociality". Across its many operations, it performs historical tasks that it would be hard to live without: socially dividing labour processes, calling up cooperative labour in production and provision, facilitating economies of scale (not always a bad thing), sharing and circulating knowledge and ingenuity (let's calls it the general intellect), collectivizing wealth into a credit system (yes, it is possible to have credit without debt or interest—just think about it!).

If value is the movement of wealth socially produced and captured as private property, it is also a placeholder for socially produced wealth freed from its capitalist integument: wealth-in-kind, socially produced wealth that is socially controlled and socially consumed, the rational production provision of useful things (rational because reproducible without doing harm or further damage), desirable things, life-sustaining things at a surplus scale (i.e. enough for all), and so on. Here's where our onerous debts meet our last hopes, where the wishful thinking of consumers and investors meets the irrepressible need for something like communism. Only at this bewitched crossroads can we recognize that value, and its derivative, surplus value, are essential categories (thought objects) for seeing the outlines of a "higher form of society" in the muck of the present one.[1]

At least, this is Marx's critique of value. Let's stick with the credit system in order to think it through. Finance, a system of lending out money capital for a price (interest), is endemic to capitalist production circulation because the circuitry of the value machine (M–C–M') comes apart. The metamorphosis of money into commodities is disjointed from the metamorphosis of commodities into money. Buying and selling are routinely separate activities, staggered, calling up (from the netherworld, it would seem) a thing called "paying". Value, in the form of money or commodities, may pile up over here, while being sorely lacking over there. The situation calls finance capital into existence, a value derivative; value forms beget value forms. The process of derivation is logical, of course, not chronological. Finance capital steps in to realize value piled up over here, and to fill in gaps over there, in order to keep value flowing, as it must do, to do what it does.

Finance capital demands to be paid for this service—it is somebody's property after all—and in doing so severs all perceptual ties to its origins in production and to its identity as the product of what living labour does there. This is why, for Marx, finance capital is the ultra-fetish, famously, "the mother of every insane form". The question is, can we think through capital's phantasmagoria in an aesthetic theory experiment for the sake of nourishing ordinary utopias (figures or placeholders for a higher form of society)? Does the madness of capital have something to teach us after all? In Marx's critique the analysis of the "pure irrationality" of interest serves to expose the fact that interest is payment for nothing at all. Interest is not a value magnitude; it is empty—pure form. As such, finance is a redistribution machine where the price of the service rendered is as rationally zero as it is 5, 10, or 20% on the principal. Interest is unnecessary, a potential redundancy, as is, by extension, speculation. Finance capital, partaking in the movement of abstraction that constitutes value in general, points to a system—as a possibility introduced by the same function of abstraction—where the mobility of wealth is not determined by any organic or customary relationship to its mode of production, or to its producers. In other words, utopian credit, as socialized wealth-in-kind—still a portion of surplus labour or its product—can be liberated to move where it needs to be, regardless of how it is produced, where, and by whom, determined by nothing other than the nature of need itself.

If such a credit system had an operator's manual, it might just as well say: "from each according to their abilities, to each according to their need". What is utopian about these instructions lies in the discord, inequality, and unreflexivity of abilities and needs, in the fact that abilities and needs need not, and surely will not, synch up in time, space, or species. I grow beets and you make music, and each of us enjoys both. Only the collectivizing of labour and its product can turn inequality from a problem into the best-case scenario.

Again: utopian finance presupposes collectivized labour because it will take part in what already actually exists (and which currently makes capital capital), namely the human capacity to produce surplus labour and to objectify both that labour and its product are things separable from their producer. Marx makes this simple but significant point in the third volume of *Capital*, that what is key to capitalist accumulation will be the key to any associated mode of production that may follow, by turning value inside out. Here is the ordinary utopian promise on the other side of finance capital's fantasy that $100 = 110$: the rational abundance unlocked when the collective labour of 100 can feed 110, house 110, provide healthcare for 110, and so on. If communists move to abolish the existing state of things and, consequently, the planet survives, it will depend on the mechanisms that allow a collectivity to give itself credit for what it wants to accomplish. Value is beautifully theoretical because it cannot stand still. It drives towards its own full, aesthetic sociality, despite itself.

Note

1   This is Marx's phrase.

Void | Amin Samman

Cynicism, Death, (Future), Luxury, Money

There is no proper place within economic thought for the void. It appears nowhere in the canonical texts of political economy, let alone the discourse of conventional economics. Yet one cannot shake the sense that it is implied in most if not all financial commentary. At the very least, the void exerts a magnetic pull on a range of related terms in the lexicon. Could it be that through these it grounds the aesthetics of finance in fundamental ways?

Consider the bounced cheque. Almost nobody writes cheques anymore, but no matter. The bounced cheque provides a way into the riddle of foundations. If the foundations of capitalism are legal, as John Commons maintained, then they are fleeting.[1] Unlike a commodity, which must find a market once produced or else hang around like so much junk, a transaction can be cancelled, annulled, dissolved. Among other things, this means that the sprawling web of contracts that enables the amassing of financial wealth today is held together by potential nullity. Everything is voidable.

This peculiar fact produces not only flux but also an emptiness at the core of things. Everyone knows that redacting a document leaves a blank space where something should be but is no longer, an absent presence. The same goes for accounting and therefore financial society. In a balance sheet universe, every entity is organized around what Hyman Minsky called a "survival constraint".[2] Life is solvency, and death comes when one too many cheques bounce, so to speak. Survival hinges on preventing this lack from revealing itself, from keeping the financial void at bay. That is what keeps any "going concern" going.

To call this a survival instinct would be misleading. The endless drive to acquire greater quantities of abstract wealth has more to do with morbid obsession. Fear and denial of death, but also a death-dealing drive to plug up the traumatic hole in the body economic. Money is the name for this hole.

Money has the uncanny ability to swallow everything else up. That's why John Maynard Keynes once described it as "a bottomless sink for purchasing power".[3] Who wants something when holding on to nothing means you could have anything? Yet by the same token, money is the source of all want and hollowness. Forget holding on to or hoarding it; any transaction in a money economy brings one into contact with the negative desire inscribed into money itself. The money object, says Noam Yuran, produces subjects who want what money wants, which always is nothing less than yet more money.[4]

All this puts pressure on the discourse of history. From behind, historical reality is sucked into the black hole of commodity money. The money object belongs to history only as its effacement, and it is this that enables history to assume the form of money unfolding itself.[5] Meanwhile, debt attacks historical reality from the future, dragging it forward into a world organized around the promise of payment perpetually deferred. And so bank money, too, is a vanishing point. No matter, then, which came first, medium of exchange or unit of account. Money implodes the temporal distinctions that would underpin either historical narrative, creating a vacuum of meaning, a void. Nothing but money. Nothing but the void.

***

Perhaps the only thinker to put things squarely in these terms was Jean Baudrillard, whose late writings in particular circle ceaselessly around the figure of the void. Reality slips into an abyss, accelerating in a void, proliferating through the endless circulation of signs. Writing against the backdrop of newly floating exchange rates, growing capital mobility, and rising levels of indebtedness, Baudrillard saw each of these as crucial aspects of history's undoing.

More than a simple benchmark or general equivalent, money is the "universal equivalent of nothing ... the equivalent of the universal circulation of the Nothing". Speculation, in turn, is "a sort of ecstasy of value ... a pure, empty form, the purged form of value operating on nothing but its own revolving motion". Finally, global debt—despite all the talk of repayment—is a debt that will never be redeemed, for it is the infinite promise on which everything now hangs: "Clearing the debt, settling the accounts, cancelling the payments by the Third World ... Don't even think about it!"[6]

In recent years much scorn has been heaped on the idea of a split between the financial and the real economy, and rightly so, only the reasons usually given are the wrong ones. The issue is less that financial logics order or produce the real, and more that the proliferation of monetary signs overtakes and undermines the criteria by which the former could be falsified and the latter verified. If bank money, which is to say debt-financed money, operates "like some artificial sun", the point is not that this sun is artificial; the point is that we live or die by it.[7]

***

With this new state of affairs comes yet more pressure. An economy filled with ever more claims upon claims is an economy grotesquely swollen and bloated, with no way to purge, expel, or discharge the waste building up within it. The image presented by Alfred Jarry in a sketch to accompany his 1896 play *Ubu Roi*—a mad king with a spiral scrawled across his enormous belly—was much favoured by Baudrillard in this regard, who saw it as a parable for the era of global money and finance. We live under a demonic threat that the king's distended belly will burst, voiding itself of all contents and leaving everyone up to their necks in shit. Yet this moment—the Great Unburdening—never seems to arrive, and so we continue conjuring wealth out of a void, feeding a kind of world-historical nausea that worsens with every passing day.

No wonder, then, that an overwhelming sense of decline accompanies contemporary financial life. The same was the case at the dawn of the twentieth century, which gave us Jarry's *Ubu Roi* alongside the ruinous march of a war economy fuelled by imperial finance capital. And the same again, too, in the 1970s, whose financial turbulence and mass media revolutions gave us the cultural phenomenon of punk music. Pere Ubu and Devo in the American Midwest, who foresaw the implosion of Atlantic Fordism and slow-motion devolution of humanity. Richard Hell and the Voidoids in New York, whose song "Blank Generation" featured a Hell so vacant he even omitted the word "blank" from one chorus. Then the coup de grâce: the Sex Pistols in London, with a tortured Johnny Rotten screaming out the phrase "No Future" on a loop in the outro to their Jubilee single, "God Save the Queen", before being locked out of music venues and confined to the dead zone of endless TV replays.

Today, perhaps the best illustration of this perverse dynamic would be luxury fashion house Balenciaga's Spring Show 2023. The collection was unveiled in mid-2022 on the floor of a New York Stock Exchange long ago made redundant by the automation of financial trading. Like Sex Pistols manager Malcolm McLaren in the 1980 film *The Great Rock 'n' Roll Swindle*, the models appear in latex gimp masks. Cameras flash as the faceless figures glide down a snaking runway, buffeted by screens flickering with the logos and stock prices of big tech and pharma companies. Cool money.

The list could go on, but the point it means to illustrate is this: the financial void opens out on to the problem of nihilism in all its forms. The meaning and feeling of vacuity, of emptiness and annihilation, the transparency with which anything and everything around us is grounded on and propelled by Nothing—these are recurring motifs in the aesthetics of finance. Together, they form a vortex, a swirling sinkhole that drags financial life into endless, abyssal circulation.

Notes

1   John Commons, *Legal Foundations of Capitalism* (Madison, WI: University of Wisconsin Press, 1926).
2   Hyman Minsky, *Induced Investment and Business Cycles* (Cheltenham: Edward Elgar, 2004), 96.
3   John Maynard Keynes, *The General Theory of Employment, Interest and Money* (London: Macmillan & Co, 1936), 231.
4   Noam Yuran, *What Money Wants: An Economy of Desire* (Stanford, CA: Stanford University Press, 2014).
5   Ibid., 110.
6   These quotations can be found in Jean Baudrillard, *Impossible Exchange*, trans. Chris Turner (London: Verso, 2001), 128; Jean Baudrillard, *The Transparency of Evil: Essays on Extreme Phenomena*, trans. James Benedict (London: Verso, 1993), 35; Jean Baudrillard, "Global Debt and Parallel Universe", trans. François Debrix, in *Digital Delirium*, ed. Arthur Kroker and Marilouise Kroker (Montréal: New World Perspectives, 1997), 39.
7   Baudrillard, *The Transparency of Evil*, 33.

W

Water

Whiteness

Work

Work | John MacIntosh

Animals, Disruption, Gaming, Migration, Money, Occupation, Organization, Value

1. Work resists representation.
2. The primary source of this resistance is the drudgery problem.
3. Work can be painful and abject, but what makes it difficult to represent is its alienating, eventless, and repetitive nature.
4. Work is the other of character, plot, and progression.
5. To represent work mimetically is to negate conventional narrative expectations.
6. This is why most texts only represent work intermittently, if at all.
7. If Melville were to represent the work of copying documents and comparing copies, he would be doing the exact stultifying work that Bartleby preferred not to.
8. Even the most canonical of labour novels tends to represent the lives of workers rather than representing those lives working.
9. Yet all texts are about work—desiring it, loathing it, seeking it, being coerced into it, shirking it, taking pride in it, profiting off it, the leisure afforded by someone else doing it, being ejected from it, deriving a sense of self from it, having one's self or body disfigured or destroyed by it, dying of it—even when those texts struggle to represent it directly.
10. Representation doesn't want work, aesthetics doesn't want work, but they can't fully escape it.

11. Beyond this long-standing aesthetic problem, the representation of work is also constrained by the representational hegemony of contemporary finance in culture more generally.

12. Finance is everywhere in the cultural imaginary; it represents itself largely on its own terms, a set of appearances that do not correspond to its practice.

13. One appearance: the equation of the financial industry with "the economy", in which only financial adepts have agency or importance (e.g. Tom Wolfe's popularization of bond traders as "masters of the universe").

14. A second: the notion that financial markets are detached not only from the "real" economy but outside human intervention altogether (e.g. a character in Don DeLillo's *Cosmopolis* suggesting that "money is talking to itself").

15. The first suggests that the financial industry produces value without the mediation of the production process; the second suggests that value produces itself outside of human agency.

16. While contradictory, the function of each appearance is to make work, the source of the value that finance derives its profits from, invisible.

17. This is the occlusion problem: finance needs work, but it can't acknowledge it, let alone show it.

18. In this sense finance aesthetics are simply capitalist aesthetics, focused on the noisy sphere of circulation rather than the hidden abode of production.

19. Without representations of work, which counter—in their limited way—its representational hegemony, value is ceded to capitalist aesthetics.

20. Capital doesn't want work, but it needs it.